Mirrors are filled with people.
The invisible see us.
The forgotten recall us.
When we see ourselves, we see them.
When we turn away, do they?

BORN OF DESIRE

❧

Life was alone, no name, no memory. It had hands, but no one to touch. It had a tongue, but no one to talk to. Life was one, and one was none.

Then desire drew his bow. The arrow of desire split life down the middle, and life was two.

When they caught sight of each other, they laughed. When they touched each other, they laughed again.

A FEAST ON FOOT

❧

Adam and Eve were black?

The human adventure in the world began in Africa. From there, our ancestors set out to conquer the planet. Many paths led them to many destinies, and the sun took care of handing out colors from the palette.

Now the rainbow of the earth is more colorful than the rainbow of the sky. But we are all emigrants from Africa. Even the whitest of whites comes from Africa.

Maybe we refuse to acknowledge our common origins because racism causes amnesia, or because we find it unbelievable that in those days long past the entire world was our kingdom, an immense map without borders, and our legs were the only passport required.

THE TROUBLEMAKER

❈

Separate were heaven and earth, good and bad, birth and death. Day and night never mixed. Woman was woman and man was man.

But Exû, the errant bandit of Africa, liked to entertain himself by provoking outlawed minglings. And he is still at it.

His devilish tricks erase borders, join what the gods divided. Thanks to his clever deeds the sun turns black and the night burns bright. From the pores of men sprout women and women sweat men. The dying are born, the born are dying. For everything ever created or yet to be created, backward and forward get so confused you can no longer tell boss from bossed or up from down.

Later rather than sooner, divine order reestablishes its hierarchies and geographies, and everything and everyone gets put in its place. But sooner rather than later, madness reappears.

Then the gods lament that the world is such a difficult place.

CAVES

❈

Stalactites hang from the ceiling. Stalagmites grow from the floor.

All are fragile crystals, born from the sweat of rocks in the depths of caves etched into the mountains by water and time.

Stalactites and stalagmites spend thousands of years reaching down or reaching up, drop by drop, searching for each other in the darkness.

It takes some of them a million years to touch.

They are in no hurry.

Praise for *Mirrors*

"It's often said that history is written by the victors, but Galeano has been documenting the losing side—the oppressed, the forgotten, the used—for decades. Neither weary nor desperate, these tales have a tinge of hope . . . Skip around, read one tiny story here, another a few pages later, and allow the tales to swim around your head a while and see if they change the way you see the world."

—Jessa Crispin, NPR.org

"Eduardo Galeano [is] the galvanizer, firebrand, a writer who tells readers about history that other, more powerful people don't want them to know or understand . . . His new book, *Mirrors*, reflects 5,000 years of human experience. But it does so with a keen sense of perspective. For all the past that Galeano captures, this is a writer who lives right now."

—Marie Arana, *Washington Post*

"[Eduardo Galeano is] a learned historian, a brilliant synthesizer and elegant stylist . . . [*Mirrors*] should increase Galeano's stature in the English-speaking world and enhance his reputation as unclassifiably brilliant." **—*Milwaukee Journal-Sentinel***

"The elegance of Galeano's words—they're just penetrating, so beautiful. It's a feast of words."

—Danny Glover, *San Francisco Chronicle*

"A genre-defying work that combines poetry, narrative, fiction, journalism, social analysis, and political opinion to tell the story of all the peoples who have been sacrificed for our progress."

—*Philadelphia Inquirer*

"In *Mirrors*, Galeano regales us with tales from our shared history in an inclusive manner, from cultural creation myths to major historical figures and inventions to significant current events. It is a truism that history is written by the victors; what if, Galeano seems to ask, history were told instead by the vanquished, the oppressed and the downtrodden of all cultures and times? This unpretentiously ambitious book is an answer."　　　　　　　　　　　　　　**—*Texas Observer***

"His most sweeping, cohesive, and empathetic effort to date . . . a dazzling display of literary prowess . . . While Galeano's fidelity to memory, justice, and truth are indeed remarkable, it is the grace, humor, and compassion with which he writes that set his works far beyond the realm of his contemporaries."　　　　　**—Powells.com**

"In his poetic nonfiction, Galeano performs the sort of extraordinary feats of compassion, artistry, and imagination achieved in fiction by his fellow visionary Latin American writers, especially Borges, García Márquez, and Bolaño . . . Now this historian of conscience, this humanely ironic commentator and dazzling storyteller, distills the entire wild pageant of human history into a radiant mosaic of pithy fables, essays, and portraits . . . Themes and connecting patterns rise up like waves and carry forward flotillas of essays in this gorgeously fluid and caustic chronicle of the human condition."

—*Booklist Starred Review*

"You've never learned history like this: the brevity of the mini-lessons and Galeano's sly wit and lapidary prose make for a smart yet never laborious summer diversion."

—*Publishers Weekly, Best Reads of the Summer Editor's Pick*

"A broad, global, sometimes glancing look at all the ways humans do wrong. Galeano practically holds a patent on the telling of history via feuilletonistic vignettes, most running just a few hundred words . . . a whirlwind of emperors, pharaohs, soldiers, explorers, saints and sinners."　　　　　　　　　　　　　　　　　　**—*Kirkus***

Mirrors

*

STORIES OF ALMOST EVERYONE

*

Eduardo Galeano

ENGLISH TRANSLATION BY MARK FRIED

NATION
BOOKS

NEW YORK

Copyright © 2009 by Eduardo Galeano
English translation copyright © 2009 by Mark Fried

Hardcover first published in the United States in 2009 by Nation Books
A Member of the Perseus Books Group
Paperback first published in the United States in 2010 by Nation Books

Originally published in the Spanish language in 2008 by Siglo XXI Editores
(Spain and Mexico) and Ediciones del Chanchito (Uruguay).

Engravings from the exhibit "Monstruos y seres imaginarios,"
Madrid National Library (2000). A complete list of artists can be found at
the end of the book. Copyright © Biblioteca Nacional de España, 2000.

The story of the image on the cover of this book is told in
"Origin of Modern Art," page 267.

Books published by Nation Books are available at special
discounts for bulk purchases in the United States by corporations,
institutions, and other organizations. For more information, please contact
the Special Markets Department at the Perseus Books Group, 2300 Chestnut
Street, Suite 200, Philadelphia, PA 19103, or call (800) 810-4145,
ext. 5000, or e-mail special.markets@perseusbooks.com.

TEXT DESIGN AND COMPOSITION BY JENNY DOSSIN

Library of Congress Cataloging-in-Publication Data
Galeano, Eduardo H., 1940–
[Espejos. English]
Mirrors : stories of almost everyone / by Eduardo Galeano ;
English translation by Mark Fried.
p. cm.
ISBN 978-1-56858-423-2 (alk. paper)
1. History--Miscellanea. I. Title.
D21.3.G3513 2009
909--dc22
2009004518

Paperback ISBN 978-1-56858-612-0
10 9 8 7 6 5 4 3 2 1

No footnotes, no bibliographic sources are included.

I realized in time that they would have taken up more pages than the nearly six hundred stories themselves.

Neither have I listed the many collaborators whose assistance allowed *Mirrors* to become more than just a raving notion. I cannot, however, fail to mention several who had the patience to read the final manuscript and who saved me from more than a few embarrassments: Tim Chapman, Antonio Doñate, Karl Hübener, Carlos Machado, Pilar Royo, and Raquel Villagra. This book is dedicated to them and to the innumerable friends who made this impossible task possible.

Y para Helena, muy.

Montevideo, the final days of 2007

Father, paint me the earth on my body.
—Sioux chant from South Dakota

ORIGIN OF FIRE

*

In school they taught me that way back in caveman times we discovered fire by rubbing stones or sticks together.

I've been trying ever since. I never got even a tiny spark.

My personal failure has not kept me from appreciating the favors fire did for us. It defended us from the cold and from threatening beasts. It cooked our food, lit up the night, and invited us to sit, together, at its side.

ORIGIN OF BEAUTY

*

There they are, painted on the walls and ceilings of caves.

Bison, elk, bears, horses, eagles, women, men, these figures are ageless. They were born thousands upon thousands of years ago, but they are born anew every time someone looks at them.

How could our ancestor of long ago paint so delicately? How could a brute who fought wild beasts with his bare hands create images so filled with grace? How did he manage to draw those flying lines that break free of the stone and take to the air? How could he? . . .

Or was it she?

SAHARA'S GREENERY

*

In Tassili and elsewhere in the Sahara, cave paintings offer stylized images from six thousand years ago of cows, bulls, antelope, giraffes, rhinoceroses, elephants. . . .

Were those animals simply imagined? If not, did the inhabitants of the desert drink sand? And what did they eat? Stones?

Art tells us the desert was no desert. Its lakes resembled seas and its valleys provided plenty of pasture for the animals that would later have to migrate south in search of the lost verdure.

HOW COULD WE?

❧

To be mouth or mouthful, hunter or hunted. That was the question.

We deserved scorn, or at most pity. In the hostile wilderness no one respected us, no one feared us. We were the most vulnerable beasts in the animal kingdom, terrified of night and the jungle, useless as youngsters, not much better as adults, without claws or fangs or nimble feet or keen sense of smell.

Our early history is lost in mist. It seems all we ever did was break rocks and beat each other with clubs.

But one might well ask: Weren't we able to survive, when survival was all but impossible, because we learned to share our food and band together for defense? Would today's me-first, do-your-own-thing civilization have lasted more than a moment?

AGES

❧

It happens to us before birth. In our bodies as they begin to take form, something like fins appear and also a tail of sorts. These appendages don't last; they barely show their faces before they fall off.

Do these ephemeral apparitions tell us we once were fish and once were monkeys? Fish who set out to conquer dry land? Monkeys who abandoned the jungle or who were abandoned by it?

And does the fear we feel in childhood, scared of anything, of everything, tell us we once were afraid of being eaten? Does our fear of the dark and of the anguish of solitude echo that primeval vulnerability?

Now that we've grown up a little, we who were fearful strike fear. The hunted is the hunter, the mouthful is now the mouth. Monsters that yesterday harried us are today our prisoners. They inhabit our zoos, adorn our flags, and embellish our anthems.

COUSINS

❧

Ham, the conquistador of outer space, was captured in Africa.

He became the first chimpanzee to travel far beyond the world, the first chimponaut. They put him in the space capsule *Mercury*, hooked him up with more wires than a telephone switchboard, and blasted him off.

He came back safe and sound, and the record of his bodily functions demonstrated that humans too could survive a voyage into space.

Ham was on the cover of *Life*. And he spent the rest of his own caged in a zoo.

GRANDPARENTS

❧

For many peoples of black Africa, ancestors are the spirits that live in the tree beside your house or in the cow grazing in the field. The great-grandfather of your great-great-grandfather is now that stream snaking down the mountainside. Your ancestor could also be any spirit that decides to accompany you on your voyage through the world, even if he or she was never a relative or an acquaintance.

The family has no borders, explains Soboufu Somé of the Dagara people: "Our children have many mothers and many fathers. As many as they wish."

And the ancestral spirits, the ones that help you make your way, are the many grandparents that each of you has. As many as you wish.

BRIEF HISTORY OF CIVILIZATION

❧

And we tired of wandering through the forest and along the banks of rivers.

And we began settling. We invented villages and community life, turned bone into needle and thorn into spike. Tools elongated our hands, and the handle multiplied the strength of the ax, the hoe, and the knife.

We grew rice, barley, wheat, and corn, we put sheep and goats into corrals, we learned to store grain to keep from starving in bad times.

And in the fields of our labor we worshipped goddesses of fertility, women of vast hips and generous breasts. But with the passage of time they were displaced by the harsh gods of war. And we sang hymns of praise to the glory of kings, warrior chiefs, and high priests.

We discovered the words "yours" and "mine," land became owned, and women became the property of men and fathers the owners of children.

Left far behind were the times when we drifted without home or destination.

The results of civilization were surprising: our lives became more secure but less free, and we worked a lot harder.

ORIGIN OF POLLUTION

❧

The Pygmies, who have short bodies and long memories, recall the time before time, when the earth was above the sky.

From earth to sky fell a ceaseless rain of dust and garbage that fouled the home of the gods and poisoned their food.

The gods tolerated that filthy discharge for an eternity, then their patience ran out.

They sent a bolt of lightning, which split the earth in two. Through the crack they hurled the sun, the moon, and the stars on high, and by that route they too climbed up. Way up there, far from us, safe from us, the gods founded their new kingdom.

Ever since, we are the ones underneath.

ORIGIN OF SOCIAL CLASSES

❧

In the earliest of times, times of hunger, the first woman was scratching at the earth when the sun's rays penetrated her from behind. In an instant, a baby was born.

The god Pachacamac was not at all pleased with the sun's good deed, and he tore the newborn to pieces. From the dead infant sprouted the first plants. The teeth became grains of corn, the bones became yucca, the flesh became potato, yam, squash. . . .

The sun's fury was swift. His rays blasted the coast of Peru and left it forever dry. As the ultimate revenge he cracked three eggs on the soil.

From the golden egg emerged the lords.

From the silver egg, the ladies of the lords.

And from the copper egg, those who work.

SERFS AND LORDS

❧

Cacao needs no sun, for it has its own.

From its inner glow come the pleasure and euphoria of chocolate.

The gods on high had a monopoly on the thick elixir, and we humans were condemned to live in ignorance.

Quetzalcóatl stole it for the Toltecs. While the rest of the gods slept, he took a few seeds and hid them in his beard. Then he rappelled down to earth on the long thread of a spider's web and presented them to the city of Tula.

Quetzalcóatl's offering was usurped by the princes, the priests, and the warrior chiefs.

Their palates alone were deemed worthy.

As the owners of heaven forbade chocolate to mortals, so the owners of the earth forbade it to commoners.

RULERS AND RULED

*

The Bible of Jerusalem says that the people of Israel were God's chosen, the children of God.

According to the second psalm, the chosen people were given the world to rule:

> *Ask of me, and I shall give thee the heathen for thine inheritance, and the uttermost parts of the earth for thy possession.*

But the people of Israel gave Him much displeasure, ungrateful were they and sinful. And after many threats, curses, and punishments, God lost patience.

Ever since, other peoples have claimed the gift for themselves.

In the year 1900, Senator Albert Beveridge of the United States revealed: "Almighty God has marked us as His chosen people, henceforth to lead in the regeneration of the world."

ORIGIN OF THE DIVISION OF LABOR

*

They say it was King Manu who bestowed divine prestige on the castes of India.

From his mouth emerged the priests. From his arms, the kings and warriors. From his thighs, the merchants. From his feet, the serfs and craftsmen.

And on that foundation arose the social pyramid, which in India has over three thousand stories.

Everyone is born where he should be born, to do what he should do. In the cradle lies the grave, origin is destiny: our lives are just recompense or fair punishment for our past lives, and heritage dictates our place and our role.

To correct deviations, King Manu recommended: "If a person from a lower caste hears the verses of the sacred books, he shall have molten lead poured in his ears; and if he recites them, he shall have his tongue cut out." Such pedagogy is no longer fashionable, but anyone who departs from his place, in love, in labor, in whatever, still risks a public flogging that could leave him dead or more dead than alive.

The outcasts, one in five Indians, are beneath those on the bottom. They are called "Untouchables" because they contaminate: damned among the damned, they cannot speak to others, walk on their paths, or touch their glasses or plates. The law protects them, reality banishes them. Anyone can humiliate the men, anyone can rape the women, which is the only time the untouchables are touchable.

At the end of 2004, when the tsunami trampled the coasts of India, they collected the garbage and the dead.

As always.

ORIGIN OF WRITING

❧

When Iraq was not yet Iraq, it was the birthplace of the first written words.

The words look like bird tracks. Masterful hands drew them in clay with sharpened canes.

Fire annihilates and rescues, kills and gives life, as do the gods, as do we. Fire hardened the clay and preserved the words. Thanks to fire, the clay tablets still tell what they told thousands of years ago in that land of two rivers.

In our days, George W. Bush, perhaps believing that writing was invented in Texas, launched with joyful impunity a war to exterminate Iraq. There were thousands upon thousands of victims, and not all of them were flesh and blood. A great deal of memory was murdered too.

Living history in the form of numerous clay tablets were stolen or destroyed by bombs.

One of the tablets said:

> *We are dust and nothing*
> *All that we do is no more than wind.*

BORN OF CLAY

❧

The ancient Sumerians believed the entire world was a land between two rivers and between two heavens.

In heaven above lived the gods who ruled.

In heaven below the gods who worked.

And thus it was, until the gods below wearied of working all the time and staged the first strike in history.

Panic ensued.

To keep from dying of hunger, the gods above modeled women and men out of clay and put them to work.

These women and men were born on the banks of the Tigris and Euphrates rivers.

From that clay, too, were made the books that tell their story.

The books say that to die is "to return to the clay."

ORIGIN OF THE DAYS

❧

When Iraq was Sumeria, time had weeks, weeks had days, and days had names.

The priests drew the first celestial maps and baptized the heavenly bodies, the constellations, and the days.

We have inherited those names, passed on from tongue to tongue, from Sumerian to Babylonian, from Babylonian to Greek, from Greek to Latin, and so on.

They named the seven stars that move across the sky for their gods. And thousands of years later we invoke those same gods for the seven days that move across time. With slight variations, the days of the week still answer to their original names: Saturn, Sun, Moon, Mars, Mercury, Jupiter, Venus. *Saturday, Sunday, Monday* . . .

ORIGIN OF THE TAVERN

❧

When Iraq was Babylonia, female hands ran the table:

> *May beer never be lacking,*
> *the house be rich in soups,*
> *and bread abound.*

In the palaces and the temples, the chef was male. Not so at home. Women made the many beers, sweet, fine, white, golden, dark, aged, as well as the soups and the breads. Any leftovers were offered to the neighbors.

With the passing of time, some houses put in counters and guests became clients. The tavern was born. This tiny kingdom ruled by women, this extension of the home, became a meeting place and a haven of freedom.

Taverns hatched conspiracies and kindled forbidden loves.

More than 3,700 years ago, in the days of King Hammurabi, the gods gave the world two hundred and eighty laws.

One of those laws ordered priestesses to be burned alive if they took part in barroom plots.

RITES OF THE TABLE

❧

When Iraq was Assyria, the king offered a palace banquet in the city of Nimrod, with twenty main dishes accompanied by forty side dishes lubricated by rivers of beer and wine. According to chronicles from 3,000 years ago, the guests numbered 69,574, all of them men, nary a woman, plus the gods who also ate and drank.

From other palaces even more ancient came the first recipes written by the masters of the kitchen. Chefs had as much power and prestige as priests, and their holy formulae have survived the shipwrecks of time and war. Their recipes are precise ("the dough shall rise four fingers in the pot") or imprecise ("eyeball the salt"), but they all end by saying: "ready to eat."

Three thousand five hundred years ago, Aluzinnu the jester left us his recipes. Among them, this herald of fine dining:

"For the last day of the next to last month of the year, no nectar compares to tripe from a mule's ass stuffed with fly shit."

BRIEF HISTORY OF BEER

❦

One of the earliest proverbs, written in the language of the Sumerians, exonerates drink in case of accident:

> *Beer is good.*
> *What's bad is the road.*

As the oldest of all books tells it, King Gilgamesh's friend Enkidu was a savage brute until he discovered beer and bread.

Beer traveled to Egypt from the land we now call Iraq. Because it gave the face new eyes, the Egyptians believed it was a gift from their god Osiris. And since barley beer was the twin sister of bread, they called it "liquid bread."

In the Andes, it is the oldest of offerings: from the beginning, the earth has asked for a few drops of *chicha*, corn beer, to cheer up its days.

BRIEF HISTORY OF WINE

❦

Reasonable doubt keeps us wondering if Adam was tempted by an apple or by a grape.

But we know with certainty there has been wine in this world ever since the Stone Age, when grapes fermented on their own.

Ancient Chinese canticles prescribed wine to alleviate the pangs of sadness.

The Egyptians believed the god Horus had one eye that was sun and one that was moon. The moon-eye cried teardrops of wine, which the living drank to put themselves to sleep and the dead drank in order to awaken.

A grapevine was the emblem of Cyrus the great, king of the Persians, and wine bathed the festivals of the Greeks and the Romans.

To celebrate human love, Jesus turned six vessels of water into wine. It was his first miracle.

THE KING WHO WANTED TO LIVE FOREVER

❧

Time, our midwife, will be our executioner. Yesterday time suckled us and tomorrow it will devour us.

So it goes, and well we know it.

Or do we?

The very first book born in the world recounts the adventures of King Gilgamesh, who refused to die.

This epic, passed on by word of mouth beginning five thousand years ago, was written down by the Sumerians, the Akkadians, the Babylonians, and the Assyrians.

Gilgamesh, monarch of the banks of the Euphrates, was the son of a goddess and a man. Divine will, human destiny: from the goddess he inherited power and beauty, from the man he inherited death.

To be mortal meant nothing to him until his friend Enkidu reached his final day.

Gilgamesh and Enkidu had shared astonishing feats. Together they entered the Cedar Forest, home of the gods, and defeated the giant guardian whose bellow made the mountains tremble. And together they humiliated the Bull of Heaven who, with a single roar, opened a hole that swallowed a hundred men.

The death of Enkidu crushed Gilgamesh and terrified him. He discovered that his valiant friend was made of clay, and that he too was made of clay.

So he set off in search of eternal life. The pursuer of immortality wandered through steppes and deserts,

he crossed light and darkness,

he navigated great rivers,

he arrived in the garden of paradise,

he was served by a masked barmaid, possessor of secrets,

he reached the other side of the sea,

he discovered the ark that survived the flood,

he found the plant that gives youth to the aged,

he followed the route of the northern stars and the route of the southern stars,

he opened the door through which the sun enters, and closed the door through which the sun departs.

And he became immortal.

Until he died.

ANOTHER ADVENTURE IN IMMORTALITY

❧

Maui, founder of the Polynesian Islands, was born half man, half god, like Gilgamesh.

His divine half obliged the sun, always in a great hurry, to walk slowly across the sky. And with a fishhook he caught the islands of New Zealand, Hawaii, Tahiti, raised them one after another from the bottom of the sea, and placed them where they now lie.

But his human half sentenced him to death. Maui knew it, and his feats did not help him forget it.

In search of Hine, the goddess of death, he traveled to the underworld.

And there he found her: immense, asleep in the mist. She looked like a temple. Her raised knees formed an arch over the hidden door to her body.

To achieve immortality, he would have to go right inside death, travel all the way through her, and exit by her mouth.

At the door, a great half-open slit, Maui let fall his clothes and his weapons. Naked, in he went, and bit by bit he slithered along the path of moist and burning darkness that his progress disclosed in the depths of the goddess.

Halfway through the journey, the birds sang and she awoke and felt

Maui excavating her innards.

And she closed the passage and never let him out

BORN OF TEARS

❦

Before Egypt was Egypt, the sun created the sky and the birds that fly through it. He created the Nile and the fish that swim in it. And he painted its black banks green with the teeming life of plants and animals.

Then the sun, maker of life, sat back to contemplate his work.

The sun felt the deep breathing of the newborn world as it opened before his eyes and he heard the first voices.

Such tremendous beauty hurt.

The sun's tears fell to earth and made mud.

And from that mud came people.

NILE

❦

The Nile obeyed the Pharaoh. It was he who opened the way for the floods that year by year ensured Egypt's astonishing fertility. After death too: when the first ray of sun filtered through the grate on Pharaoh's tomb and lit up his face, everyone knew the earth would offer three harvests.

Thus it was.

Not anymore.

Of the seven arms of the delta only two remain, and of the holy cycles of fertility, which are no longer holy or cycles, all that remains are the ancient hymns of praise for the longest river:

> *Thou quenchest the thirst of the flocks.*
> *Thou drinkest the tears of all eyes.*
> *Rise up Nile, may thy voice resound!*
> *May thy voice be heard!*

STONE THAT SPEAKS

❧

When Napoleon invaded Egypt, one of his soldiers found on the banks of the Nile a great black stone entirely engraved with symbols.

They called it Rosetta.

Jean François Champollion, a student of dead languages, spent his youth going round and round that stone.

Rosetta spoke three languages. Two had been deciphered. Not the Egyptian hieroglyphs.

The writing of the creators of the pyramids remained an enigma. A scripture much commented upon: Herodotus, Strabo, Diodorus, and Horapollo all pretended to translate it, making it up as they went along, as did the Jesuit Athanasius Kircher, who published four tomes of nonsense. All of them believed hieroglyphs were a system of symbolic images, and the meanings varied according to the fantasy of each translator.

Mute symbols or deaf men? For years and years, Champollion peppered the Rosetta Stone with questions, and received only obstinate silence in response. The poor fellow was wasting away from hunger and discouragement when one day he thought of a possibility that had occurred to no one before: suppose the hieroglyphs were sounds as well as symbols? Suppose they were something like the letters of an alphabet?

That day the tombs opened and the dead kingdom spoke.

WRITING, NO

❧

Some five thousand years before Champollion, the god Thoth traveled to Thebes and offered King Thamus of Egypt the art of writing. He explained hieroglyphs and said that writing was the best remedy for poor memory and feeble knowledge.

The king refused the gift: "Memory? Knowledge? This invention will encourage forgetting. Knowledge resides in truth, not in its appearance. One cannot remember with the memory of another. Men will record, but they won't recall. They will repeat, but they will not live. They will learn of many things, but they won't understand a thing."

'WRITING, YES

❧

Ganesha is stout, thanks to his love of candy, and he has the ears and trunk of an elephant. But he writes with human hands.

He is the master of initiations, the one who helps people begin their work. Without him, nothing in India would ever get under way. In the art of writing as in everything else, the first step is what counts. Any beginning is a grand moment in life, so Ganesha teaches, and the first words of a letter or a book are as fundamental as the first bricks of a house or a temple.

OSIRIS

❧

Egyptian scripture tells us the story of the god Osiris and his sister Isis.

Osiris was murdered in one of those family quarrels that occur frequently on earth and in the heavens, then he was quartered and scattered in the depths of the Nile.

Isis, his sister and lover, dove down and collected the pieces. One by one, she joined his parts with seams of clay, and out of clay she modeled whatever was missing. When the body was complete, she lay him down on the bank of the river.

That clay, stirred and mixed by the Nile, contained grains of barley and seeds of other plants.

The sprouting body of Osiris stood up and walked.

ISIS

*

Like Osiris, Isis was privy to the mysteries of perpetual birth.

We know her image: a mother goddess breastfeeding her son Horus, as the Virgin Mary suckled Jesus much later on. But Isis was never what we might call a virgin. She began making love to Osiris when they were growing together inside their mother's womb. And she practiced the world's oldest profession for ten years in the city of Tyre.

In the thousands of years that followed, Isis traveled the world resuscitating whores, slaves, and others among the damned.

In Rome, she founded temples for the poor alongside bordellos. The temples were razed by imperial order, their priests crucified, but like stubborn mules they came back to life again and again.

And when Emperor Justinian's soldiers demolished the sanctuary of Isis on the island of Philae in the Nile, and built the very Catholic church of Saint Stephen on the ruins, Isis's pilgrims continued paying homage to their errant goddess at the Christian altar.

SAD KING

*

According to Herodotus, Pharaoh Sesostris III dominated all of Europe and Asia. He rewarded valiant peoples by bestowing on them a penis as their emblem, and humiliated cowardly ones by engraving a vulva on their stellae. As if that weren't enough, he tread on the bodies of his own children to save himself from the fire set by his brother, who kindly wished to roast him alive.

All this seems incredible, and it is. But several facts are indisputable: this pharaoh extended the network of irrigation canals and turned deserts into gardens. When he conquered Nubia he enlarged the empire beyond the second cataract of the Nile. The kingdom of Egypt had never been so vigorous or so envied.

However, the statues of Sesostris III are the only ones to show a somber face, anguished eyes, puckered lips. The other pharaohs immortalized by imperial sculptors watch us serenely from a state of celestial peace.

Eternal life was a privilege of the pharaohs. Perhaps that privilege could also be a curse.

ORIGIN OF THE HEN

❧

Pharaoh Tuthmosis was returning from Syria after completing one of the crushing campaigns that extended his power and glory from the Nile Delta to the Euphrates River.

As was the custom, the body of the vanquished king hung upside down on the prow of the flagship, and the entire fleet was filled with tributes and offerings.

Among the gifts was a female bird never before seen, fat and ugly. The giver had delivered the unpresentable present himself: "Yes, yes," he confessed, eyes on the floor. "This bird is not beautiful. It does not sing. It has a blunt beak, a silly crest, and stupid eyes. And its wings of sad feathers have forgotten how to fly."

Then he swallowed. And he added, "But it sires a child a day."

He opened a box where seven eggs lay. "Here are last week's children."

The eggs were submerged in boiling water.

The pharaoh tasted them, peeled and dressed with a pinch of salt.

The bird traveled in his chambers, lying by his side.

HATSHEPUT

❧

"Her splendor and her form were divine; she was a maiden beautiful and blooming."

Thus was the modest self-portrait of Hatsheput, the eldest daughter of Tuthmosis. When the warrior daughter of a warrior came to occupy his throne, she decided to call herself "king" and not "queen."

Queens were the women of kings, but Hatsheput was unique, the daughter of the sun, the greatest of the great.

This pharaoh with tits used a man's helmet and mantle, wore a stage-prop beard, and gave Egypt twenty years of prosperity and glory.

The little nephew she raised, who learned from her the arts of war and good government, wiped out all memory of her. He ordered the usurper of male power erased from the list of pharaohs, her name and image removed from paintings and stellae, and the statues she had erected to her own glory demolished.

But a few statues and inscriptions escaped the purge, and thanks to that oversight we now know there was once a female pharaoh disguised as a man, a mortal who did not want to die, one who announced: "My falcon rises high above the kingly banner into all eternity."

Thirty-four hundred years later, her tomb was found. Empty.

THE OTHER PYRAMID

❧

The construction of a pyramid could take more than a century. Brick by brick, day after day, thousands upon thousands of men worked to erect the immense resting place where each pharaoh would spend eternity surrounded by the treasures of his funerary array.

Egyptian society not only built pyramids, it was one.

At the base lay the landless peasant. During the flooding of the Nile he built temples, raised dikes, dug canals. And when the waters returned to their channel, he worked the lands of others.

Four thousand years ago, the scribe Dua-Khety portrayed him:

> *The farmer wears his yoke.*
> *His shoulders sag under the weight.*
> *On his neck he has a festering sore.*
> *In the morning, he waters leeks.*
> *In the evening, he waters coriander.*
> *At midday, he waters palm trees.*
> *Sometimes he sinks down and dies.*

No funerary monuments for him. Naked he lived and in death, dirt was his home. He was laid out by the roadside in the desert with the reed mat on which he had slept and the clay jug from which he had drunk.

In his fist they placed a few grains of wheat, in case he felt like eating.

GOD OF WAR

✷

Face on or in profile, one-eyed Odin inspired fear. The divinity of war's glory, father of massacres, lord of evildoers and the hanged, was the godliest god of the Vikings.

His two trusted ravens, Hugin and Munin, were his master spies. Every morning they took off from their perch on his shoulders and flew over the world. At dusk they returned to tell him all they had seen and heard.

The Valkyries, angels of death, also flew for him. They circled battlefields and chose the best soldiers from among the cadavers and recruited them for the army of ghosts Odin commanded on high.

On earth, Odin offered fabulous booty to the princes he protected, and he armed them with invisible shields and invincible swords. But when he decided he wanted them at his side in heaven he would send them to their deaths.

Though he had a fleet of a thousand ships and galloped on eight-legged horses, Odin preferred to stay put. This prophet of the wars of our times fought from afar. His magic lance, grandmother of the remote-controlled missile, flew from the sky and found its way straight to the enemy's breast.

THEATER OF WAR

Japan's Prince Yamato Takeru, born a couple of millennia ago, child number eighty of the emperor, began his career by chopping his twin brother into little pieces for being late to the family supper.

He then annihilated the rebellious peasants of the island of Kyûshû. Dressed as a woman, coiffed and made up as a woman, he seduced the leaders of the uprising and at a party his sword split them open like melons. Elsewhere he attacked other poor wretches who dared to challenge the imperial order, and by making hamburger of them he pacified the enemy, as was said then, as is said now.

His most famous exploit put an end to the infamous renown of a bandit who wreaked havoc in the province of Izumo. Prince Yamato offered him pardon and peace, and the troublemaker responded with an invitation to ride with him through his domain. Yamato brought along a wooden sword in a luxurious scabbard, a sheathed sham. At noon, the prince and the bandit cooled off in a river. While the other swam, Yamato switched swords. He slipped the wooden one in the bandit's scabbard, keeping the bandit's metal blade for himself.

At dusk, he challenged him.

ART OF WAR

Twenty-five centuries ago, General Sun Tzu of China wrote the first treatise on military tactics and strategy. His sage advice is still heeded today not just on battlefields but in business, where blood tends to flow more freely.

> *If you are able, appear unable.*
> *If you are strong, appear weak.*
> *When you are near, appear distant.*

Never attack when the enemy is powerful.
Always avoid battles you cannot win.
If you are weaker, retreat.
If your enemies are united, divide them.
Advance when they are unprepared
and attack where they least expect it.
To know your enemy, know yourself.

HORROR OF WAR

❦

On the back of a blue ox rode Lao Tse.

He was traveling the paths of contradiction, which led to the secret place where water and fire fuse.

In contradiction all meets nil, life meets death, near meets far, before meets after.

Lao Tse, village philosopher, believed that the richer a nation is, the poorer it becomes. He believed that knowing war teaches peace, because suffering inhabits glory:

Every action provokes reactions.
Violence always returns.
Only thistles and thorns grow where armies encamp.
War summons hunger.
He who delights in conquest, delights in human pain.
Every victory should be celebrated with a funeral.

YELLOW

❦

The most fearful river in China is called Yellow, thanks either to a dragon's recklessness or to human folly.

Before China was China, the dragon Kau Fu tried to cross the sky mounted on one of the ten suns.

By noon he could no longer bear the heat.

Set ablaze by the sun, crazed by thirst, the dragon dropped into the first river he saw. From the heights he plummeted to the depths and drank the water down to the last drop, leaving nothing but a long bed of yellow clay where the river had been.

Some say this version is not scientific. They say it is a historical fact that the Yellow River has been called as such for about two thousand years, since the forests on its banks were felled and could no longer afford protection from avalanches of snow, mud, and garbage. Then the river, formerly jade green, lost its color and gained its name. With the passing of time, things got worse until the river became one huge sewer. In 1980, four hundred river dolphins lived there. In 2004, only one was left. It didn't last long.

YI AND THE DROUGHT

❦

All ten suns had gone haywire and were spinning about the sky.

The gods summoned Yi, the unbeatable bowman, master of masters in the art of the arrow.

"The earth is roasting," they told him. "People are dying, and animals and plants are dying too."

As night came to an end, Yi the archer lay in wait. At dawn he let fly.

One after another the suns were snuffed out.

Only the sun that now lights our days survived.

The gods mourned the deaths of their glowing sons. And though the gods themselves had called on Yi, they expelled him from heaven.

"If you love the earthlings so, go live with them."

Forced into exile, Yi became mortal.

YU AND THE FLOOD

❧

After drought came flood.

The rocks groaned, the trees howled. The Yellow River, nameless still, swallowed people and crops, drowned valleys and mountains.

Yu, the lame god, came to rescue the world.

Hobbling along, Yu ventured into the flood and with his shovel opened canals and tunnels to drain the furious waters.

Yu was assisted by a fish that knew the river's secrets, by a dragon that went first and deflected the current with his tail, and by a tortoise that went last and carried away all the mud.

ORIGIN OF THE CHINESE BOOK

❧

Cang Jie had four eyes.

He earned his living reading stars and telling fortunes.

After much study of the design of constellations, the profile of mountains, and the plumage of birds, he created the symbols that spell words.

In one of the oldest of books, made of bamboo tablets, the ideograms invented by Cang Jie tell the story of a kingdom where men lived longer than eight centuries and women were the color of light because they ate sunshine.

The Lord of Fire, who ate stones, challenged royal authority and sent his troops to march on the throne. His magic powers wrapped the palace in a dense curtain of fog, leaving the king's guard dumbstruck. Soldiers teetered in the darkness, blind, aimless, when the Black Woman with bird feathers flew down from the heights, invented the compass, and presented it to the desperate king.

The fog was defeated, and the enemy too.

FAMILY PORTRAIT IN CHINA

❦

In ancient times, Shun, Lord Hibiscus, reigned over China. Hou Ji, Lord Millet, was his minister of agriculture.

The two had faced a number of difficulties in childhood.

Right from birth, Shun's father and his older brother detested him. They set fire to the house when he was a baby, but he was not even singed. So they put him in a hole in the ground and threw in enough dirt to bury him completely, but he was not bothered in the least.

His minister, Hou Ji, also managed to survive his family's tenderness. His mother, convinced that the newborn would give her bad luck, abandoned him in the countryside, hoping that hunger would kill him. And when it did not, she ditched him in the woods for the tigers to eat. When the tigers paid no heed, she tossed him into a snowdrift so the cold would put an end to him. A few days later she found him in good humor and slightly overheated.

SILK THAT WAS SPITTLE

❦

Queen Lei Zu, wife of Huang Di, founded the Chinese art of silk making.

As memory's storytellers would have it, Lei Zu reared the first worm. She gave it white mulberry leaves to eat, and soon threads of the worm's spittle were weaving a cocoon around its body. Bit by tiny bit, Lei Zu's delicate fingers unraveled that mile-long thread. Thus the cocoon that was to become a butterfly became silk instead.

And silk became transparent gauze, muslin, tulle, and taffeta. It dressed ladies and lords in plush velvets and sumptuous brocades embroidered with pearls.

Outside the kingdom, silk was a forbidden luxury. Its trade routes passed over snow-capped mountains, fiery deserts, and seas populated by mermaids and pirates.

FLIGHT OF THE CHINESE WORM

Much later on, scores of fearsome enemies no longer lay in wait along the silk routes. Yet those who attempted to take mulberry seeds or the eggs of the thread-making worm out of China still lost their heads.

In the year 420, Xuan Zang, the king of Yutian, asked for the hand of a Chinese princess. He had spied her just once, but from then on he saw her wherever he looked.

The princess, Lu Shi was her name, was given to him.

An ambassador traveled on the king's behalf to retrieve her.

There was an exchange of gifts and interminable banquets and ceremonies.

At one point, when they could be alone, the ambassador warned the princess of the worries that beset the husband who awaited her. Yutian had always used jade to pay for China's silk, but little jade remained in the kingdom.

Lu Shi said nothing, and nothing was revealed by her full-moon face.

And they set off. The caravan accompanying her, thousands of camels, thousands of tinkling bells, crossed the vast desert and reached the border at Yumenguan Pass.

The inspection lasted several days. Not even the princess herself was spared a search.

At last, the nuptial cortege arrived at its destination.

Lu Shi had traveled without saying a word, without so much as a gesture.

She ordered them all to stop at a monastery. There she was bathed and perfumed. To the strains of music she ate, and in silence she slept.

When her king arrived, Lu Shi gave him the mulberry seeds she had hidden in her medicine chest. She then introduced him to three maids from among her servants, who were neither maids nor servants, but experts in the arts of silk making. Then she removed from her head the great headdress made of cinnamon-tree leaves, and parted her long black hair. There lay the eggs of the silkworm.

From China's point of view, Lu Shi was a traitor to her country of birth.

From Yutian's point of view, she was a heroine of the country she ruled.

THE EMPEROR WHO DEDICATED HIS LIFE TO BUILDING HIS DEATH

❧

China comes from Chin, Chin Shi Huang, its first emperor.

Through blood and fire, he transformed a collection of warring fiefdoms into a nation. He imposed a common language and a common system of weights and measures, and he created a single currency of bronze coins with a hole in the center. To protect his domain he raised the Great Wall, an endless crest of stone that crossed the map and is still, twenty-two hundred years later, the most visited defensive barricade in the world.

But he never lost sleep over such minutiae. The project of his life was his death: his sepulchre, his palace for the afterlife.

Construction began the day he first sat on the throne at the age of thirteen, and year by year the mausoleum grew until it was larger than a city. The army that was to guard it also grew, to more than seven thousand horsemen and infantrymen, their uniforms the color of blood and their armor black. Those clay warriors, modeled by the very best sculptors, were born exempt from aging and incapable of treason. Today, they astonish the world.

The funerary monument was the task of prisoners, who were worked to death and thrown to the desert. The emperor directed even the smallest details and he urged them to work faster and faster. Several times his enemies had tried to kill him. He traveled in disguise and every night he slept in a different house. He was terrified of dying without the great grave he deserved.

The day arrived when the colossal undertaking was finished. The army was complete, the gigantic mausoleum too, and it was a masterpiece. Any change would have insulted its perfection.

Then, when the emperor was about to complete half a century of living, death came for him and he let himself go.

The great theater was ready, the curtain rose, the performance was about to begin. He could not possibly fail to show up. It was an opera composed for solo voice.

FOOT MURDERERS

❧

A couple of centuries ago, Li Ju-chen invented an upside-down China. His novel, *The Flowers in the Mirror,* took place in a country of women, where women ruled.

In the story, she was he, and he, she. The men, sentenced to pleasing women, were obliged to perform a great variety of services. Among other humiliations, they had to accept having their feet atrophied.

No one took seriously that flight of fancy. And things continued as before, with men binding female feet until they turned into something like the hooves of goats.

For over a thousand years, until well into the twentieth century, the canons of beauty would not allow a girl's foot to grow. The first version of Cinderella, written in ninth-century China, gave literary form to the male fetish for the diminutive female foot, and at the same time, give or take a year, the custom of binding daughters' feet from infancy took root.

It was about more than aesthetic ideals. Bound feet also bind: they were shields of virtue. By preventing women from walking freely, they foiled any indecent escapades that might have put the family honor at risk.

WORD SMUGGLERS

❧

Yang Huanyi, whose feet were crippled in infancy, stumbled through life until the autumn of the year 2004, when she died just shy of her hundredth birthday.

She was the last to know Nushu, the secret language of Chinese women.

This female code dated from ancient times. Barred from male

language, which they could not write, women founded a clandestine one, out of men's reach. Fated to be illiterate, they invented an alphabet of symbols that masqueraded as decorations and was indecipherable to the eyes of their masters.

Women sketched their words on garments and fans. The hands that embroidered were not free. The symbols were.

MALE PANIC

In the most ancient of nights, they lay together for the very first time, woman and man. Then he heard a threatening rumble in her body, a gnashing of teeth between her legs, and fear cut short their embrace. Anywhere in the world, even the most macho of machos still trembles when he recalls, without knowing what he recalls, that fear of being devoured. And he wonders, without knowing what he wonders, could woman be an entrance with no exit? Could it be that he who enters her, in her will remain?

A DANGEROUS WEAPON

In more than thirty countries, tradition insists the clitoris be severed.

That slash confirms the husband's right of property over his woman or his women.

The mutilators call this crime against female pleasure "purification," and they explain that the clitoris

is a poison dart
is a scorpion's tail
is a termites' nest
kills men or makes them ill
excites women
poisons their milk
and makes them insatiable
and crazy as can be.

To justify mutilation, they cite the Prophet Mohammed, who never spoke of this matter, and the Koran, which does not mention it either.

NINE MOONS

❧

Gútapa spent his life drowsing in a hammock, while his wife, who had not even a name, scratched his head, waved away mosquitoes, and fed him with a spoon. Once in a while, he would get up and give her a good beating, to keep her in line and himself in shape.

When the woman fled, Gútapa went looking for her in the deep gorges of the Amazon, pounding a club on every possible hiding place. With all his heart and soul, he struck a mighty blow in one spot, unaware that therein lay a wasps' nest.

The wasps, a furious whirlwind, stung him a thousand times on the knee.

The knee swelled up and kept on swelling, moon after moon, until it was the size of a huge balloon. Inside, many tiny men and women began to take form and move about, weaving baskets, stringing necklaces, and carving arrows and blowguns.

Under the ninth moon, Gútapa gave birth. From his knee were born the first Tikunas, welcomed with great huzzahs by the blue-winged, red-lored, and grape-eating parrots, and other commentators.

VICTORIOUS SUN, MOON VANQUISHED

❧

The moon lost her first battle against the sun when he spread word that it wasn't the wind who was impregnating women.

Then history brought more sad news:

the division of labor assigned nearly all tasks to the females so that we males could dedicate ourselves to mutual extermination,

the right to property and the right to inheritance allowed women to be owners of nothing, the organization of the family enclosed them in the cage of father, husband, and son,

and along came the state, which was like the family, only bigger.

The moon shared in her daughters' downfall.

Left far behind were the times when the Egyptian moon would devour the sun at dusk and sire him at dawn,

when the Irish moon kept the sun in line by threatening him with perpetual night,

and when the kings of Greece and Crete would dress up as queens with taffeta tits, and in sacred ceremonies unfurl the moon as their standard.

In the Yucatan, moon and sun lived in matrimony. When they fought, it caused an eclipse. The moon was lady of the seas and the springs, and goddess of the earth. With the passing of time, she lost her powers. Now she only reigns over births and illnesses.

On the coasts of Peru, we can date her humiliation. Shortly before the Spanish invasion, in the year 1463, the moon of the Chimú kingdom, the most powerful of moons, surrendered to the army of the Incan sun.

MEXICANS

❦

Tlazoltéotl, Mexico's moon, goddess of the Huasteca night, managed to elbow her way into the macho pantheon of the Aztecs.

She was the most mothering of mothers, who protected women in labor and their midwives, and guided seeds on their voyage to becoming plants. Goddess of love and also of garbage, condemned to eat shit, she embodied fertility and lust.

Like Eve, like Pandora, Tlazoltéotl bore the guilt for men's perdition. Women born in her times lived condemned to seek pleasure.

And when the earth trembled, in soft vibrations or devastating earthquakes, no one doubted: "It is she."

EGYPTIANS

*

Herodotus the Greek proved that the river and the sky of Egypt were unlike any other river or any other sky, and the same was true of its customs. Funny people, the Egyptians: they kneaded dough with their feet, and clay with their hands, and they mummified their dead cats and kept them in sacred chests.

But most remarkable was the place women held among men. Whether nobles or plebeians, they married freely without surrendering their names or their possessions. Education, property, work, and inheritance were theirs by right, not only for men, and women were the ones who shopped in the market while men stayed home weaving. According to Herodotus, who was not entirely trustworthy, women peed standing up and men on their knees.

HEBREWS

*

According to the Old Testament, the daughters of Eve were to suffer divine punishment forever.

Stoning could be the fate of adulteresses and witches and brides who were not virgins,

to the stake marched the daughters of priests who became prostitutes,

and off with the hand of any woman who grabbed a man by the balls, even in self-defense or in defense of her husband.

For forty days a woman giving birth to a son remained impure. Eighty days of filth if the child was a girl. Impure was the menstruating woman for seven days and nights, and her impurity infected all who touched her or touched the chair on which she sat or the bed in which she slept.

HINDUS

❧

Mitra, mother of the sun and the water and of all sources of life, was a goddess from birth. When she arrived in India from Babylonia or Persia, the goddess had to become a god.

A number of years have passed since Mitra's arrival, and women are still not very welcome in India. There are fewer women than men, in some regions eight for every ten. Many are those who never arrive because they die in their mothers' wombs, and countless more are smothered at birth.

Prevention is the best medicine, since women can be very dangerous. As a sacred text of the Hindu tradition warns: "A lascivious woman is poison, serpent, and death, all in one."

Others are virtuous, though proper habits are being lost. Tradition orders widows to throw themselves into the fire where the dead husband's body burns, but today few if any are willing to obey that command.

For centuries or millennia they were willing, and they were many. In contrast, there is no instance ever in the whole history of India of a husband leaping into the pyre of his deceased wife.

CHINESE

❧

About a thousand years ago, Chinese goddesses stopped being goddesses.

Male power, which by then had taken over the earth, was also aligning the heavens. The goddess Xi He was split in two and the goddess Nu Gua was relegated to the status of mere woman.

Xi He had been mother of the suns and the moons. She gave comfort and succor to her sons and daughters at the end of their exhausting voyages through day and night. When she was divided into Xi and He, each of them a he-god, she was no longer a she and she disappeared.

Nu Gua did not disappear but she was reduced to a mortal.

In other times she had been the founder of all that lives:

she had cut off the legs of the great cosmic tortoise to give the world and the sky columns to rest on,

she had saved the world from disasters of fire and water,

she had invented love, lying with her brother behind a tall screen of grasses,

and she had created nobles and plebeians by modeling the higher ones of yellow clay and the lower ones of mud from the river.

ROMANS

❧

Cicero explained that women ought to be ruled by male guardians "due to the weakness of their intellect."

Roman women went from one pair of male hands to another. The father who married off his daughter could cede her to her husband as property or tender her to him as a loan. In either case, what counted was the dowry, the patrimony, the inheritance. For pleasure there were slave women.

Like Aristotle, Roman physicians believed that women, all of them, patricians, plebeians, or slaves, had fewer teeth and smaller brains than men, and that on the days they menstruated, their mirrors darkened with a reddish tinge.

Pliny the Elder, the empire's greatest scientific authority, demonstrated that a menstruating woman soured new wine, sterilized crops, caused seeds and fruits to wither, killed grafted plants and swarms of bees, tarnished bronze, and made dogs go crazy.

GREEKS

❧

A headache may give birth to a goddess. Athena sprouted from the throbbing head of her father, Zeus, whose temples split open to deliver her. She was born without a mother.

Some time later she cast the deciding vote when a tribunal of the gods on Olympus had to judge a difficult case: to avenge their father, Electra and her brother Orestes had chopped off their mother's head with an ax.

The Furies prosecuted. They demanded the murderers be stoned to death because the life of a queen is sacred, and killing one's mother cannot be forgiven.

Apollo took up the defense. He maintained that the accused were children of an unworthy mother and that maternity did not matter in the least. A mother, argued Apollo, is nothing more than an inert furrow where the man throws his seed.

Of the thirteen gods of the jury, six voted to condemn and six to absolve.

Athena would break the tie. She voted against the mother she never had and gave eternal life to the power of men in Athens.

AMAZONS

❧

The Amazons, fearsome women, fought against Hercules when he was Heracles, and against Achilles in the Trojan War. They hated men and cut off their right breasts so their arrows would fly true.

The great river that cuts across the body of America from one side to the other is called Amazon, thanks to Spanish conquistador Francisco de Orellana.

He was the first European to navigate its length, from the inner depths of the land to the outer reaches of the sea. He returned to Spain minus an eye and said women warriors, who fought in the nude and roared like wild beasts, had riddled his brigantines with arrows. When they hungered for love, they kidnapped men, kissed them all night long, and strangled them at dawn.

And to burnish his story with the luster of the Greeks, Orellana said they were the very Amazons who worshipped the goddess Diana, and with their name he baptized the river where they reigned.

Centuries have passed. The Amazons were never heard from again. But the river still bears their name, and though poisoned daily by pesticides, chemical fertilizers, mercury from mines, and oil from ships, its waters are still the richest in the world in fish, birds, and stories.

'WHEN THE LIVER
WAS THE HOME OF THE SOUL

❧

In earlier times, long before cardiologists and balladeers, matters of the heart could well have been called matters of the liver.

The liver lay at the heart of everything.

The Chinese believed the liver was where the soul slept and dreamt.

In Egypt, its custody was in the hands of Amset, son of the god Horus, and in Rome none less than Jupiter, father of the gods, cared for it.

The Etruscans read the future in the livers of the animals they sacrificed.

In Greek tradition, Prometheus stole fire from the gods for us mortals. Then Zeus, top dog on Mount Olympus, punished him by chaining him to a rock where every day a vulture devoured his liver. Not his heart, his liver. Every day Prometheus's liver grew back and that was proof of his immortality.

ORIGIN OF MISOGYNY

❧

As if such torment were not enough, Zeus also punished Prometheus's betrayal by creating the first woman. And he sent us the present.

According to the poets of Olympus, her name was Pandora. She was lovely and curious and rather harebrained.

Pandora arrived on earth holding in her arms a large box. Inside the box, captive, were the sorrows. Zeus forbade her to open it, but barely had she arrived among us than she succumbed to temptation and took off the lid.

Out flew the woes and stung us. Thus came death to the world, as did old age, illness, war, work . . .

According to the priests of the Bible, a woman named Eve, created by another god on another cloud, also brought us nothing but calamities.

HERACLES

❧

Zeus was quite the punisher. For behaving badly, he sold his son Heracles into slavery.

Heracles, who in Rome would be called Hercules, was bought by Omphale, queen of Lydia, and in her service he destroyed a giant serpent, not a tall order for one who had been chopping up snakes since he was a baby. And he captured the twins who turned into flies at night and robbed people of their sleep.

Queen Omphale was unimpressed by such feats. She wanted a lover, not a bodyguard.

They almost always stayed indoors. The few times they emerged, he wore a pearl necklace, gold bracelets, and brightly colored underwear that did not last because his muscles burst the seams. And she wore the skin of the lion he had strangled with his bare hands in Nemea.

Word went around the kingdom that when he misbehaved she slapped him on the ass with her sandal. And that in his free time Heracles lay at his owner's feet and busied himself sewing and weaving, while the women of the court fanned him, groomed him, perfumed him, spoon-fed him, and served him wine by the sip.

The vacation lasted three years, until Zeus the father ordered Heracles back to work to finish the twelve labors of the strongest man in the world.

ORIGIN OF THE
WORLD TRADE ORGANIZATION

❧

They needed a god of trade. From his throne on Olympus, Zeus surveyed his family. He did not have to ponder long. Hermes was the god for the job.

Zeus gave him sandals with little gold wings and put him in charge of promoting the exchange of goods, the signing of treaties, and the safeguarding of free trade.

Hermes, who would become Mercury in Rome, was chosen because he was the best liar.

ORIGIN OF THE POSTAL SERVICE

❧

Two thousand five hundred years ago, horses and cries carried messages to far-off lands.

Cyrus the Great, son of the house of Achaemenes, prince of Anzan, king of Persia, organized a postal system in which the Persian cavalry's best horsemen rode relay night and day.

The express service, the most expensive, worked by shouts. From voice to voice, words crossed the mountains.

ECHO

❧

In earlier times, the nymph Echo knew how to speak. And she spoke with such grace that her words seemed always new, never before spoken by any mouth.

But the goddess Hera, Zeus's legal spouse, cursed her during one of her frequent fits of jealousy. And Echo suffered the worst of all punishments: she was deprived of her own voice.

Ever since, unable to speak, she can only repeat.

Nowadays, that curse is looked on as a virtue.

THALES

§

Two thousand six hundred years ago in the city of Miletus, an absentminded genius named Thales liked to go for a stroll at night to gaze at the stars, and as a result he frequently fell into the ditch.

Perhaps by asking the stars, Thales discovered that death is not an end but a transformation, and that water is the origin and meaning of all life. Not gods, water. Earthquakes happen because the sea moves and disturbs the land, not because of Poseidon's tantrums. The eye sees not by divine grace, but by reflecting reality the way the river reflects the bushes on its banks. And eclipses occur, not because the sun hides from the wrath of Olympus, but because the moon covers the sun.

Thales, who had learned to think in Egypt, accurately predicted eclipses, measured with precision the distance to approaching ships on the high seas, and calculated the exact height of the Keops Pyramid by the shadow that it cast. One of the most famous theorems is attributed to him, as well as four more, and it is even said that he discovered electricity.

But perhaps his greatest feat was of a different kind: to live godless, naked of any religious comfort, never giving an inch.

ORIGIN OF MUSIC

§

When Orpheus caressed the strings of the lyre, the oak trees in the woods of Thrace danced by virtue of his melodies.

When Orpheus embarked with the Argonauts, the rocks heard his music, a language where all languages meet, and their vessel was saved from shipwreck.

When the sun rose, Orpheus's lyre greeted it from the peak of Mount Pangaeum and the two chatted as equals, light to light, because his music also set the air on fire.

Zeus sent a bolt of lightning to punish the author of such audacities.

DIVINE MONOPOLY

❧

The gods will not abide competition from vulgar and common earthlings.

We owe them humility and obedience. We were made by them, they claim; heavenly censors quashed the rumor that they were made by us.

When the Mayan gods realized we could see beyond the horizon, they threw dust in our eyes. And the Greek gods blinded Phineus, king of Salmydessus, when they learned he could see beyond time.

Lucifer was the favorite archangel of the god of the Jews, the Christians, and the Muslims. When he tried to raise his throne higher than the stars, that god turned him to ash, consuming him in the fire of his own beauty.

The same god banished Adam and Eve, the first people, the ones with no belly buttons, because they wanted to know divine glory. And he punished the builders of the Tower of Babel for committing the insolence of trying to reach up to heaven.

THANKS FOR THE PUNISHMENT

❧

The tower that symbolized the sin of human arrogance rose in Babylon, the cursed city known in the Bible as "harlot and mother of harlots."

Heaven's wrath did not delay: God condemned Babylonians to speak in many tongues so no one would ever understand them, and the tower was left half-finished for all time.

According to the ancient Hebrews, the flowering of human languages was divine punishment.

Perhaps, but in his desire for rebuke, God saved us from the boredom of a single tongue.

ORIGIN OF LANGUAGES

*

According to the ancient Mexicans, the story was different.

They told of the mountain Chicomóztoc, which stood where the sea split in two, and had seven caves in its bowels.

In each of the seven caves reigned a god.

Each of the first peoples of Mexico were modeled from the dirt of one of the seven caves, kneaded with blood from that cave's god.

Little by little, these peoples sprouted from the mountainside.

Each still speaks the language of the god of its cave.

That is why languages are sacred, and diverse are the melodies of speech.

ALL THE RAINS

*

The god of the Hebrews was displeased by the behavior of his children. As retribution, a flood engulfed all human flesh and the beasts of the field and the birds of the sky.

Noah, the only just man, had the privilege of building an ark of wood three stories high to save his family and a male-female couple from each of the species that populated the world.

The great flood drowned the rest.

Those expelled from the ark also merited death: abnormal couples like the horse and the mule, or the bitch in love with the wolf, and the males who ignored nature's hierarchy and were dominated by females.

RELIGIOUS ORIGIN OF RACISM

*

Noah got drunk celebrating the ark's arrival at Mount Ararat.

When he came to, he was incomplete. According to one of the many versions of the Bible, his son Ham had castrated him as he slept. In that version God then cursed Ham and his sons, and the sons of his sons, condemning them to slavery for centuries upon centuries.

But none of the many versions of the Bible say Ham was black. Africa did not sell slaves when the Bible was written, and Ham's skin did not begin to darken until much later on, perhaps in the eleventh or twelfth century, after the Arabs launched the slave trade in the southern part of the desert. By the sixteenth or seventeenth centuries, once slavery had become the biggest business of Europe, Ham was utterly black.

The slave trade enjoyed divine sanction and eternal life from that point forward. Reason in the service of religion, religion in the service of oppression: since the slaves were black, Ham must have been black. And his children, also black, were born to be slaves because God is never wrong.

And Ham and his sons, and the sons of his sons, would have kinky hair, bloodshot eyes, and swollen lips. They would go about nude, exposing their scandalous penises. They would have a taste for theft, would hate their owners, would never tell the truth. And they would dedicate the time they should be sleeping to nasty things.

SCIENTIFIC ORIGIN OF RACISM

❦

"Caucasian race" is the name of the white minority that sits at the summit of humanity's hierarchy.

The christening occurred in 1775 at the hands of Johann Friedrich Blumenbach.

The zoologist believed the Caucasus was the cradle of human civilization and that all intelligence and beauty originated there. Against all evidence, the term remains in use to this day.

Blumenbach collected two hundred and forty-five skulls, which provided the justification for the European right to humiliate all others.

He saw humanity as a five-story pyramid.

On top, the whites.

Over the next three floors, the races of dirty skin marred original purity: Australian Aborigines, American Indians, yellow Asians. Underneath them all, deformed without and within, were the blacks of Africa.

Big-S Science has always put black people in the basement.

In 1863, the Anthropological Society of London concluded that blacks were intellectually inferior to whites, and only Europeans had the ability to "humanize and civilize" them. Europe dedicated its best energies to this noble mission but did not succeed. Nearly a century and a half later, in 2007, an American, James Watson, winner of the Nobel Prize in medicine, confirmed that blacks were still less intelligent.

THE LOVE OF LOVES

❦

King Solomon sang to the most womanly of his women. He sang to her body and to the door to her body and to the lushness of the shared bed.

The Song of Songs is not the least like the other books of the Bible of Jerusalem. Why is it there?

According to the rabbis, it is an allegory of God's love for Israel. According to the priests, a jubilant homage to Christ's marriage to the Church. But not a single verse mentions God, much less Christ or the Church, which emerged long after the Song was sung.

It seems more likely that this encounter between a Jewish king and a black woman was a celebration of human passion and of the diversity of our colors.

"Better than wine are the kisses of your lips," the woman sang.

And in the version that has lasted to our days, she also sang:

"I am black, but I am beautiful,"

and she excused herself, attributing her color to her work in the sun, in the vineyards.

Other versions, however, insist the "but" was snuck in. She sang:

"I am black, and I am beautiful."

ALEXANDER

❧

Demosthenes mocked him:

"This boy wants altars. Well, that much we'll give him."

The boy was Alexander the Great. He claimed descent from Heracles and Achilles. He liked to call himself "the invincible god." By then he had been wounded eight times and was still conquering the world.

He began by crowning himself king of Macedonia, after killing all his relatives. Anxious to become king of everything else, he lived the few years of his brief life continuously at war.

His black horse outpaced the wind. He was always first to attack, sword in hand, plume of white feathers on his head, as if each battle were a personal matter:

"I will not steal a victory," he said.

How well he recalled the lesson of his teacher Aristotle:

"Humanity is divided into those born to rule and those born to obey."

With an iron hand, he snuffed out rebellions and crucified or stoned the disobedient, but he was an unusual conqueror who respected those he conquered and was even willing to learn their customs. The king of kings invaded lands and seas from the Balkans to India by way of Persia and Egypt and everywhere in between, and wherever he went he sowed matrimony. His astute idea of marrying Greek soldiers to local women was unpleasant news for Athens, which heartily disapproved, but it consolidated Alexander's prestige and power across his new map of the world.

Hephaestion always accompanied him in his warrings and wanderings. He was his right-hand man on the battlefield and his nighttime lover in victory. With thousands of invincible horsemen, long lances, flaming arrows, and Hephaestion by his side, Alexander founded seven cities, the seven Alexandrias, and it seemed as if he might go on forever.

When Hephaestion died, Alexander drank alone the wine they had shared. At dawn, thoroughly drunk, he ordered up a bonfire so immense it scorched the heavens, and he outlawed music throughout the empire.

Soon thereafter he too died, at the age of thirty-three, without having conquered all the kingdoms the world possessed.

HOMER

❧

There was nothing, no one. Not even ghosts. Nothing but mute stones, and a sheep or two looking for grass amidst the ruins.

But the blind poet could see the great city that was no more. He saw it surrounded by walls, high on a hill overlooking the bay. And he heard the shrieks and thunder of the war that leveled it.

And he sang to it. It was the second founding of Troy, born anew by Homer's words four and a half centuries after its destruction. And the Trojan War, consigned to oblivion, became the most famous war of all.

Historians say it was a trade war. The Trojans controlled the entrance to the Black Sea and were charging dear. The Greeks annihilated Troy to open up the route to the Orient via the Dardanelles. But all the wars ever fought, or nearly all, have been trade wars. Why did this war, so like the others, become worthy of remembering? The stones of Troy were turning to sand and nothing but sand as fated by nature, when Homer saw them and heard them speak.

Did he simply imagine what he sang?

Was it just fancy, that squadron of twelve hundred ships launched to rescue Helen, the queen born from a swan's egg?

Did Homer make up the bit about Achilles dragging the vanquished Hector behind a chariot as he drove several times around the walls of the besieged city?

And the story of Aphrodite wrapping Paris in a mantle of magic mist when she saw he was losing, could that have been delirium or drunkenness?

And Apollo guiding the fatal arrow to Achilles's heel?

Was it Odysseus, alias Ulysses, who built the immense wooden horse that fooled the Trojans?

What truth is there in the end of Agamemnon, the victor who returned from ten years of war to be murdered by his wife in the bath?

Those women and those men, and those goddesses and those gods who are so like us, jealous, vengeful, treasonous, did they exist?

Who knows if they existed?

All that's certain is that they exist.

LITERARY ORIGIN OF THE DOG

❧

Argos was the name of a hundred-eyed giant and of a Greek city four thousand years ago.

Also named Argos was the only one to recognize Odysseus when he returned to Ithaca in disguise.

Homer tells us that after plenty of war and plenty of sea Odysseus came back home dressed as a decrepit, bedraggled beggar.

No one realized it was he.

No one, except for a friend who could no longer bark or walk or even get up. Argos lay in the doorway of a shed, abandoned, tormented by ticks, awaiting death.

When he saw or perhaps smelled the beggar approach, he raised his head and wagged his tail.

HESIOD

❧

Of Homer, nothing is known. Seven cities swear they were his birthplace. In each, perhaps, Homer recited one night in exchange for a roof and a meal.

Of Hesiod, it is said he was born in a village named Asera and that he lived in Homer's time.

But he did not sing to the glory of warriors. His heroes were the peasants of Boeotia. He took up the lives and labors of men who wrested meager harvests from the hard earth, fulfilling the curse of merciless gods.

His poetry counseled chopping wood when Sirius first appears,
picking grapes when Sirius moves south,
threshing when Orion rises,

harvesting when the Pleiades appear,
plowing when the Pleiades disappear,
working in the nude,
and never trusting the sea, thieves, women, restless tongues, or evil
days.

THE SUICIDE OF TROY

❧

According to Homer, it was the goddess Athena who whispered the
idea in Odysseus's ear. And the city of Troy, for ten years impervious
to the Greek siege, was defeated by a horse made of wood.

Why did Priam, the Trojan king, let it in? As soon as that strange,
enormous figure showed up outside the walls, smoke from the kitchens
turned red and statues wept, laurels withered and the sky emptied of
stars. Princess Cassandra threw a lit torch at the horse and the priest
Laocoön stuck a lance in its flank. The king's advisers counseled
opening it to see what it might contain, and in all Troy there was no
one who did not suspect the beast was some sort of trick.

Priam chose his downfall. He wanted to believe the goddess Athena
had sent him an offering as a sign of peace. Not to offend her, he
ordered the gates thrown open, and the horse was received with
chants of praise and gratitude.

From its innards emerged the soldiers who razed Troy to its final
stone. And the vanquished became their slaves, and the women of the
vanquished became their women.

THE HERO

❧

How would the Trojan War have been told by an unknown soldier?
A Greek foot soldier, ignored by the gods and desired only by the
vultures that circled the battlefields? A farmer-fighter, hymned by no
one, sculpted by no one? A nobody, an everybody, obliged to kill and
without the slightest interest in being killed to win Helen's eyes?

Would that soldier have predicted what Euripides later confirmed? That Helen never was in Troy, only her shadow? That ten years of butchery occurred for the sake of an empty tunic?

And if that soldier survived, what would he recall?

Who knows.

Maybe the smell. The smell of pain, and only that.

Three thousand years after the fall of Troy, war correspondents Robert Fisk and Fran Sevilla tell us that wars stink. They have been in several, on the inside, and they know the hot, sweet, sticky stench of decay that gets into your pores and takes up residence in your body. The nausea never goes away.

FAMILY PORTRAIT IN GREECE

❧

The sun moved backward across the heavens and set in the east. While that strangest of days withered away, Atreus was conquering the throne of Mycenae.

Atreus felt the crown teeter on his head. He watched his relatives out of the corner of his eye. Thirst for power shone in his nephews' gaze. Just to be sure, he cut off their heads, chopped them to bits, cooked them up, and served them as a casserole at the banquet he offered his brother Thyestes, father of the deceased.

Atreus's son Agamemnon inherited the throne. He fancied Clytemnestra, his uncle's wife, and wanted her for his queen. Agamemnon had to kill his uncle. Years later he had to slit the throat of his prettiest daughter, Iphigenia. The goddess Artemis demanded as much if her host of satyrs, centaurs, and nymphs was to provide favorable winds to the ships heading off to fight the kingdom of Troy.

At the end of that war, under a full moon, Agamemnon returned triumphantly to his palace at Mycenae. Queen Clytemnestra welcomed him and drew him a hot bath. When he stepped out of the bath, she wrapped him in a cloak she herself had woven. That cloak became Agamemnon's shroud. Aegisthus, Clytemnestra's lover, buried a double-edged sword in his body, and she decapitated him with an ax.

With that same ax, some time later, Electra and Orestes avenged their father's death. The children of Agamemnon and Clytemnestra chopped up their mother and her lover, and gave inspiration to the poet Aeschylus and to Dr. Freud.

STRIKE OF CLOSED THIGHS

In the midst of the Peloponnesian War, the women of Athens, Sparta, Corinth, and Boeotia went on strike against the war.

It was the first strike of closed thighs in the history of the world. It occurred onstage, born of the imagination of Aristophanes, and of the rant he placed in the mouth of Lysistrata, an Athenian matron:

"I will not point my feet at the heavens, neither will I squat on all fours with my ass in the air!"

The strike went on without a truce, until the love-fast forced the warriors to acquiesce. Weary of fighting without solace and alarmed by the female insurgency, they had no choice but to bid the battlefield goodbye.

This was more or less how it was told by Aristophanes, a conservative playwright who defended traditions as if he believed in them, but in his heart held nothing sacred but the right to laugh.

And peace reigned on the stage.

Not in reality.

The Greeks had been fighting for twenty years when this play was first performed, and the butchery continued for another seven.

Women still had no right to strike, no right to an opinion, no right at all, except to submit to the duties assigned to their sex. Acting was not one of them. Women could attend plays in the worst seats, but not appear onstage. There were no actresses. In Aristophanes's production, Lysistrata and the other protagonists were played by men wearing masks.

THE ART OF DRAWING YOU

❧

In a bed by the Gulf of Corinth, a woman contemplates by firelight the profile of her sleeping lover.

On the wall, his shadow flickers.

The lover, who lies by her side, will leave. At dawn he will leave to war, to death. And his shadow, his traveling companion, will leave with him and with him will die.

It is still dark. The woman takes a coal out of the embers and draws on the wall the outline of his shadow.

Those lines will not leave.

They will not embrace her, and she knows it. But they will not leave.

SOCRATES

❧

Several cities fought on one side or the other. But this Greek war, the war that killed more Greeks than any other, was the war between Sparta and Athens: the oligarchy of the few, proud to be few, against the democracy of the few pretending to be all.

In the year 404 BC, to the trilling of flutes, Sparta took her cruel time demolishing the walls of Athens.

Of Athens, what remained? Five hundred ships at the bottom of the sea, eighty thousand dead from plague, innumerable warriors disemboweled, and a city humbled, filled with the mutilated and the insane.

Then Athenian justice condemned to death the most just of her men.

The great teacher of the Agora, who pursued truth by thinking out loud while strolling in the public square, who fought in three battles in the war just ended, was found guilty. "Corruptor of the young," the judges declared, though perhaps they meant to say he was guilty of teasing and criticizing their sacred city, and never mindlessly adoring her.

OLYMPICS

❧

The Greeks loved to kill each other, but they also played other sports.

They competed at the sanctuary of Olympia, and when the Olympics were on, they forgot all about war for a while.

Everyone was naked: the runners, the athletes who threw the javelin and the discus, the ones who jumped, boxed, wrestled, galloped, or competed by singing. None of them wore brand-name sneakers or spandex tights or anything but their own skin, glistening with oils.

The champions received no medals. They won a laurel wreath, a few vessels of olive oil, the right to eat for free for the rest of their lives, and the respect and admiration of their neighbors.

The first Olympic winner, someone named Korebus, earned his living as a cook and continued to do so thereafter. At the inaugural Olympics, he ran farther than his rivals and faster than the fearsome north winds.

The Olympics were ceremonies of shared identity. By playing sports, those bodies were saying wordlessly: "We hate each other, we fight each other, but we are all Greeks." And thus it was for a thousand years, until triumphant Christianity outlawed these pagan nudities that offended the Lord.

In the Greek Olympics, women, slaves, and foreigners never took part.

Not in Greek democracy either.

PARTHENON AND AFTER

❧

Phidias, the most envied sculptor of all time, died of a broken heart after his insufferable talent landed him a jail sentence.

Many centuries later, Phidias was punished again, this time by usurpation.

His best works, the sculptures of the Parthenon, are no longer in Athens but in London. And they are called not the Phidias Marbles, but the Elgin Marbles.

Lord Elgin was not exactly an artist. As British ambassador a couple of centuries ago, he shipped these marvels home and sold them to his government. Since then, they sit in the British Museum.

When Lord Elgin filched what he filched, the Parthenon had already been devastated by weather and war. Erected to the eternal glory of the goddess Athena, it endured the invasion of the Virgin Mary and her priests, who eliminated several figures, rubbed out many faces, and mutilated every penis. Many years later came the Venetian invasion and the temple, used as a powder house, got blown to pieces.

The Parthenon was left in ruins. While the sculptures that Lord Elgin took were broken and remain so, they speak to us about what they once were:

that tunic is just a piece of marble, but in its folds sways the body of a woman or a goddess,

that knee walks on in the absent leg,

that torso, decapitated, bears an invisible head,

that bristling mane conveys the missing horse in full whinny, and those galloping legs how it thunders on.

In the little there is, lies all that was.

HIPPOCRATES

❦

They call him the father of medicine.

New doctors take their oath in his name.

Two thousand four hundred years ago, he cured and he wrote.

These are a few of the aphorisms born, he said, of his experience:

Experience can fool you, life is short, the art of treatment long, the moment fleeting, and judgment difficult.

Medicine, the most noble of all arts, falls far behind others thanks to the ignorance of those who practice it.

There is a circulation common to all, a respiration common to all. Everything is related to everything else.

The nature of the parts of the body cannot be understood without grasping the nature of the organism as a whole.

Symptoms are the body's natural defenses. We call them diseases, but in reality they are the treatment for the disease.

Eunuchs do not go bald.

Bald men do not suffer from varicose veins.

May meals be your food, and food your medicine.

What cures one will kill another.

If a woman has conceived a boy, she has good color. If she has conceived a girl, then her color is poor.

ASPASIA

✿

In the time of Pericles, Aspasia was the most famous woman in all Athens.

This could be said otherwise: in the time of Aspasia, Pericles was the most famous man in all Athens.

Her enemies never forgave her for being a woman and a foreigner. To add insult to injury they saddled her with an unmentionable past and said that the school of rhetoric she ran was a breeding ground for girls of easy virtue.

They accused her of scorning the gods, an offense that might have cost her life. Before a tribunal of fifteen hundred men, Pericles took up the defense. Aspasia was absolved, although in his three-hour speech Pericles forgot to say that rather than scorning the gods, she believed the gods scorn us and spoil our ephemeral human joys.

By then, Pericles had already tossed his wife out of his bed and his house, and was living with Aspasia. He sired a son with her, and to defend the child's rights he broke a law he himself had decreed.

Socrates interrupted his classes to listen to Aspasia, and Anaxagoras cited her opinions.

Plutarch wondered: "What artful power did that woman possess that allowed her to inspire philosophers and dominate the most eminent political figures?"

SAPPHO

❧

Of Sappho not much is known.

They say she was born twenty-six hundred years ago on the island of Lesbos, thus giving lesbians their name.

They say she was married, that she had a son, and that she threw herself off a cliff because a sailor paid her no heed. They also say she was short and ugly.

Who knows? We men do not like it when a woman prefers another woman instead of succumbing to our irresistible charms. In the year 1703, the Catholic Church, bastion of male power, ordered all of Sappho's books burned.

A handful of poems survived.

ᵀEPICURIUS

❧

In his garden in Athens, Epicurius spoke out against fear. Against fear of the gods, death, pain, and failure.

It is simply vanity, he said, to believe the gods care about us. From their bastion of immortality, their perfection, they offer neither prizes nor punishments. Why fear the gods when we fleeting, sorry beings merit no more than their indifference?

Death is not frightening either, he said. While we exist, death does not, and when death exists, we no longer do.

Fear pain? Fear of pain is what hurts most, and nothing gives more pleasure than pain's departure.

Fear failure? What failure? Nothing is enough if enough is too little, but what glory could compare to the delight of conversing with friends on a sunny afternoon? What power equals the urge to love, to eat, to drink?

Let's turn our inescapable mortality, Epicurius suggested, into an eternal feast.

ORIGIN OF INSECURITY

❧

Greek democracy loved freedom but lived off its prisoners. Slaves, male and female, worked the land,
    built the roads,
    mined the mountains in search of silver and stone,
    erected the houses,
    wove the clothes,
    sewed the shoes,
    cooked,
    washed,
    swept,
    forged lances and shields, hoes and hammers,
    gave pleasure at parties and in brothels,
    and raised the children of their owners.

A slave was cheaper than a mule. Slavery, despicable topic, rarely appeared in poetry or onstage or in the paintings that decorated urns and walls. Philosophers ignored it, except to confirm it as the natural fate of inferior beings, and to sound the alarm. Watch out, warned Plato. Slaves, he said, unavoidably hate their owners and only constant vigilance can keep them from murdering us all.

And Aristotle maintained that military training for the citizenry was crucial, given the climate of insecurity.

SLAVERY ACCORDING TO ARISTOTLE

❧

One who is a human being belonging by nature not to himself but to another is by nature a slave; and being a man he is an article of property, and an article of property is an instrument . . . The slave is a living tool, just as a tool is an inanimate slave.

Hence there are by nature various classes of rulers and ruled. For the freeman rules the slave, the male the female, and the man the child.

The art of war includes hunting, an art which we ought to practice against wild beasts and against men who, though intended by nature to be governed, refuse to submit; for war of such a kind is naturally just.

Bodily service for the necessities of life is forthcoming from both, from slaves and from domestic animals alike. The intention of nature therefore is to make the bodies of freemen and of slaves different.

WATCH OUT FOR THE BACCHANALIA

❦

In Rome, too, slaves were the sunshine of every day and the nightmare of every night. Slavery stoked the empire's life and its dread.

Even the festivals of Bacchus posed a threat to stability, for in those nighttime rituals the walls between slaves and freemen crumbled, and wine allowed what the law forbade.

Subversion of hierarchies by lust: those wild parties, people suspected, people knew, had a lot to do with the slave rebellions breaking out in the south.

Rome did not stand put. A couple of centuries before Christ, the Senate accused the followers of Bacchus of conspiracy and gave two consuls, Marcius and Postumius, the mission to extinguish all trace of bacchanalia throughout the empire.

Blood flowed.

The bacchanalia continued. The rebellions as well.

ANTIOCHUS, KING

❦

His owner used him as a jester at banquets.

The slave Eunus would fall into a trance and blow smoke and fire and prophecies from his mouth, sending the guests into fits of laughter.

At one of these big feasts, after the flames and delight died down, Eunus announced solemnly that he would be king of this island. Sicily will be my kingdom, he said, and he said he was told as much by the goddess Demeter.

The guests laughed so hard they rolled on the floor.

A few days later, the slave was king. Breathing fire from his mouth, he slit his owner's throat and unleashed a slave revolt that engulfed towns and cities and crowned Eunus king of Sicily.

The island was ablaze. The new monarch ordered all prisoners killed, save those who knew how to make weapons, and he issued coins stamped with his new name, Antiochus, beside the likeness of the goddess Demeter.

The reign of Antiochus lasted four years, until he was betrayed, deposed, jailed, and devoured by fleas.

Half a century later, Spartacus arrived.

SPARTACUS

❧

He was a shepherd in Thrace, a soldier in Rome, a gladiator in Capua.

He was a runaway slave who fled armed with a kitchen knife. At the foot of Mount Vesuvius he formed a legion of free men that gathered strength as it roamed and soon became an army.

One morning, seventy-two years before Christ, Rome trembled. The Romans saw that Spartacus's men saw them. At dawn, the crests of the hills bristled with lances. From there, the slaves contemplated the temples and palaces of the queen of cities, the one that had the world at her beck and call: within reach, touched by their eyes, was the place that had torn from them their names and their memories, and had turned them into things to be lashed, sold, or given away.

The attack did not occur. It was never known if Spartacus and his troops had really been that close, or if they were specters conjured up by fear. For at the time, the slaves were humiliating the legions on the battlefield.

A guerrilla war kept the empire on edge for two years.

Then the rebels, surrounded in the mountains of Lucania, were at last annihilated by soldiers recruited in Rome under a young officer named Julius Caesar.

When Spartacus saw he was beaten, he leaned against his horse, head to head, his forehead pressed to the forelock of his companion in every battle. He thrust in the long blade and sliced open the horse's heart.

Crucifixions lined the entire Via Appia from Capua all the way to Rome.

ROME TOUR

❧

Manual labor was for slaves.

Thought not enslaved, day laborers and artisans practiced "vile occupations." Cicero, who practiced the noble occupation of usury, defined the labor hierarchy:

"The least honorable are all that serve gluttony, like sausage-makers, chicken and fishmongers, cooks . . . "

The most respectable Romans were warlords, who rarely went into battle, and landowners, who rarely set foot on their land.

To be poor was an unpardonable crime. To dissemble their disgrace, the formerly wealthy went into debt and, if lucky, pursued successful careers in politics, which they undertook in the service of their creditors.

The sale of sexual favors was a reliable source of wealth. So was the sale of political or bureaucratic favors. These activities shared a single name. Pimps and lobbyists were both called *proxenetas*.

JULIUS CAESAR

❧

They called him "the bald whorer," said he was the husband of every woman and the wife of every man.

Those in the know contend he spent several months in Cleopatra's bedroom without even peeking out.

He returned to Rome from Alexandria with her, his trophy. Crowning his victorious campaigns in Europe and Africa, he paid homage to his own glory by ordering a multitude of gladiators to fight to the death, and by showing off the giraffes and other rarities Cleopatra had given him.

Rome dressed him in the only purple toga in the entire empire, and wrapped his forehead in a laurel wreath. And Virgil, the official poet, celebrated his divine lineage, descending from Aeneas, Mars, and Venus.

Not long after, from the height of heights, he proclaimed himself dictator for life and announced reforms that threatened the sacrosanct privileges of his own class.

And his people, the patricians, decided that an ounce of prevention was worth a pound of cure.

Marked for death, all-powerful Caesar was surrounded by his intimates, and his beloved Brutus, who may have been his son, embraced him first and plunged the first knife into his back.

Other knives riddled him and were raised, red, to the heavens.

And there he lay on the stone floor. Not even his slaves dared to touch him.

SALT OF THE EMPIRE

✿

In the year 31 before Christ, Rome went to war against Cleopatra and Mark Anthony, inheritor of Caesar's fame and Caesar's dame.

That was when Emperor Augustus bought popularity by handing out salt.

The patricians had already given the lower orders the right to salt, but Augustus increased the ration.

Rome loved salt. There was always salt, either rock salt or sea salt, near the cities the Romans founded.

"Via Salaria" was the name of the first imperial road, built to bring salt from the beach at Ostia, and the word "salary" comes from the payment in salt, which the legionaries received during military campaigns.

CLEOPATRA

✿

Her courtiers bathe her in donkey's milk and honey.

After anointing her with nectar of jasmine, lily, and honeysuckle, they place her naked body on silk pillows filled with feathers.

On her closed eyelids lie thinly sliced discs of aloe. On her face and neck, plasters made of ox bile, ostrich eggs, and beeswax.

When she awakens from her nap, the moon is high in the sky.

The courtiers impregnate her hands with essence of roses and perfume her feet with elixirs of almonds and orange blossoms. Her nostrils exhale fragrances of lime and cinnamon, while dates from the desert sweeten her hair, shining with walnut oil.

And the time for makeup arrives. Beetle dust colors her cheeks and lips. Antimony dust outlines her eyebrows. Lapis lazuli and malachite paint a veil of blue and green shadows around her eyes.

In her palace at Alexandria, Cleopatra begins her final night.

The last of the pharaohs,

who was not as beautiful as they say,

who was a better queen than they say,

who spoke several languages and understood economics and other male mysteries,

who astonished Rome,

who challenged Rome,

who shared bed and power with Julius Caesar and Mark Anthony,

now dresses in her most outlandish outfit and slowly sits down on her throne, while the Roman troops advance against her.

Julius Caesar is dead, Mark Anthony is dead.

The Egyptian defenses crumble.

Cleopatra orders the straw basket opened.

The rattle resounds.

The serpent slithers.

And the queen of the Nile opens her tunic and offers it her bare breasts, shining with gold dust.

CONTRACEPTIVE METHODS OF
PROVEN EFFECTIVENESS

❧

In Rome, many women avoided having children by sneezing immediately after making love, but the professionals preferred shaking their hips at the moment of climax to divert the seed. Pliny the Elder recounted how poor women avoided having children by hanging from their necks before dawn an amulet made of worms extracted from the head of a furry spider, wrapped in elk skin. Upper-class women warded off pregnancy by carrying a small ivory tube containing a slice of the uterus of a lioness or the liver of a cat.

A long time later, in Spain, believers practiced an infallible prayer:

Saint Joseph, you who had without doing
make it so that I do without having.

SHOW BUSINESS

❦

Silence. The priests consult the gods. They slice open a white bull, read his entrails. Suddenly the band strikes up and the stadium howls: yes, the gods say yes. They too are burning with desire for the revelry to begin.

The gladiators, who are going to die, raise their weapons to salute the emperor's box. Mostly they are slaves or criminals sentenced to death, though a few are professionals who trained long for a short career that ends the day the emperor gives the thumbs-down.

Cameos, badges, and clay pots decorated with the faces of the most popular gladiators sell like hotcakes in the stands, while the crowd goes wild making bets and hurling abuse and praise.

The show might last several days. Private entrepreneurs sell the tickets and prices are high, but sometimes politicians put on the killings for free. That's when the stands fill up with pennants and banners exhorting all to vote for the friend of the people, the only one who keeps his promises.

Arena of sand, sodden with blood. A Christian named Telemaco won sainthood for leaping between two gladiators in the midst of a fight. The crowd made mincemeat of him, pelting him with stones for interrupting the show.

FAMILY PORTRAIT IN ROME

❧

For three centuries, hell was Rome and devils were its emperors. To the delight of the public, they threw Christians to hungry lions in the pits of the Coliseum. Those luncheons were not to be missed.

According to Hollywood's historians, Nero was worst of all. They say he had the apostle Saint Peter crucified upside down, and that he set fire to Rome in order to lay blame on the Christians. And he kept up the imperial tradition of exterminating his own family.

He gave his Aunt Lepida, who had raised him, a lethal laxative, and with poison mushrooms he bid goodbye to his half-brother Britannicus.

After marrying his half-sister Octavia, he sent her into exile and ordered her strangled. Widowed and free, he openly wooed the incomparable beauty Poppaea, whom he made empress until he tired of her and with one kick sent her on to the other world.

Agrippina was the toughest to kill. Nero owed her because he was the fruit of her womb, and also because she had poisoned her husband, Emperor Claudius, so that he, her little boy, could ascend to the throne. But Agrippina, beloved mother, did not let him rule and at every chance slipped into his bed and feigned sleep. Getting rid of her was no easy task. Happily, you have but one mother. Nero toasted her health with toxic potions, previously tested on slaves and animals, he made the roof over her bed fall in, he knocked holes in the hull of her ship . . . At last he was able to grieve for her.

Afterward he killed Poppaea's son Rufrius Crispinus, who was vying to become emperor.

And then, sticking a knife in his own throat, he did in the only relative he had left.

THE POET WHO POKED FUN AT ROME

❧

Spain was his place of birth and death, but the poet Martial lived and wrote in Rome.

It was the age of Nero, and in fashion were wigs made of the hair of barbarians, as Germans were called:

> *That blond hair is all her own.*
> *So she says, and she won't lie.*
> *Where she bought it knows none but I.*

And false eyelashes:

> *Keep on winking with that eyelid*
> *you pulled from a drawer this morning.*

Death improved poets, then as now:

> *Only the dead do honors gain.*
> *I prefer to carry on*
> *alive and without acclaim.*

A doctor's house call could prove fatal:

> *Before you came, a fever I had not.*
> *But then you saw me, thanks a lot.*

And justice could be unjust:

> *Who said the adulterer's nose one should snip?*
> *To betray you he did not use that tip.*

LAUGH THERAPY

❧

Galen, hero of doctors everywhere, started out healing the wounds of gladiators and ended up as physician to Emperor Marcus Aurelius. He believed in experience and distrusted speculation: "I prefer the long hard road to the short easy path." In his years of working with the sick, he came to see that habit is second nature and that health and illness are ways of life. He advised patients who were ill by nature to change their habits.

He discovered or described hundreds of afflictions and cures, and by testing remedies he concluded:

"Laughter is the best medicine."

JOKES

❧

The Andalusian emperor of Rome, Hadrian, said farewell to his soul when he knew his last morning had arrived:

> *Little soul,*
> *fragile wanderer,*
> *my body's guest and companion,*
> *where will you go now?*
> *To what pale, tough, barren places will you go?*
> *You won't be telling jokes anymore.*

THE LOOKING-GLASS WORLD
MOCKED THE REAL ONE

❧

Roman women enjoyed one day of absolute power. During the festival of Matronalia, the she's gave the orders, and the he's took them.

The Saturnalia, descended from Sacaea of ancient Babylon, lasted a week and were, like the Matronalia, an occasion to let loose. Hierarchies were inverted: the rich served the poor, who invaded their homes, wore their clothes, ate at their tables, and slept in their beds. Saturnalia, homage to the god Saturn, culminated on December 25. That was the day of *Sol Invictus,* Unconquered Sun, which centuries later became Christmas by Catholic decree.

During Europe's Middle Ages, the Day of Innocent Saints turned power over to children, idiots, and the demented. In England reigned the Lord of Misrule, and fighting for Spain's throne were the King of Roosters and the King of Pigs, each of them denizens of the insane asylum. A child decked out in miter and crosier played Pope of the Crazies and made people kiss his ring, while another child mounted on a mule pronounced the bishop's sermons.

Like all fiestas of the looking-glass world, those fleeting spaces of liberty had a beginning and an end. They were brief. When the captain's around, the sailors pipe down.

FORBIDDEN TO LAUGH

The ancient festivals that marked the cycles of nature now called Christmas and Easter are no longer homages to pagan gods, but rather solemn rituals that venerate the divinity who kidnapped their days and hijacked their symbols.

The Hilaria, a festival either inherited or invented by Rome, greeted the arrival of spring. The goddess Cybele would bathe in the river, calling for rain and fertility in the fields, while the Romans, dressed in bizarre clothes, laughed themselves silly. Everyone made fun of everyone else, and there was no person or thing in the world undeserving of a good ribbing.

By decision of the Catholic Church, this pagan festival, which celebrated with hilarity the resurrection of spring, was deemed to coincide each March, more or less, with the resurrection of Jesus, of whom the scriptures record not a single laugh.

And by decision of the Catholic Church, the Vatican was built in the exact location where the festival of glee used to reach its zenith. Now, in that vast plaza where the guffaws of the multitudes once resonated, we hear the grave voice of the pope reciting passages from the Bible, a book where no one ever laughs.

THE SMILING DIVINITY

❧

Images of him show him smiling, serenely ironic, as if mocking the paradoxes that defined his life and afterlife.

Buddha did not believe in gods or in God, but his devotees made him one.

Buddha did not believe in miracles, nor did he perform them, but his devotees attribute to him miraculous powers.

Buddha did not believe in any religion, nor did he found one, but the passing of time turned Buddhism into one of the most popular religions in the world.

Buddha was born on the banks of the Ganges, but Buddhists make up less than 1 percent of the population of India.

Buddha preached asceticism, the renunciation of passion, and the negation of desire, but he died from eating way too much pork.

A FATHER WHO NEVER LAUGHS

❧

Jews, Christians, and Muslims worship the same divinity, the god of the Bible who answers to three names, Yahweh, God, and Allah, depending on who happens to be calling. Jews, Christians, and Muslims kill one another on His orders, they say.

In other religions, the gods are or were many. Greece, India, Mexico, Peru, Japan, China all boast or boasted numerous Olympians. Yet the God of the Bible is jealous. Jealous of whom? Why is He so worried about the competition if He is the only true god?

Thou shalt not bow thyself down to any other god, nor serve them; for I the Lord thy God am a jealous God. (Exodus 20:5)

Why does He punish several generations of offspring for the disloyalty of their parents?

I the Lord thy God will visit the iniquity of the fathers upon the children unto the third and fourth generation of them that hate me. (Exodus 20:5)

Why is He so insecure? Why does He mistrust his devotees so? Why must He threaten them to get them to obey? Speaking live and direct, or by the mouths of the prophets, He warns:

If thou wilt not hearken unto the voice of the Lord thy God . . . the Lord shall smite thee with consumption, and with fever, and with inflammation, and with extreme burning, and with drought . . . A wife wilt thou betroth, and another man shall lie with her . . . The Lord shall give as the rain of thy land powder and dust . . . Much seed wilt thou carry out into the field, yet but little shalt thou gather in; for the locust shall consume it. Vineyards wilt thou plant and dress, but wine shalt thou not drink nor lay up; for the worms shall eat them . . . Ye will offer yourselves for sale unto our enemies for bondmen and bondwomen, without any one to buy you. (Deuteronomy 28)

Six days may work be done; but on the seventh is the sabbath of rest, holy to the Lord; whoever doeth any work on the sabbath day shall surely be put to death. (Exodus 31:15)

He that blasphemeth the name of the Lord, he shall surely be put to death, and all the congregation shall certainly stone him. (Leviticus 24:16)

The stick works better than the carrot. The Bible is a catalogue of harrowing punishments meted out to the unbelieving:

I will send out against you the beasts of the field . . . I will chastise you, sevenfold for your sins. And ye shall eat the flesh of your sons, and the flesh of your daughters shall ye eat . . . I will draw out after you the sword; and your land shall be a desolate wild, and your cities shall be a waste. (Leviticus 26)

This perpetually angry God rules the world in our days by means of His three religions. He is not what we might call nice:

God is jealous, and the Lord revengeth; the Lord revengeth, and is furious; the Lord will take vengeance on his adversaries, and he reserveth wrath for his enemies. (Nahum 1:2)

His ten commandments do not outlaw war. On the contrary, He orders it done. And His is a war without pity for anyone, not even babes:

Now go and smite Amalek, and utterly destroy all that they have, and spare them not; but slay both man and woman, infant and suckling, ox and sheep, camel and ass. (Samuel 15:3)

Daughter of Babel, devastator: Happy shall he be, that taketh and dasheth thy little ones against the stones. (Psalms 137:9)

THE SON

❧

No one knows how: Yahweh, the one god who never made love, fathered a son.

According to the scriptures, the son came into the world when Herod reigned in Galilee. Since Herod died four years before the beginning of the Christian era, Jesus must have been born at least four years before Christ.

What year, nobody knows. Or what day or what time. Jesus had spent nearly four centuries without a birthday when Saint Gregory Nazianzen issued him a birth certificate in the year 379. Jesus was born on December 25. Thus the Catholic Church once again draped itself in the illustrious robes of idolatry. According to pagan tradition, that was the day the sacred sun initiated its march against night through the winter's darkness.

Whenever it may have occurred, that first silent night of peace and love was certainly not celebrated as it is now in many lands, with the deafening battle roar of firecrackers. For sure, there were no little pins showing the golden-curled babe which that newborn was not. Any more than the ones who followed a star no one else ever saw to a manger in Bethlehem were either three or kings. And certainly that first Christmas, which foretold such bad news for the merchants in the temple, was not and was never intended to be a promise of spectacular sales for the merchants of the world.

WANTED

❧

> WANTED
>
> NAME, JESUS.
>
> AKA, MESSIAH.
>
> NO JOB OR FIXED ADDRESS.

He claims to be the son of God, who came down from heaven to set fire to the world.

An outlaw from the desert, he gets townspeople all riled up.

He promises paradise to the destitute, to slaves, crazies, drunks, and prostitutes.

He fools the common people by curing lepers, multiplying loaves and fishes, and performing other tricks of magic and sorcery.

He does not respect Rome's authority or Jewish tradition.

He has always lived outside the law.

For thirty-three years he has been running from the death sentence he received at birth.

The cross awaits him.

THE ASS

❧

He gave warmth to newborn Jesus in the manger, and that's why he is in all the pictures, posing with his big ears beside the bed of straw.

On the back of an ass, Jesus escaped Herod's sword.

On the back of an ass, he wandered all his life.

On the back of an ass, he preached.

On the back of an ass, he entered Jerusalem.

Perhaps the ass is not such an ass after all?

RESURRECTION OF JESUS

❧

In Oaxaca, the Mazatecos say Jesus was crucified because he gave the poor a voice and made the trees speak.

And they say that after long suffering, they took him down from the cross.

And he was already buried, asleep in his death, when a cricket began to sing.

And the cricket awakened him.

And Jesus said he wished to leave death behind.

And the cricket told the mole, who then dug a long tunnel underground until he reached the casket where Jesus lay.

And the mole sought the help of the mouse, who then broke open the casket with his sharp teeth.

And Jesus got out.

And with one finger he pushed aside the immense boulder that the soldiers had put in his way.

And he thanked the cricket, the mole, and the mouse who had been so kind.

And he rose up to heaven, though he had no wings.

And above the open tomb he left the immense boulder floating in the air with an angel seated on it.

And the angel told all this to lady Mary, mother of Jesus.

And lady Mary could not keep the secret and she told her neighbors in the market.

And that is how we know.

MARYS

❦

In the scriptures, Mary seldom appears.

The Church ignored her too until about a thousand years ago. Then the mother of Jesus was consecrated as the mother of humanity and the symbol of the purity of the faith. In the eleventh century, while the Church was inventing purgatory and obligatory confession, in France eighty churches and cathedrals sprang up in homage to Mary.

Virginity was the source of her prestige. Mary, nourished by angels, impregnated by a dove, was never touched by a man. The husband, Saint Joseph, said hello from afar. And she became even more holy after 1854, when the infallible Pope Pius IX revealed that Mary had been conceived without sin, which in translation means that the mother of the Virgin was also a virgin.

Today Mary is the most adored and miraculous divinity in the world. Eve brought ruin to all women. Mary redeems them. Thanks to her, the sinning daughters of Eve have the chance to repent.

And that is what happened to the other Mary, the one who appears in the pictures at the foot of the holy cross, beside the immaculate one.

According to tradition, that other Mary, Mary Magdalene, was a whore and became a saint.

Believers humiliate her by offering forgiveness.

RESURRECTION OF MARY

❈

Mary was reborn in Chiapas.

It was announced by an Indian from the town of Simojovel, a cousin of hers, and by a hermit who was unrelated and lived under a tree in Chamula.

And in the town of Santa Marta Xolotepec, Dominica López was harvesting corn when she saw her. The mother of Jesus asked her to build her a chapel because she was tired of sleeping in the woods. Dominica paid heed, but in a few days the bishop turned up and arrested her along with Mary and all her followers.

Then Mary escaped from jail and went to the town of Cancuc and spoke out of the mouth of a girl who was also named Mary.

The Tzetzal Mayas never forgot what she said. She spoke in their language and in a hoarse voice she ordered:

that women should not deny their bodily desires, because these cheered her;

that women who wished to get married to other men should do so, because marriages performed by Spanish priests were no good;

and that the prophecy that the yoke would be thrown off and lands and freedom restored had come to pass, and there was no longer any need for tribute or king or bishop or high mayor.

And the Council of Elders heard her and obeyed. And in the year 1712, thirty-two indigenous towns rose up in arms.

ORIGIN OF SANTA CLAUS

❈

The first rendering of Santa Claus, published in 1863 in *Harper's* of New York, showed a hefty little gnome entering a chimney. He issued from the hand of the artist Thomas Nast, vaguely inspired by the legend of Saint Nicholas.

Christmas of 1930 saw Santa Claus working for Coca-Cola. Before then he did not wear a suit and generally preferred to wear blue or green. The artist Haddon Sundblom dressed him in the company colors, bright red with white piping, and gave him the features familiar to us all. Every child's friend has a white beard, laughs all the time, travels by sleigh, and is so plump that no one can figure out how he gets down the world's chimneys loaded with presents and carrying a Coke in each hand.

Neither can anyone figure out what he has to do with Christ.

ORIGIN OF HELL

The Catholic Church invented hell and also invented the devil.

The Old Testament makes no mention of the perpetual barbecue, neither do its pages feature an appearance by the monster reeking of sulfur, who carries a trident and sports horns and a tail, claws and hooves, goat's legs and dragon's wings.

But the Church asked itself: what will become of reward without punishment? What will become of obedience without fear?

And it wondered: what will become of God without the devil? What will become of good without evil?

And the Church concluded that the threat of hell is more effective than the promise of heaven, and from then on ministers and holy fathers have terrorized us with sermons about torture in the fiery abyss where the evil one reigns.

In the year 2007, Pope Benedict XVI confirmed it:

"There is a hell. And it is eternal."

PRISCILLIAN

❧

And the time of the catacombs ended.

In the Coliseum, the Christians ate the lions.

Rome became the global capital of the faith and the Catholic religion became the official religion of the empire.

And in the year 385, when the Church condemned Bishop Priscillian and his followers, it was the Roman emperor who killed them as heretics.

Heads rolled.

The Christians led by Bishop Priscillian had been guilty:

they danced and sang and celebrated darkness and fire,

they turned the mass into a pagan festival from Galicia, the suspicious land where Priscillian was born,

they lived in community and in poverty,

they repudiated the alliance of the Church with the powers that be,

they condemned slavery,

and they allowed women to preach, as priests.

HYPATIA

❧

"She'll go off with anybody," they said, to denigrate her freedom.

"She is not like a woman," they said, to praise her intelligence.

But numerous professors, magistrates, philosophers, and politicians came from afar to the School of Alexandria to hear her words.

Hypatia studied the enigmas that defied Euclid and Archimedes, and she spoke out against blind faith unworthy of divine love or human love. She taught people to doubt and to question. And she counseled:

"Defend your right to think. Thinking wrongly is better than not thinking at all."

What was that heretical woman doing giving classes in a city run by Christian men?

They called her a witch and a sorcerer. They threatened her with death.

And one March day in the year 415, a crowd set upon her at noon.

And she was pulled from her carriage and stripped naked and dragged through the streets and beaten and stabbed. And in the public square a bonfire disposed of whatever was left of her.

"It will be investigated," said the prefect of the city.

THEODORA

The city of Ravenna owed allegiance to Emperor Justinian and Empress Theodora, but the city's sharp tongues delighted in digging up the empress's murky past: dancing in the slums of Constantinople as the geese pecked grains of barley off her nude body, her moans of pleasure, the roars of the audience . . .

But the sins which puritan Ravenna could not forgive were others, the ones she committed after her coronation. Theodora was the reason why the Christian empire of Byzantium became the first place in the world where abortion was a right,

adultery was not punished by death,

women had the right to inherit,

widows and illegitimate children were protected,

a woman's divorce was not an impossibility,

and the marriage of Christian nobles to women of lower class or different religion was no longer prohibited.

Fifteen hundred years later, the portrait of Theodora in the Church of Saint Vitale is the most famous mosaic in the world.

This masterpiece of stonework is also the symbol of the city that loathed her and now lives from her.

URRACA

She was the first queen of Spain.

Urraca ruled for seventeen years, though Church records say her reign lasted no more than four.

Fed up with insults and beatings, she divorced the husband of a forced marriage, booting him out of her bed and her palace, though Church records say he left her.

To show the Church who was in charge and teach it to respect the female throne, Queen Urraca locked up the archbishop of Santiago de Compostela and seized his castles, something unheard of in such a Christian land, though Church records say that was but "an explosion of womanly spirit, easily unhinged, and of womanly mind, filled as it is with pestiferous poison."

She had dalliances, affairs, lovers, and she flaunted them cheerfully, though Church records say they were "behaviors that would make one blush to speak of."

AYESHA

Six centuries after the death of Jesus, Mohammed died.

The founder of Islam, who by Allah's permission had twelve wives nearly all at the same time, left nine widows. By Allah's prohibition, none of them remarried.

Ayesha, the youngest, had been the favorite.

Some time later, she led an armed uprising against the caliph, Imam Ali.

In our times, many mosques refuse entry to women, but back then mosques were where Ayesha's fiery speeches roused people to anger. Mounted on her camel, she attacked the city of Basra. The lengthy battle caused fifteen thousand casualties.

That bloodletting launched the enmity between Sunnis and Shiites, which to this day takes lives. And certain theologians decreed it irrefutable proof that women make a mess of things when they escape the bedroom and the kitchen.

MOHAMMED

❦

When Ayesha was defeated, someone suddenly recalled what Mohammed had suggested twenty-eight years earlier:

"Hang up your lash where your woman can see it."

And other disciples of the Prophet, also given to timely recollections, remembered that he had said paradise is filled with the poor and hell filled with women.

Time passed, and by a few centuries after Mohammed's death the sayings attributed to him by Islam's theocracy numbered over six hundred. A good many of those phrases, especially the ones that curse women, have become religious truths received from heaven and untouchable by human doubt.

Yet the Koran, the holy book dictated by Allah, says that man and woman were created equal and that Eve had no art or part in Adam's seduction by the serpent.

MOHAMMED'S BIOGRAPHER

❦

He was an evangelical pastor, but not for long. Religious orthodoxy was not for him. An open-minded man, a passionate polemicist, he traded the church for the university.

He studied at Princeton, taught in New York.

He was a professor of Oriental languages and author of the first biography of Mohammed published in the United States.

He wrote that Mohammed was an extraordinary man, a visionary blessed with irresistible magnetism, and also an impostor, a charlatan, a purveyor of illusions. But he thought no better of Christianity, which he considered "disastrous" in the epoch when Islam was founded.

That was his first book. Later on, he wrote others. In the field of Middle Eastern affairs, few academics could compare.

He lived indoors surrounded by towers of strange books. When he wasn't writing, he read.

He died in New York in 1859.

His name was George Bush.

SUKAINA

❃

For women in some Muslim nations, the veil is a jail: a peripatetic prison that travels wherever they go.

But Mohammed's women did not cover their faces, and the Koran never mentions the word "veil," though it does recommend that women cover their hair with a shawl outside the home. Catholic nuns, who do not follow the Koran, cover their hair, and in many places in the world non-Muslim women wear shawls or wraps or kerchiefs on their heads.

But a shawl worn by choice is one thing, and a veil worn by male dictum, obliging women to hide their faces, is something else.

One of the most implacable enemies of face-covering was Sukaina, Mohammed's great-granddaughter, who not only refused to wear one, but denounced it at the top of her lungs.

Sukaina married five times, and in each of her five marriage contracts she refused to pledge obedience to her husband.

MOTHER OF ALL STORYTELLERS

❃

To avenge a woman who betrayed him, a king killed them all.

At dusk he married and at dawn he widowed.

One after another, the virgins lost their virginity and their heads.

Scheherazade was the only one to survive the first night, and then she continued trading a story for each new day of life.

Stories she heard, read, or imagined saved her from decapitation. She told them in a low voice, in the darkness of the bedroom, with no light but that of the moon. In the telling she felt pleasure and gave pleasure, but she tread carefully. Sometimes, in the middle of a tale, she felt the king's eyes studying her neck.

If he got bored, she was lost.

From fear of dying sprang the knack of narrating.

BAGHDAD

❦

Scheherazade lived her thousand and one nights in a palace in Baghdad on the banks of the Tigris River.

Her thousand and one stories were born in that land or had migrated there from Persia, Arabia, India, China, or Turkistan, just as the thousand and one marvels brought by merchant caravans from far-off lands ended up in the city's market stalls.

Baghdad was the center of the world. All roads, of words and of things, met in that city of plazas and fountains, baths and gardens. The most famous physicians, astronomers, and mathematicians also met in Baghdad, at an academy of sciences known as the House of Wisdom.

Among them was Muhammed al-Khwarizmi, the inventor of algebra, which got its name from the first word of the title of one of his books, *al-jabr*.

VOICE OF WINE

❦

Omar Khayyam wrote treatises on algebra, metaphysics, and astronomy. And he was the author of underground poems that spread by word of mouth throughout Persia and beyond.

Those poems were hymns to wine, sinful elixir condemned by the powers of Islam.

Heaven has not learned of my arrival, the poet said, and my departure will not in the least diminish its beauty and grandeur. The moon, which seeks me out tomorrow, will continue rising even if it no longer finds me. I will sleep underground, with neither woman nor friend. For us ephemeral mortals, the only eternity is the moment, and drinking to the moment is better than weeping for it.

Khayyam preferred the tavern to the mosque. He feared neither earthly powers nor celestial threats, and he felt pity for God, who could never get drunk. The word "supreme" is not written in the Koran, but on the lip of a wineglass. It is read not with the eyes, but with the mouth.

CRUSADES

In the span of just over a century and a half, Europe sent eight Crusades to the infidel lands of the East.

Islam, which had usurped the sacred sepulchre of Jesus, was a remote enemy. So along the way these warriors of the faith took advantage to wipe other maps clean.

The holy war began at home.

The First Crusade set fire to synagogues and left not a Jew alive in Mainz and other German cities.

The Fourth Crusade left for Jerusalem but never arrived. The Christian warriors stopped over in Christian Constantinople, an opulent city, and for three days and nights they pillaged, sparing neither churches nor monasteries, and when there were no women left to rape or palaces to sack they stayed on to enjoy the booty, and forgot all about the final destination of their sacred enterprise.

A few years later, in 1209, another Crusade began by exterminating Christians on French soil. The Cathars, puritan Christians, refused to acknowledge the power of the king or the pope and believed all wars offended God, including those, like the Crusades, that were waged in God's name. This very popular heresy was torn out by the roots. From city to city, castle to castle, village to village. The most ferocious massacre took place in Béziers. There everyone got the knife: Cathars and Catholics alike. Some sought refuge in the cathedral. In vain, no one escaped the butchery. There wasn't time to figure out who was whom.

According to some versions, papal legate Arnaud-Amaury, later archbishop of Narbonne, did not hesitate. He ordered: "Kill them all; for the Lord knoweth them that are His."

DIVINE COMMANDMENTS

❧

The literacy rate among the armed services of Christianity was not exactly high. That may explain why they were unable to read the commandments on Moses's tablets.

They read that God ordered his name taken in vain, and in God's name they did what they did.

They read that God ordered them to lie, and they violated nearly every agreement they signed in their holy war against the infidels.

They read that God ordered them to steal, and they pillaged everything in their path to the Orient, buttressed by the standard with the cross and by the blessing of the pope, which guaranteed their debts would be pardoned and their souls saved for eternity.

They read that God ordered them to commit carnal acts, and the hosts of the Lord fulfilled that duty not only with the numerous professionals hired by the Army of Christ, but also with the captured heathens who formed part of the booty.

And they read that God ordered them to kill, and entire towns underwent the knife, children included: out of Christian duty to purify lands soiled by heresy, or out of simple necessity, as in the case of Richard the Lionhearted, who had to slit the throats of his prisoners because they slowed his pace.

"They walk spattering blood," a witness said.

CRAZY ABOUT FRENCH WOMEN

❧

Imad ad-Din was the right-hand man of Sultan Saladin. In addition, he was a poet of florid hand.

From Damascus he described the three hundred French prostitutes who accompanied the warriors of Christ on the Third Crusade:

They all were wild fornicators, proud and scornful, who took and gave, sinners of firm flesh, crooners and flirts, available but haughty, impetuous, ardent, dyed and painted, desirable, delectable, exquisite, grateful, who rent and mended, destroyed and rebuilt, lost and found, stole and consoled, wantonly seductive, languid, desired and desirous, dizzy and dizzying, ever-changing, practiced, rapturous adolescents, amorous, offering of themselves, loving, passionate, shameless, of abundant hips and narrow waist, fleshy thighs, nasal voices, black eyes, blue eyes, ashen eyes. And oh so dumb.

POET PROPHET

❦

Mohammed's descendants dedicated themselves to fighting each other, Sunnis against Shiites, Baghdad against Cairo, and the Islamic world fractured into bits bent on mutual hatred.

At war with itself, the Muslim army disintegrated and the crusaders, finding no obstacle, marched on the holy sepulchre at the pace of conquerors.

An Arab poet, who wrote about the Arabs from the Arab point of view, described it thus:

> *There are two kinds of people in this land:*
> *those who have brains but no religion*
> *and those who have religion but no brains.*

And also:

> *Fate smashes us as if we were made of glass,*
> *and never again will our pieces come together.*

The author was Abu Ali al-Ma'arri. He died in the year 1057 in the Syrian city of Ma'arrat, forty years before the Christians demolished it stone by stone.

The poet was blind. So they say.

TROTULA

※

While the Crusades leveled Ma'arrat, Trotula di Ruggiero was dying in Salerno.

Since History was busy recording the feats of Christ's warriors, not much is known of her. We know that a cortege forty blocks long accompanied her to the cemetery, and that she was the first woman to write a treatise on gynecology, obstetrics, and child development.

"Women do not dare uncover their intimate parts before a male doctor, due to shame and innate reserve," wrote Trotula. Her treatise distilled her experience as a woman helping other women in delicate matters. They opened up to her, body and soul, and told her secrets that men would neither understand nor deserve to know.

Trotula taught women how to face widowhood, how to simulate virginity, how to get through childbirth and its troubles, how to avoid bad breath, how to whiten skin and teeth, and "how to repair the irreparable abuse of time."

Surgery was in fashion, but Trotula did not believe in the knife. She preferred other therapies: hands, herbs, ears. She gave gentle massages, prescribed infusions, and knew how to listen.

SAINT FRANCIS OF ASSISI

※

The crusaders laid siege to the Egyptian city of Damietta. In the year 1219, in the midst of the assault, Father Francis left his post and began walking, barefoot, alone, toward the enemy bastion.

The wind swept the ground and buffeted the earth-colored tunic of this skinny angel, fallen from heaven, who loved the earth as if from the earth he had sprouted.

From afar they saw him coming.

He said he had come to speak of peace with the sultan, Al-Kamil.

Francis represented no one, but the walls parted.

The Christian troops were of two minds. Half thought Father

Francis was crazy as a loon. The other half thought he was dumb as an ass.

Everybody knew that he talked to birds, that he liked to be called "God's minstrel," that he preached and practiced laughter, and that he told his brother monks:

"Try not to look sad, stern, or hypocritical."

People said that in his garden in the town of Assisi the plants grew upside down, their roots pointing up. And people knew that the opinions he voiced were upside down too. He thought war, the passion and profession of kings and popes, was good for winning riches, but useless for winning souls, and that the Crusades were launched not to convert Muslims, but to subdue them.

Moved by curiosity or who knows what, the sultan received him.

The Christian and the Muslim crossed words, not swords. In their long dialogue, Jesus and Mohammed did not come to terms. But they listened to each other.

ORIGIN OF SUGAR

❧

King Darius of Persia praised "this cane that makes honey without bees," and long before him the Indians and the Chinese knew of it. But Christian Europeans only discovered sugar when the crusaders saw cane fields on the plains of Tripoli and tasted the flavorful juices that saved the besieged Arab populations of Elbarieh, Marrah, and Arkah from hunger.

Mystical fervor did not blind their good eye for business, so the crusaders seized plantations and mills in the lands they conquered, from the kingdom of Jerusalem all the way to Akkra, Tyre, Crete, and Cyprus, including a place near Jericho named for good reason Al-Sukkar.

From that point forward, sugar became "white gold," sold by the gram in the apothecaries of Europe.

THE LITTLE CRUSADE AGAINST DOLCINO

❧

In the archives of the Inquisition lies the story of the final Crusade, launched at the beginning of the fourteenth century against a heretic named Dolcino and his initiates:

Dolcino had a girlfriend named Margarita who accompanied him and lived with him. He claimed he behaved toward her with utter chastity and honesty, treating her like a sister in Christ. And when she was found to be in a state of pregnancy, Dolcino and his men pronounced her with child by the Holy Ghost.

The inquisitors of Lombardy, according to the bishop of Verceil, recommended a Crusade with absolute dispensation for any sins committed therein, and they organized a significant expedition against the abovementioned Dolcino. The subject, after contaminating numerous disciples and initiates with his sermons against the faith, retreated with them to the mountains of Novarais.

There, as a consequence of the inclement temperature, it occurred that many grew weak and perished from hunger and cold, thus they died not disabused of their mistaken ways. Moreover, by scaling the mountains, the army captured Dolcino and about forty of his men. Those killed and those dead of cold and hunger numbered more than four hundred.

Along with Dolcino, the heretic and charmer Margarita was likewise captured on Holy Thursday of the year 1308 of the incarnation of Our Lord. Said Margarita was sliced up before Dolcino's eyes, and then he too was cut to pieces.

SAINTS VISITED FROM HEAVEN

❧

Saint Mechtilde of Magdeburg: "Lord, love me with strength, love me long and often. Ablaze with desire, I call to you. Your ardent love enflames me night and day. I am just a naked soul, and You within it are a guest richly adorned."

Saint Margaret Mary Alacoque: "One day when Jesus lay on me with all his weight, he responded to my protests thusly: 'I want you to be the object of my love, without any resistance on your part, so that I can take pleasure in you.'"

Saint Angela of Foligno: "It was as if I were possessed by a device that penetrated me and withdrew, scraping my entrails. My members were aching with desire . . . And by this time God wished my mother, who for me was a huge impediment, to die. Soon my husband and all my children died. I felt great solace. God did this for me, so that my heart could be in his heart."

SAINTS PORTRAY
THE DAUGHTERS OF 'EVE

❧

Saint Paul: "The head of woman is man."

Saint Augustine: "My mother blindly obeyed the one designated to be her spouse. And when women came to the house with the scars of marital anger on their faces, she told them, 'You are to blame.'"

Saint Jerome: "Woman is the root of all evil."

Saint Bernard: "Women hiss like snakes."

Saint John Chrysostom: "When the first woman spoke, it caused the original sin."

Saint Ambrose: "If women are allowed to speak again, it will bring ruin once more to man."

'FORBIDDEN TO SING

❧

In the year 1234, the Catholic religion prohibited women from singing in churches.

Women, impure thanks to Eve, befouled sacred music, which only boys or castrated men could intone.

The pain of silence lasted seven centuries, until the beginning of the twentieth.

A few years before their mouths were shut, back in the twelfth century, the nuns of Bingen convent on the banks of the Rhine still sang freely to the glory of paradise. Luckily for our ears, the liturgical music Abbess Hildegard created to rise on the wings of female voices has survived intact, unblemished by time.

In her convent at Bingen and in others where she preached, Hildegard did more than make music. She was a mystic, a visionary, a poet, and a physician who studied the personality of plants and the curative powers of waters. She also worked miracles to carve out space where her nuns could be free, despite the masculine monopoly of the faith.

FORBIDDEN TO FEEL

❈

"Oh feminine figure! How glorious you are!"

Hildegard of Bingen believed that "blood that stains is the blood of war, not the blood of menstruation," and she openly invited all to celebrate the joy of being born a woman.

In her writings on medicine and natural sciences, she dared to stand up for female pleasure in terms that were remarkable for her church and unique in the Europe of her day. Surprisingly sagacious for a puritan abbess who lived in and by strict habits, a virgin among virgins, Hildegard declared that the pleasure of love that smolders in the blood is more subtle and profound in a woman than in a man:

"In women, it is comparable to the sun and its sweetness, which delicately warms the earth and makes it fertile."

A century before Hildegard, the celebrated Persian physician Avicenna included in his *Canon of Medicine* a more detailed description of the female orgasm, "from the moment when the flesh around her eyes begins to redden, her breath quickens, and she begins to stammer."

Since pleasure was man's business, European translations of Avicenna's works omitted that page.

AVICENNA

✷

s measured by its intensity, not by its duration," he said, but he lived nearly seventy years, not bad for the eleventh century.

He was taken care of by the best doctor in Persia: himself.

For centuries his *Canon of Medicine* was the work to consult in the Arab world, in Europe, and in India.

This treatise on diseases and remedies not only collected the legacies of Hippocrates and Galen, it also drank from the springs of Greek philosophy and oriental knowledge.

At the age of seventeen, Avicenna had already set up a clinic.

Long after his death, he was still taking care of patients.

A FEUDAL LADY EXPLAINS HOW TO CARE FOR EARTHLY GOODS

✷

When it comes to sex, every churchman, from the pope in Rome to the most humble parish priest, dictates lessons on good behavior. How can they know so much about an activity they are not allowed to pursue?

As early as 1074, Pope Gregory VII warned that only those married to the Church were worthy of practicing divine service:

"Priests ought to escape the clutches of their wives," he decreed.

Soon thereafter, in 1123, the Letran Council imposed obligatory celibacy. The Catholic Church has warded off carnal temptation with a vow of chastity ever since, and it is the only enterprise run by single men in the entire religious world. The Church demands of its priests exclusive dedication, a 24/7 routine that protects the peace of their souls from conjugal strife and babies' shrieks.

Perhaps, who knows, the Church also wished to preserve its earthly goods, and thus placed them safely beyond the reach of women's and children's claims to inheritance. A trifling detail, but nevertheless it is worth recalling that at the beginning of the twelfth century the Church owned one-third of all the lands of Europe.

A FEUDAL LORD EXPLAINS HOW TO CARE
FOR THE PEASANTS

❧

At the end of the twelfth century, Bertrand de Born, lord of Péri-gord, warrior and troubadour of violent verse and valiant curse, defined his peasants thus:

By reason of his species and his manners, the peasant comes below the pig. He finds moral life profoundly repugnant. If by chance he achieves great wealth, he loses all sense. So you see, his pockets must be kept empty. He who fails to dominate his peasants only augments their vileness.

FOUNT OF THE FOUNTAIN

❧

Peasants did not tire of displeasing their lords.

The fountain of the city of Mainz offers artistic testimony to that fact.

"Don't miss it," the tourist guides insist. This German renaissance treasure, displayed in all its golden splendor in the market square, is the symbol of the city and the hub of its celebrations.

It was born of a celebration: the fountain, crowned by the Virgin and child, was a gift from the archbishop of Brandenburg to give thanks to heaven for the victory of the princes.

Desperate peasants had stormed the castles whose opulence they had paid for with their sweat, a multitude of pitchforks and hoes defying the power of cannon, spears, and swords.

Thousands of men hanged or beheaded gave mute testimony to the reestablishment of order. The fountain as well.

PLAGUES

❧

In the medieval division of labor, priests prayed, knights killed, and peasants fed all and sundry. In times of famine, peasants abandoned ruined crops and fruitless harvests, too much rain or none at all, and took to the road, fighting over carcasses and roots. And when their skin turned yellow and their eyes bugged out, they took to assaulting castles or convents.

In normal times, the peasants worked and, moreover, they sinned. When plagues occurred, the peasants caught the blame. Misfortune did not strike because the priests prayed poorly, but because their faithful were unfaithful.

From the pulpits, God's functionaries cursed them:

"Slaves to the flesh! You deserve divine punishment!"

Between 1348 and 1351, divine punishment liquidated one out of every four Europeans. The plague razed fields and cities, did in sinners and virtuous alike.

According to Boccaccio, the Florentines had breakfast with their relatives and supper with their ancestors.

WOMEN AGAINST THE PLAGUE

❧

Because the land was offended, the plague spread across Russia, annihilating animals and humans. Men had forgotten to bring offerings in gratitude for the last harvest, or they had wounded the pregnant land by driving shovels or posts into it while it slept under the snow.

Then women enacted a ritual passed down from the dark night of time. The earth, origin and destiny of all who live upon it, received her daughters, fecund like her, and not a single man dared show his face.

A woman yoked herself to the plow, oxlike, and set off to make the furrow. Others followed, sowing seeds. All walked naked, barefoot, their hair down. They banged pots and pans and laughed great big belly laughs, scaring off fear and cold and the plague.

CURSED WATER

*

We know Nostradamus from his predictions, which are still hot tickets all over the world.

We may not know that Nostradamus was also a physician, an extraordinary one who did not believe in leeches. For the plague he prescribed air and water: ventilating air, cleansing water.

Though filth incubated disease, water had a bad reputation in Christian Europe. Except in baptism, bathing was avoided because it felt good and invited sin. In the tribunals of the Holy Inquisition, frequent bathing was proof of Mohammedan heresy. When Christianity was imposed on Spain as the only truth, the crown ordered the many public baths left by the Muslims razed, because they were sources of perdition.

Not a single saint, male or female, ever set foot in a bath, and kings rarely bathed since that's what perfume was for. Queen Isabella of Castile had a soul that was sparkling clean, but historians debate whether she bathed two or three times in her entire life. The elegant Sun King of France, the first man to wear high heels, bathed only once between 1647 and 1711. And that time it was on doctor's orders.

SAINTS OF THE MIDDLE AGES PRACTICED MEDICINE ON AN INDUSTRIAL SCALE

*

According to contemporary testimony, Saint Dominic of Silos "opened the closed eyes of the blind, cleansed the filthy bodies of lepers, afforded the sick the longed for gift of health, granted the deaf their lost hearing, straightened hunchbacks, made the lame leap with glee, made the crippled jump for joy, made the mute shout . . . "

Father Bernard of Toulouse "cured twelve blind men, three deaf men, seven cripples, four hunchbacks, and healed other sick people numbering more than thirty."

Saint Louis "brought back to health an innumerable quantity of people suffering from tumefactions, gout, paralysis, blindness, fistulas, tumors and lameness."

Death did not reduce the saints' therapeutic powers. In France, cemeteries kept strict account of the miracles that healed visitors to sacred sepulchres: "41% hemiplegics and paraplegics, 19% blind, 12% demented, 8% deaf, mutes, and deaf-mutes, and 17% suffering from fevers and other maladies."

ORIGIN OF CHILDHOOD

❧

If the plague didn't get them, cold or hunger did. Execution by hunger could occur early in a poor child's life, if not enough milk was left over in Mother's breasts after nursing the infants of the rich.

But not even babes of a comfortable cradle looked out on an easy life. All over Europe, adults helped boost the infant mortality rate by subjecting their children to an education that tended toward the severe side.

The educational process started with turning babies into mummies. Every day servants wrapped them from head to foot in cloths tightly secured by straps and ties.

That way their pores were closed to plagues and to the satanic vapors that permeated the air, and what's more the infants would not be a bother. Held prisoner, they could barely breathe, never mind cry, and with arms and legs pinioned they could not kick or fuss.

If bedsores or gangrene did not finish them off, these human packages moved on to the next stage. With belts holding them upright, they learned how to stand and walk as God commands, thus avoiding the animal habit of crawling on all fours. Once they were a bit bigger, they began an intensive course in the many uses of the cat-o-nine-tails, the cane, the paddle, the wooden or iron rod, and other pedagogical tools.

Not even kings were safe. Louis XIII of France was crowned king on his eighth birthday, and he began the day by receiving his quota of lashes.

The king survived childhood.

Other children also survived, who knows how, and became adults well schooled to educate their own children.

GOD'S LITTLE ANGELS

When Flora Tristán traveled to London, she was astounded to find that English mothers never caressed their children. Children occupied the lowest rung on the social ladder, below that of women. They were as deserving of trust as a broken sword.

Nevertheless, three centuries earlier it was an Englishman who became the first high-ranking European to champion children as persons worthy of respect and enjoyment. Thomas More loved them and defended them, spent time with them every chance he got, and shared with them the desire for a life of never-ending play.

His example did not last long.

For centuries, and until very recently, corporal punishment was legal in British schools. Democratically, without regard to social class, adult civilization had the right to correct childhood barbarity by beating girls with straps and striking boys with rods or canes. In the name of morals, for many generations these disciplinary instruments corrected the vices and deviations of those who had gone astray.

Not until 1986 were straps, rods, and canes outlawed in British state schools. Later on, the private schools followed suit.

To keep children from being children, parents may still punish them as long as the blows are applied "in reasonable measure and without leaving a mark."

FATHER OF THE OGRE

The best-known children's stories, terrorist creations that they are, also merit inclusion in the arsenal of adult weaponry against little people.

Hansel and Gretel tips you off that your parents are likely to abandon you. Little Red Riding Hood teaches you that every stranger could be the wolf who will eat you up. Cinderella compels you to distrust stepmothers and stepsisters. But the character who most effectively teaches obedience and spreads fear is the Ogre.

The child-eating Ogre in Perrault's stories was based on an illustrious gentleman, Gilles de Retz, who fought alongside Joan of Arc at Orléans and in other battles.

This lord of several castles, the youngest marshal in France, was accused of torturing, raping, and killing wayward children caught wandering about his estates in search of bread or perhaps a job in one of the choruses that sang to the glory of his accomplishments.

Under torture, Gilles confessed to hundreds of infanticides, and gave detailed accounts of his carnal delights.

He ended up on the gallows.

Five and a half centuries later, he was absolved. A tribunal in the French Senate reviewed the trial, decreed it was a travesty, and revoked the sentence.

He was unable to celebrate the good news.

THE TATAR OGRE

❧

Genghis Khan, the Antichrist who led the Mongolian hordes sent by Satan, was the Ogre of the stories that for many years terrorized Europe's adults.

"They aren't men! They are demons!" shrieked Frederick II, king of Sicily and of Prussia.

In reality, Europe was offended because Genghis Khan thought the continent not worth invading. He scorned it as backward, and stuck to Asia. Using rather indelicate methods, he conquered an enormous empire that stretched from the Mongolian plateau to the Russian steppes, encompassing China, Afghanistan, and Persia.

His reputation rubbed off on the entire Khan clan.

Yet Genghis's grandson Kublai Khan did not devour raw the Europeans who turned up from time to time before his throne in Beijing. He feted them, listened to them, hired them.

Marco Polo worked for him.

MARCO POLO

%

He was in prison in Genoa when he dictated the book of his travels. His fellow inmates believed every word. While they listened to the adventures of Marco Polo, twenty-seven years wandering on the roads of the Orient, each and every prisoner escaped and traveled with him.

Three years later, the former prisoner from Venice published his book. "Published" is a manner of speaking, because the printing press had yet to appear in Europe. Several handmade copies circulated. The few readers Marco Polo found did not believe a thing.

He must have been hallucinating: how could glasses of wine float up untouched to the lips of the great Khan? How could a melon from Afghanistan cost as much as a woman? The most generous among them said the merchant writer was not well in the head.

By the Caspian Sea, on the road from Mount Ararat, this delirious raver had seen burning oils, then in the mountains of China he'd seen flaming rocks. Ridiculous at best were his claims about the Chinese having paper money bearing the seal of the Mongolian emperor, and ships that carried over a thousand people. The unicorn from Sumatra and the singing sands of the Gobi Desert evoked guffaws, and those textiles that laughed at fire, which Marco Polo found beyond Takla-makan, were simply unbelievable.

Centuries later it all came out:

the oils that burned were petroleum,

the stone that burned was coal,

the Chinese had been using paper money for five hundred years, and their ships, ten times the size of European ones, had gardens that provided sailors with fresh vegetables to prevent scurvy,

the unicorn was a rhinoceros,

the wind made the tops of the dunes in the desert whine,

and the fire-resistant fabric was made of asbestos.

At the time of Marco Polo, Europe knew nothing of petroleum, coal, paper money, large ships, rhinoceroses, high dunes, or asbestos.

'WHAT DID THE CHINESE NOT INVENT?

When I was a child, I knew China as the country on the other side of the world from Uruguay. You could get there if you had the patience to dig a hole deep enough.

Later on, I learned something about world history, but world history was the history of Europe and it remains so today. The rest of the world lay, and still lies, in darkness. China too. We know little or nothing of the past of the country that invented practically everything.

Silk began there, five thousand years ago.

Before anyone else the Chinese discovered, named, and cultivated tea.

They were the first to mine salt from below ground and the first to use gas and oil in their stoves and lamps.

They made lightweight iron plows and machines for planting, threshing, and harvesting two thousand years before the English mechanized their agriculture.

They invented the compass eleven hundred years before Europe's ships began to use them.

A thousand years before the Germans, they discovered that water-driven mills could power their iron and steel foundries.

Nineteen hundred years ago, they invented paper.

They printed books six centuries before Gutenberg, and two centuries before him they used mobile type in their printing presses.

Twelve hundred years ago, they invented gunpowder, and a century later the cannon.

Nine hundred years ago, they made silk-weaving machines with bobbins worked by pedals, which the Italians copied after a two-century delay.

They also invented the rudder, the spinning wheel, acupuncture, porcelain, soccer, playing cards, the magic lantern, fireworks, the pinwheel, paper money, the mechanical clock, the seismograph, lacquer, phosphorescent paint, the fishing reel, the suspension bridge, the wheelbarrow, the umbrella, the fan, the stirrup, the horseshoe, the key, the toothbrush, and other things hardly worth mentioning.

THE GREAT FLOATING CITY

❧

On the coast of Ceylon at the beginning of the fifth century, Admiral Zheng, commander of the Chinese fleet, etched in stone an homage to Allah, Shiva, and Buddha. And in three languages he asked the threesome to bless his sailors.

Zheng, a eunuch loyal to the empire that mutilated him, commanded the largest fleet ever to sail the seven seas.

At the center lay the gigantic ships with their gardens of fruits and vegetables, and around them a forest of a thousand masts:

"The sails catch the wind like clouds in the sky . . . "

The ships traveled to and fro between the ports of China and the coasts of Africa, passing by way of Java and India and Arabia. The mariners left China carrying porcelain, silk, jade, and they returned loaded with stories and magic plants, and giraffes, elephants, and peacocks. They discovered languages, gods, customs. They learned the ten uses of the coconut and the unforgettable flavor of the mango. They discovered horses painted in black and white stripes, and long-legged birds that ran like horses. They found incense and myrrh in Arabia, and in Turkey rare stones like amber, which they called "dragon's drool." In the southern islands they were astonished by birds that talked like men and by men who wore a rattle hanging between their legs to announce their sexual prowess.

The voyages of the great Chinese fleet were missions of exploration and commerce. They were not enterprises of conquest. No yearning for domination obliged Zheng to scorn or condemn what he found. What was not admirable was at least worthy of curiosity. And from trip to trip, the imperial library in Beijing continued growing until it held four thousand books that collected the wisdom of the world.

At the time, the king of Portugal had six books.

A GENEROUS POPE

❧

Seventy years after those voyages by the Chinese fleet, Spain launched the conquest of America and placed a Spaniard on the throne in the Vatican.

Valencia-born Rodrigo Borgia became Pope Alexander VI, thanks to the cardinals' votes he bought with four mule loads of gold and silver.

The Spanish pope then issued a bull which gave the king and queen of Spain and their inheritors, in the name of God, the islands and lands which a few years later would be named America.

The pope also confirmed that Portugal was owner and lord of the islands and lands of black Africa, from which she had been taking gold, ivory, and slaves for half a century.

His intentions were not precisely the same as those that guided Admiral Zheng's navigations. The pope gave away America and Africa "so that barbarian nations might be overpowered and converted to the Catholic faith."

At that point, America had fifteen times the population of Spain, and Africa a hundred times that of Portugal.

EVIL COPIES GOOD

❧

In one of his frescoes in a chapel in Padua, Giotto painted the torments that demons inflict on sinners in hell.

As in other artistic works of the period, the instruments of infernal torture, which provoked shock and fear, were the very tools used by the Holy Inquisition to impose the Catholic faith. God inspired his worst enemy: in hell Satan imitated the technology of pain that the inquisitors applied on earth.

Punishment confirmed that this world was but a dress rehearsal for hell. In the here and now and in the Great Beyond, disobedience merited the same reward.

ARGUMENTS OF THE FAITH

❧

For six centuries and in several countries, the Holy Inquisition punished rebels, heretics, witches, homosexuals, pagans . . .

Many ended up at the stake, sentenced to roast over a slow fire fed with green wood. Many more were subjected to torture. Here are some of the instruments utilized to extract confessions, modify beliefs, and sow panic:

the barbed collar,

the hanging cage,

the iron gag that stifled unwanted screams,

the saw that cut you slowly in two,

the finger-stretching tourniquet,

the head-flattening tourniquet,

the bone-breaking pendulum,

the seat of pins,

the long needle that perforated the devil's moles,

the iron claw that shredded flesh,

the pincer and tongs heated to fiery red,

the sarcophagus lined with sharp nails,

the iron bed that extended until arms and legs got pulled out of their sockets,

the whip with a nail or knife at the tip,

the barrel filled with shit,

the shackles, the stocks, the block, the pillory, the gaff,

the ball that swelled and tore the mouths of heretics, the anuses of homosexuals, and the vaginas of Satan's lovers,

the pincer that ground up the tits of witches and adulterers,

and fire on the feet,

among other weapons of virtue.

THE TORTURER'S CONFESSION

In the year 2003, Al-Qaeda leader Ibn al-Shaykh was tortured until he confessed that Iraq had trained him in the use of chemical and biological weaponry. Immediately, the government of the United States joyfully blandished his words as proof that Iraq deserved to be invaded.

Not long thereafter, the truth came out: as usual, the tortured said what the torturer wanted to hear.

But any discomfiture from that revelation did not impede the United States government from practicing or preaching torture around the world, calling it by its many stage names: alternative means of coercion, intensive interrogation technique, pressure and intimidation tactic, method of convincing . . .

With less and less dissembling, the biggest of the mass media now exalt the merits of the machinery for grinding human flesh, while more and more people applaud or at least accept it. Don't we have a right to defend ourselves from the terrorists and criminals threatening us?

But the inquisitors of yesteryear knew only too well, as do the country snatchers of today: torture is useless for protecting people. It is only good for terrorizing them.

The bureaucracy of pain tortures in order to perpetuate the power of the powers it serves. A confession extracted by torture is worth little or nothing. But in the torture chamber the powerful do drop their masks. By torturing, they confess that fear is their daily bread.

WE WERE ALL EXECUTIONERS

Little or no change has come to Bòria Street in Barcelona, although now it devotes itself to serving other needs.

During a good part of the Middle Ages, it was one of the settings where European justice was turned into public spectacle.

The jester and the musicians headed up the procession. The condemned man or woman left the jail on the back of an ass, naked or nearly so, and while getting the lash he or she was subjected to showers of abuse, blows, saliva, shit, rotten eggs, and other homages from the crowd.

The most enthusiastic punishers were also the most enthusiastic sinners.

MERCENARIES

❧

Now they are called contractors.

In Italy, centuries ago, they were called *condottieri*. They were killers for hire, and *condotta* was the word for contract.

Paolo Ucello painted these warriors dressed so elegantly and so graciously arranged that his paintings look more like fashion shows than bloody battles.

But the *condottieri* were men with hair on their chests, who feared nothing, except peace.

In his youth Duke Francisco Sforza had been one, and he never forgot it.

One afternoon when the duke was riding about Milan, he tossed a coin to a beggar from high up on his horse.

The beggar wished him the best:

"May peace be with you."

"Peace?"

A sword's blow knocked the coin from the beggar's hand.

OUR LADY OF THE IMPOSSIBLE

❧

Because she believed in peace, she was called Our Lady of the Impossible.

Saint Rita worked the miracle of peace in times of war,

war between neighbors,

war between families,

war between kingdoms,

war between gods.

She also performed other miracles, the last one on her deathbed. Rita asked the figs to ripen in the middle of winter and she asked the rosebush to bloom under the snow. And thus she managed to die with the taste of figs in her mouth and the scent of fresh roses in her nose, while the bells of all the churches in Cascia, her hometown, rang all by themselves.

HOLY WARRIOR

No man could best her, neither with plow nor sword.

In the silence of her garden at noon, she heard voices. Angels and saints spoke to her, Saint Michael, Saint Margaret, Saint Catherine, and even the supreme voice in heaven:

"No one in the world can liberate the kingdom of France. Except you."

And she repeated it everywhere, always citing the source:

"God told me."

Thus this unschooled peasant girl, born to harvest children, came to lead a great army that grew as it advanced.

The warrior damsel, a virgin by divine mandate or male panic, pressed on in battle after battle.

Lance in hand, charging on her steed against the English troops, she was unbeatable. Until she was beaten.

The English took her prisoner and decided to let the French deal with the lunatic.

She had battled in the name of God for France and its king, and the functionaries of God and the king sent her to the stake.

Head shaven, in chains, she had no lawyer. The judges, the prosecutor, the experts from the Inquisition, the bishops, the priors, the canonists, the notaries, and the witnesses all agreed with the learned University of the Sorbonne, which decreed that the accused was schismatic, apostate, lying, suspected of heresy, errant in her faith, and blasphemous of God and the saints.

She was nineteen when she was tied to a stake in the marketplace of Rouen and the executioner lit the fire.

Later, the fatherland and the church that roasted her changed their minds. Now Joan of Arc is a heroine and a saint, symbol of France, emblem of Christianity.

WHEN SHIPS NAVIGATED BY LAND

❧

Emperor Constantine gave his name to the city of Byzantium and that strategic meeting point of Asia and Europe became known as Constantinople.

Eleven hundred years later, when Constantinople succumbed to the Turkish siege, another emperor, another Constantine, died with her, fighting for her, and Christianity lost its open door to the Orient.

The Christian kingdoms had promised assistance, but at the moment of truth, besieged, suffocated Constantinople died alone. The enormous eight-meter cannons known as wall-busters, and the bizarre voyage of the Turkish fleet, were decisive in the final collapse. The Turkish ships had been unable to break the underwater chains that blocked their way, until Sultan Mehmet gave an unheard-of order: navigate on dry land. Riding on rolling platforms and pulled by many oxen, the ships slid over the hill that separated the Bosporus from the Golden Horn, up one side and down the other in the silence of the night. At dawn, sentries in the port discovered to their horror that the Turkish fleet, by some form of magic, was sailing the outlawed waters right under their noses.

From that point forward, the siege, which had been by land, was also by sea, and the final massacre reddened the rain.

Many Christians sought refuge in the immense cathedral of Saint Sophia, which nine centuries previous had sprung from Empress Theodora's delirium. That throng of Christians expected an angel to come down from heaven and chase the invaders out with his fiery sword.

No angel came.

Sultan Mehmet did. He entered the cathedral mounted on his white horse and turned it into the main mosque of the city now known as Istanbul.

THE DEVIL IN DISGUISE

❧

A number of years had passed since the fall of Constantinople when Martin Luther warned that Satan resided not only among the Turks and Moors, but "in our own home: in the bread we eat, in the water we drink, in the clothes we wear, and in the air we breathe."

Thus it was and thus it remains.

Centuries later, in the year 1982, the devil, in the form of a housewife who howled and slithered along the floor, dared to visit the Vatican, obliging Pope John Paul II to wage hand-to-hand combat with the evil one. He warded off the intruder by reciting the demon-killing exorcisms of another pope, Urban VIII, who chased from the head of Galileo Galilei the devilish notion that the earth revolved around the sun.

When the devil appeared in the form of an intern in the Oval Office, President Bill Clinton spurned such an antiquated Catholic methodology. He frightened off the evil one by unleashing a three-month torrent of missiles on Yugoslavia.

SHE WALKS LIKE AN ANGEL

❧

Venus turned up one morning in the city of Sienna. They found her lying naked in the sun.

The city paid homage to the marble goddess buried during the Roman Empire, who had favored them by emerging from the depths of the earth.

She was offered the pinnacle of the city's principal fountain as her home.

No one tired of gazing at her; everyone wanted to touch her.

But soon came war and its horrors, and Sienna was attacked and looted. In its session of November 7, 1357, the municipal council decided Venus was to blame. God had sent misfortune as punishment for the sin of idolatry. And the council ordered Venus, that invitation to lust, destroyed, and the pieces buried in the hated city of Florence.

In Florence, a hundred and thirty years later, another Venus was born from the hand of Sandro Botticelli. The artist painted her rising from the foam of the sea, with no more clothing than her skin.

And a decade later, when the monk Savonarola built his great bonfire of purification, it is said that Botticelli himself, repenting the sins of his brushes, fed the flames with some of the diabolical pranks he had painted in his youth.

With Venus, he could not.

DEVILCIDE

❦

The great beak of a bird of prey crowned his figure wrapped in a long black cloak. Underneath the cloak, a horsehair shirt tormented his skin.

God's wrath roared in his sermons. Father Girolamo Savonarola terrified, threatened, punished. His eloquence set the churches of Florence ablaze: he exhorted children to inform on their sinning parents, he denounced homosexuals and adulterous women hiding from the Inquisition, and he demanded that carnival be turned into a time of penance.

Pulpits burned with his holy ire, and in the piazza of the seigniory burned the bonfire of the vanities, stirred up night and day by his words. Ladies renounced pleasure and threw their jewelry, perfumes, and potions into the fire, alongside lascivious paintings and books that exalted the libertine life.

At the end of the fifteenth century, Savonarola too was tossed into the flames. Unable to control him, the Church burned him alive.

LEONARDO

❧

When he was twenty-five, the watchdogs of public morality known as the Officers of the Night took Leonardo from the workshop of his teacher Verrocchio and plunked him in a cell. Two months he spent there, unable to sleep or breathe, terrified by the prospect of the stake. Homosexuality was punished by fire, and an anonymous tip accused him of "committing sodomy in the person of Jacopo Saltrelli."

He was absolved for lack of evidence, and restored to life.

Then he painted master works, nearly all of them unfinished, which were the first to make use of sfumato and chiaroscuro,

he wrote fables, legends, and recipes,

he sketched the organs of the body perfectly for the first time, having studied anatomy from cadavers,

he proved that the world turned,

he invented the helicopter, the airplane, the bicycle, the submarine, the parachute, the machine gun, the grenade, the mortar, the tank, the moving crane, the floating dredger, the spaghetti-making machine, the bread mill . . .

and on Sundays he bought birds in the market and opened their cages.

Those who knew him said he never embraced a woman. Yet from his hand was born the most famous portrait of all times. A woman.

BREASTS

❧

To avoid punishment, some homosexuals dressed up as women and passed themselves off as prostitutes.

At the end of the fifteenth century, Venice approved a law that obliged the professionals to show their tits. Bared breasts had to be displayed in the windows where they offered their services to clients walking by. They worked beside a bridge over the Rialto, which is still called the Ponte delle Tette.

ORIGIN OF THE FORK

❧

They say Leonardo wished to perfect the fork by giving it three tines, but it ended up looking just like the trident of the king of hell.

Centuries previous, Saint Pietro Damiani decried that novelty from Byzantium:

"God would not have given us fingers if he wanted us to use that instrument of Satan."

Queen Elizabeth of England and the Sun King of France ate with their hands. When the writer Michel de Montaigne ate in a hurry, he bit his fingers. Every time the musician Claudio Monteverdi felt obliged to use a fork, he purchased three masses to pay for the sin.

VISIT TO THE VATICAN

❧

On the off chance he'll answer, I ask Michelangelo:

"Why does the statue of Moses have horns?"

"In the fresco *The Creation of Adam* in the Sistine Chapel, we all fix our gaze on the finger that gives Adam life, but who is that naked girl God is casually yet lovingly caressing with his other hand?"

"In the fresco *The Creation of Eve*, what are broken branches doing in Eden? Who cut them? Was logging allowed?"

"And in the fresco *The Last Judgment*, who is the pope who has been punched by an angel and is tumbling down to hell carrying the pontifical keys and a bulging purse?"

"The Vatican concealed forty-one little penises that you painted in that fresco. Did you know that your friend and colleague Daniele da Volterra was the one who covered those crotches with cloths of shame by order of the pope, and for that reason earned the nickname *Il Braghettone*, the Underwear Man?"

BOSCH

❦

A condemned man shits gold coins.
Another hangs from an immense key.
The knife has ears.
The harp plays the musician.
Fire freezes.
The pig wears a nun's habit.
Inside the egg lives death.
Machines run people.
Each nut dwells in his own world.
No one meets up with anyone.
All are running nowhere.
They have nothing in common, save fear of each other.
"Five centuries ago, Hieronymus Bosch painted globalization," to quote John Berger.

PRAISED BE BLINDNESS

❦

In Siracusa, Sicily, back around the year 300, Saint Lucy gouged out her eyes, or had them gouged out, for refusing to accept a pagan husband. She lost her sight to win entry to heaven, and pictures show the saint holding a platter on which she offers her eyes to Our Lord Jesus Christ.

Twelve hundred and fifty years later, Saint Ignatius of Loyola, founder of the Jesuits, published in Rome his spiritual exercises. There he wrote this testimony of blind submission:

"Take, Lord, and receive all my freedom, my memory, my understanding, and my will."

And as if that were not enough:

"To get everything right, I must always believe that what I see as white is black, if the Church hierarchy so determines."

FORBIDDEN TO BE CURIOUS

❧

Knowledge is sin. Adam and Eve ate the fruit of that tree and look what happened to them.

Some time later, Nicolaus Copernicus, Giordano Bruno, and Galileo Galilei were punished for having shown that the earth moves around the sun.

Copernicus did not dare publish his scandalous revelation until he felt death approaching. The Catholic Church included his work in the Index of Forbidden Books.

Bruno, wandering poet, spread the word about Copernicus's heresy: the earth was but one of the planets of the solar system, not the center of the universe. The Holy Inquisition locked him up in a dungeon for eight years. Several times he had the chance to repent, and several times Bruno refused. In the end, this obstinate mule was set aflame before a crowd in the Roman market at Campo de' Fiori. While he burned, they brought a crucifix to his lips. He turned away.

A few years later, exploring the heavens with the thirty-two lenses of his telescope, Galileo confirmed that the condemned man was right.

He was imprisoned for blasphemy.

He broke down during the interrogation.

In a loud voice, he swore that he cursed any who believed the earth moved around the sun.

And under his breath, they say, he murmured the phrase that made him famous for all time.

THE DANGEROUS VICE OF ASKING

❧

Which is worth more? Experience or doctrine?

By dropping stones and pebbles, big balls and little balls, Galileo Galilei proved that velocity remains the same no matter the weight. Aristotle was wrong, and for nineteen centuries no one had noticed.

Johannes Kepler, another curious fellow, discovered that plants do not rotate in circles when they follow the light over the course of a day. Wasn't the circle supposed to be the perfect path of everything that revolves? Wasn't the universe supposed to be the perfect work of God?

"This world is not perfect, not nearly," Kepler concluded. "Why should its paths be perfect?"

His reasoning seemed suspicious to Lutherans and Catholics alike. Kepler's mother had spent four years in prison accused of practicing witchcraft. They must have been up to something.

But he saw, and helped others to see in those times of obligatory gloom:

he deduced that the sun turns on its axis,

he discovered an unknown star,

he invented a unit of measure he called the "diopter" and founded modern optics.

And when his final days were drawing near, he let it be known that just as the sun determined the route of plants, the seas obeyed the moon.

"Senile dementia," his colleagues diagnosed.

RESURRECTION OF SERVET

❧

In 1553 in Geneva, Miguel Servet was reduced to ashes along with his books. At the request of the Holy Inquisition, John Calvin had him burned alive using green wood.

As if that were not fire enough, French inquisitors burned him again, in effigy, a few months later.

Servet, a Spanish physician, lived his life in flight, changing names, changing kingdoms. He did not believe in the Holy Trinity or in baptism before reaching the age of reason. And he committed the unpardonable insolence of showing that blood does not lie still, rather it flows through the body and is purified in the lungs.

That is why he is known today as the Copernicus of physiology.

Servet wrote: "In this world there is no truth, only passing shadows."

And his shadow passed.

Centuries later, it returned. It was stubborn, like him.

EUROEVERYTHING

❧

On his deathbed, Copernicus published the book that founded modern astronomy.

Three centuries before, Arab scientists Mu'ayyad al-Din al-'Urdi and Nasir al-Din Tusi had come up with the theorems crucial to that development. Copernicus used their theorems but did not cite the source.

Europe looked in the mirror and saw the world.

Beyond that lay nothing.

The three inventions that made the Renaissance possible, the compass, gunpowder, and the printing press, came from China. The Babylonians scooped Pythagoras by fifteen hundred years. Long before anyone else, the Indians knew the world was round and had calculated its age. And better than anyone else, the Mayans knew the stars, eyes of the night, and the mysteries of time.

Such details were not worthy of Europe's attention.

SOUTH

❧

Arab maps still showed the south on top and the north below, but by the thirteenth century Europe had reestablished the natural order of the universe.

According to the rules of that order, dictated by God, north was up and south was down.

The world was a body. In the north lay the limpid countenance, eyes raised to heaven. In the south lay the musky nether parts, populated by filth and by dark beings named antipodes, the reverse image of the luminous inhabitants of the north.

In the south, rivers ran backward, summers were cold, day was night, and the devil was God. The sky was black, empty. All the stars had fled north.

BESTIARY

❦

Beyond Europe, monsters swarmed, the sea bellowed, and the earth burned. A few travelers had been able to overcome their fear. Upon their return, they told their stories.

Odoric of Pordenone, who set forth in the year 1314, saw two-headed birds and hens covered in wool instead of feathers. In the Caspian Sea, live lambs emerged from the buds of plants. In Africa, Pygmies married and had children when they reached six months of age.

John Mandeville visited some of the islands of the Orient in 1356. There he saw headless people who ate and spoke through an open mouth in their chests, and he also saw people with a single foot that was sometimes used as a parasol or an umbrella. The inhabitants of the island of Tacorde, who ate nothing but raw snakes, did not speak. They hissed.

In 1410, Cardinal Pierre d'Ailly described Asia according to the tales of travelers. On the island of Taprobane there were mountains of gold, guarded by dragons and by ants as large as dogs.

Antonio Pigafetta went around the world in 1520. He saw trees that sprouted leaves with feet, and during the day they leapt from the branches and went for a stroll.

ORIGIN OF SEA BREEZES

❦

According to the stories of ancient mariners, the sea was once still, an immense lake without waves or ripples, and it could only be navigated by paddle.

Then a canoe, lost in time, arrived from the

other side of the world and found the island where the breezes lived. The mariners captured them and carried them off and obliged them to blow. The canoe rode on the captive breezes, and the mariners, who had spent centuries paddling and paddling, could at last lie down to sleep.

They never awakened.

The canoe crashed against a rocky cliff.

Ever since, the breezes wander the globe in search of their lost island home. Trade winds and monsoons and hurricanes roam the seven seas, in vain. To avenge that long-ago kidnapping, they sometimes sink the ships that cross their path.

AFTERMAP

❧

A couple of millennia ago, Seneca foretold that someday the map of the world would extend beyond Iceland, known then as Thule.

Seneca the Elder, who was a Spaniard, wrote:

> *In the later years of the world, will come*
> *certain times in which the ocean sea will release*
> *the meekness of things.*
> *And a great land will open.*
> *And a new mariner,*
> *like the one who guided Jason*
> *and who went by the name Tiphys,*
> *will discover a new world*
> *and the island of Thule will no longer be the last of the lands.*

COLUMBUS

❧

Defying the fury of the winds and the hunger of ship-eating monsters, Admiral Christopher Columbus set sail.

He did not discover America. The Polynesians had arrived a century previous, and the Vikings four centuries before that. And three hundred centuries before them all came the oldest inhabitants of these lands, people whom Columbus called Indians, believing he had entered the Orient by the back door.

Since he did not understand what they said, Columbus was convinced the natives did not know how to speak. Since they went about naked, were docile, and gave up everything in return for nothing, he believed they were not thinking beings.

Although he died insisting his travels had taken him to Asia, Columbus did begin to harbor doubts on his second voyage. When his ships anchored off the Cuban coast in the middle of June 1494, the admiral dictated a statement affirming that he was in China. He left written evidence that his crew agreed: anyone saying the contrary was to receive a hundred lashes, be fined ten thousand maravedies, and have his tongue cut out.

At the bottom of the page, the few sailors who knew how to write signed their names.

FACES

❧

The caravels left the port of Palos heading the same way as the birds, toward the void.

Four and a half centuries after the first voyage, Daniel Vázquez Díaz painted the walls of the Rábida Monastery, next door to the port, in homage to the discovery of America.

Although the artist intended a celebration, involuntarily he disclosed the rotten mood Columbus and his sailors were in. No one smiles in those paintings, and the long, somber faces portend nothing good. They sensed the worst. Perhaps those poor devils, pulled from prison or kidnapped from the docks, knew they were to do the dirty work Europe needed to become what it is today.

DESTINIES

❦

On his third crossing of the ocean sea, Christopher Columbus was clapped in chains and, in the name of the Spanish Crown, returned to Spain a prisoner.

In the name of the Crown, Vasco Núñez de Balboa lost his head.

In the name of the Crown, Pedro de Alvarado was tried and imprisoned.

Diego de Almagro was strangled to death by Francisco Pizarro, who was then stabbed sixteen times by the son of his victim.

Rodrigo de Bastidas, the first Spaniard to navigate the Magdalena River, ended his days on the point of his lieutenant's knife.

Cristóbal de Olid, conquistador of Honduras, lost his head by order of Hernán Cortés.

Hernán Cortés, the luckiest conquistador, died a marquis and in bed, but could not avoid being tried by the King's envoy.

AMERIGO

❦

Botticelli's Venus was a girl named Simonetta, who lived in Florence and married not Amerigo Vespucci, but his cousin. Lovesick, Amerigo drowned his sorrows in seawater rather than tears. And he sailed all the way to the land that now bears his name.

Under a sky of stars never before seen, Amerigo found people who had neither king nor property nor clothing, who valued feathers more than gold, and with whom he traded a brass bell for a hundred and fifty-seven pearls worth a thousand ducats. He got along well with these untrustworthy innocents, though he slept with one eye open in case they decided to roast him on a grill.

And he also feared losing his faith. Up to then he had believed, literally, in everything the Bible said. But seeing what he saw in America, Amerigo could never again believe the story of Noah's ark, because no ship, no matter how immense, could hold all those birds of a thousand plumages and a thousand calls, and the outrageously prodigious diversity of beasts, bugs, and brutes.

ISABELLA

*

Columbus left from the tiny port of Palos, not from Cádiz as planned, because it was filled to bursting. Thousands upon thousands of Jews were being expelled from the land of their forebears and the forebears of their forebears.

Columbus made his voyage thanks to Queen Isabella. So did the Jews.

And after the Jews, it was the Muslims' turn.

For ten years, Isabella battled the final bastion of Islam in Spain. When Granada fell and her Crusade ended, she did all she could to save those souls condemned to eternal hellfire. In her infinite compassion, she offered them pardon and conversion. They answered her with sticks and stones. At that point she had no choice: she ordered the sacred books of Mohammed burned in the central square of the conquered city, and she expelled the infidels who persisted in their false religion and insisted on speaking Arabic.

Other expulsion decrees, signed by other monarchs, completed the purge. Spain sent into everlasting exile her children of befouled blood, Jews and Muslims, and thus emptied herself of her finest artisans, artists, and scientists, of her most advanced farmers, and of her most experienced bankers and merchants. In exchange, Spain multiplied her beggars and her warriors, her parasitic nobles, and her fanatical monks, all of untainted Christian blood.

Isabella, born on Holy Thursday and a devotee of Our Lady of Anguishes, founded the Spanish Inquisition and named as her confessor the celebrated Supreme Inquisitor, Torquemada.

Her last will and testament, inflamed with mystical ardor, emphasized defending the purity of the faith and the purity of the race. Of the kings to come she begged and commanded them "never to cease fighting for the faith against the infidels and always to give great favor to matters of the Holy Inquisition."

THE AGES OF JUANA LA 'LOCA

❧

At the age of sixteen, she marries a Flemish prince. Her parents, the Catholic Monarchs, marry her off to a man she has never met.

At eighteen, she discovers the bath. An Arab maiden shows her the delights of water. Juana, thrilled, bathes every day. A shocked Queen Isabella comments: "My daughter is abnormal."

At twenty-three, she tries to regain her children, who for reasons of state she rarely sees. "My daughter has lost her marbles," remarks her father, King Ferdinand.

At twenty-four, on a trip to Flanders, her ship sinks. Unflappable, she demands her food be served. Her husband, stuffed into an enormous lifesaver and kicking wildly in fear, screams, "You're crazy!"

At twenty-five, scissors in hand, she hovers over several ladies of the court suspected of marital infidelity, and clips their curls.

At twenty-six, she is a widow. Her husband, recently proclaimed king, drank a glass of ice-cold water. She suspects it was poisoned. She sheds not a tear, but from then on dresses perpetually in black.

At twenty-seven, she spends her days seated on the throne in Castile, staring into space. She refuses to put her signature to laws, letters, or anything else they place before her.

At twenty-nine, her father declares her insane and locks her up in a castle on the banks of the Duero River. Catalina, the youngest of her daughters, stays with her. The girl grows up in the cell next door, and from her window watches other children play.

At thirty-six, she is alone. Her son Charles, soon to become emperor, has taken Catalina away. She refuses to eat until they bring her daughter back. They tie her up, beat her, oblige her to eat. Catalina does not return.

At seventy-six, after nearly half a century of prison life, the queen who never reigned dies. For a long time she has been immobile, gazing at nothing.

CHARLES

❧

a la Loca was a king of seventeen crowns, inherited,
ght.

in 1519, in Frankfurt, having convinced the electors of the Holy
Roman Empire with two tons of gold, he became emperor of all Europe.

This persuasive argument was lent to him by bankers: the Germans
Fugger and Welser, the Genovese Fornari and Vivaldo, and the Floren-
tine Gualterotti.

Charles was nineteen years old and already a prisoner of the bankers.
He reigned in reins.

LEGACY DENIED

❧

One night in Madrid I asked a taxi driver:

"What did the Moors bring to Spain?"

"Trouble," he answered without a trace of hesitation or doubt.

The Moors were Islamic Spaniards who called Spain home for
eight centuries, thirty-two generations, and whose culture shone there
as nowhere else.

Many Spaniards know nothing of the light still glowing from those
lamps. The Muslim legacy includes:

religious tolerance, later crushed by the Catholic Monarchs,

windmills, parks, and aqueducts that still quench the thirst of several
cities and their surrounding fields,

the postal service,

vinegar, mustard, saffron, cinnamon, cumin, cane sugar, churros,
meatballs, dried fruits,

chess,

zero and the other digits we use,

algebra and trigonometry,

classic works by Anaxagoras, Ptolemy, Plato, Aristotle, Euclid,
Archimedes, Hippocrates, Galen, and others, which became known in
Spain and in Europe through their Arabic translations,

the four thousand Arabic words in the language of Castile,
and several cities of incredible beauty, like Granada, of which an
anonymous verse sings:

> *Please give the man a penny,*
> *Lady, you must be kind,*
> *His sorrow is worse than any,*
> *To be in Granada and be blind.*

MAIMONIDES AND AVERROES

❧

Jewish and Muslim cultures flowered side by side in Spain under the
caliphs.

Two sages, Maimonides, a Jew, and Averroes, a Muslim, were born
nearly at the same time in Córdoba in the twelfth century, and they
traveled down the same path.

Both were physicians.

The sultan of Egypt was a patient of Maimonides, and Averroes took
care of the caliph of Córdoba without ever forgetting, as he wrote, that
"most deaths are caused by medicine."

Both were jurists too.

Maimonides consolidated Hebrew law, up to that point dispersed
among many books, and he brought coherence and unity to the
myriad rabbinical writings on the subject. Averroes was the highest
judicial authority in all of Muslim Andalusia, and his decisions set
precedents under Islamic law for centuries.

And both were philosophers.

Maimonides wrote *Guide for the Perplexed* to help the Jews, who had
discovered Greek philosophy thanks to Arabic translations, overcome
the contradiction between reason and faith.

That contradiction condemned Averroes. Fundamentalists accused
him of putting human reason before divine revelation. Even worse, he
refused to limit the exercise of reason to the male half of humanity,
and said that women in several Islamic nations were treated like veg-
etables. He was banished.

Neither man died in the city of his birth. Maimonides died in Cairo, Averroes in Marrakesh. A mule took Averroes back to Córdoba. The mule carried his body and his outlawed books.

STONE

✿

When triumphant Catholics invaded the Córdoba mosque, they smashed half of the one thousand columns and filled the edifice with suffering saints.

The Córdoba Cathedral is now its official name, but no one calls it that. It remains the Mosque. This forest of stone columns, the survivors, is still a Muslim temple, even though prayers to Allah are prohibited.

At the ceremonial center, in sacred space, lies a boulder, large and unadorned.

The priests allowed it to stay.

They believed it was mute.

WATER AND LIGHT

✿

Back in the year 1600-something, sculptor Luis de la Peña wanted to sculpt light. In his workshop on an alley in Granada, he spent his entire life trying and failing.

It never occurred to him to look up. There, on the crest of a hill of red earth, other artists had sculpted light, and water too.

In the turrets and gardens of the Alhambra, crown of the Muslim kingdom, those artists had made the impossible possible.

The Alhambra is not a stationary sculpture. It breathes water and light and plays with them as they cavort with each other: liquid light, shining water.

FORBIDDEN TO BE

❧

The great-grandson of Queen Isabella, Emperor Philip II, sworn enemy of water and light, reiterated certain prohibitions against the Moors, and as the year 1567 began, he decided to implement them with an iron fist.

It was forbidden to:

speak, read, or write in Arabic,

dress in traditional garb,

celebrate holidays with Moorish instruments or song,

use Moorish names or nicknames,

bathe in public baths.

This last prohibition forbade what no longer existed.

A century before, there had been six hundred public baths in the city of Córdoba alone.

THE MOST POWERFUL MAN IN THIS WORLD LIVED IN THE OTHER

❧

Emperor Chin was the founder of China, and from him China got its name. Emperor Philip II was lord and master of half the world, stretching from America to the Philippines, and from him the Philippines got its name. Both of them lived for their deaths.

The Spanish monarch spent his weekends at El Escorial cemetery, built for his eternal rest, and he slept his finest siestas in his coffin: a rehearsal.

Everything else mattered but little. His Invincible Armada had been minced, and cobwebs had invaded the coffers of the Royal Treasury, but the promenades to his funerary temple sheltered him from the world's ingratitude.

On his final journey from throne to grave, King Philip had sixty thousand masses celebrated in homage to his own glory.

'LAST SPARK OF THE TURBANS

✼

Moorish rage exploded. Against the prohibitions, the remaining children of Mohammed in the lands of Andalusia rose up.

For over a year the soldiers of Christ were unable to stamp out the flames. Then, just as in the times of the Crusades, a decisive favor came their way: they were given exclusive rights to all booty, tax-free, as well as the right to enslave all prisoners.

The forces of order then seized the wheat and the millet, the almonds, cows, sheep, silks, gold, clothing, necklaces, girls, and women. And any men they hunted down, they auctioned off.

THE DEVIL IS MUSLIM

✼

Dante knew Mohammed was a terrorist. Not for nothing did he locate him in one of the circles of hell, condemned to be disemboweled in perpetuity. "One whom I saw ripped," the poet rejoiced in *The Divine Comedy*, "right from his chin to where we fart . . ."

More than one pope found proof that the hordes of Muslims tormenting Christians were not beings of flesh and blood, rather a great army of demons that grew larger with every blow of the lance, sword, and harquebus.

Back in the year 1564, demonologist Johannes Wier counted the number of plainclothes devils working full time for the perdition of Christian souls. There were 7,409,027, organized in seventy-nine legions.

A lot of boiling water has flowed under hell's bridge since that census was taken. How many envoys from the kingdom of darkness would there be today? Their flair for the theater makes a precise tally difficult. Those sneaks still wear turbans to hide their horns, and long tunics to cover their tails and bat's wings, not to mention the bombs they carry under their arms.

THE DEVIL IS JEWISH

❧

Hitler did not invent a thing. For two thou[sand years,] unpardonable assassins of Jesus, have been t[...]

What do you mean, Jesus was Jewish? And the twe[...] four evangelists too? Impossible. Revealed truths live outside the rea[lm] of doubt: in synagogues the devil teaches Jews to defile the host, poison holy waters, cause bankruptcies, and spread plagues.

England expelled them in 1290, leaving not a one, but that did not stop Marlowe and Shakespeare, who probably never met a Jew in their lives, from inventing characters who fit the caricature of a blood-sucking parasitic moneylender.

Accused of serving the evil one, this accursed people wandered for centuries, from expulsion to expulsion, from massacre to massacre. After England, they were tossed in succession from France, Austria, Spain, Portugal, and from several Swiss, German, and Italian cities. They had lived in Spain for thirteen centuries. When they left, they took the keys to their homes with them. Some have them still.

The colossal butchery organized by Hitler was the culmination of a long history.

Hunting Jews has always been a European sport.

Now the Palestinians, who never played it, are paying the bill.

THE DEVIL IS BLACK

❧

Like the night, like sin, black is the enemy of innocence and light.

In his renowned book of travels, Marco Polo described the inhabitants of Zanzibar: "They are quite black and go entirely naked. . . . They have big mouths, and their noses are so flattened and their lips and eyes so big that they are horrible to look at. Anyone who saw them in another country would say that they were devils."

In Spain three centuries later, a black-painted Lucifer rode a chariot of fire onstage in playhouses and at fairs.

Saint Theresa could not shake him off. He stood right beside her

e, "a very abominable shade of black." Another time, when he sat
on her prayer book, she saw a red flame emerge from his black body
as the prayers burned him.

In America, everyone knew it was Satan who pounded the drums
on the plantations, calling on the thousands of imported slaves to
disobey, and who put music and writhing and shuddering into the
bodies of his children born to sin. Even Martín Fierro, the poor and
punished gaucho, felt a little better when he compared himself to the
blacks:

"Those guys were made by the Devil," he said, "as a blight on hell."

THE DEVIL IS FEMALE

Malleus Maleficarum, also known as *The Hammer of Witches*, recom-
mends the most ruthless techniques for exorcising titty, long-haired
demons.

At the request of Pope Innocent VIII, two German inquisitors,
Heinrich Kramer and Jakob Sprenger, wrote the book that became the
juridical and theological basis for the tri-
bunals of the Holy Inquisition.

The authors demonstrate that
witches, Satan's harem, repre-
sent women in their natu-
ral state, for "all witch-
craft comes from carnal
lust, which in women is insa-
tiable." And they warn that such beings of
pleasant aspect, fetid touch, and deadly
company enchant men and attract them, serpent's hiss, scorpion's tail,
only to annihilate them.

That treatise on criminology advises torturing everyone suspected
of witchcraft. Those who confess deserve the stake; those who do not
also deserve the stake, because only a witch, fortified by her lover the
devil at the witches' Sabbath, could resist such suffering without telling
all.

Pope Honorius III decreed:

"Women should not speak. Their lips carry the stigma of Eve, who led men to perdition."

Eight centuries later, the Catholic Church still denies women the pulpit.

The same fear drives fundamentalist Muslims to mutilate women's genitalia and cover their faces.

And a sense of relief moves orthodox Jewish men to begin each day by whispering:

"Thanks be to God for not making me a woman."

THE DEVIL IS POOR

❧

Today's cities are immense jails holding prisoners of fear, where fortresses masquerade as homes and armor as clothing.

A state of siege. Do not get distracted, do not let down your guard, do not ever trust, say the lords of the world, masters of impunity who rape the environment, kidnap countries, extort wages, and murder by the throng. Watch out, they warn, the bad guys are right there, huddled in miserable slums, chewing on their envy, resentfully licking their wounds.

The poor: the ragamuffins for all bondage, the dead for all wars, the flesh for all prisons, the bargain-basement hands for all jobs.

Hunger, which kills silently, kills the silent. Experts speak for them, poorologists who tell us what the poor do not work at, what they do not eat, what they do not weigh, what height they do not reach, what they do not have, what they do not think, what parties they do not vote for, what they do not believe in.

The only question unanswered is why poor people are poor. Could it be because we are fed by their hunger and clothed by their nakedness?

THE DEVIL IS FOREIGN

*

The blame-o-meter indicates that immigrants have come to steal our jobs, and the danger-o-meter is flashing red.

If poor, young, and nonwhite, the intruder from outside is deemed guilty at first sight, guilty of indigence, of chaos, of carrying the unconcealed weapon of his skin. If neither poor nor young nor dark, a nasty welcome is justified in any case, since he or she has come prepared to work twice as hard for half as much.

Anxiety about losing one's job is among the most fearsome of all the fears that govern us in these times of fear, and immigrants are always at hand to take responsibility for unemployment, shrinking wages, crime, and other calamities.

In times past, Europe showered soldiers, prisoners, and starving peasants on the south of the world. These protagonists of colonial adventures went down in the history books as envoys of God and civilization sent to save barbaric lands.

Now comes the return voyage. Those who travel south to north, or perish in the attempt, are protagonists of colonial misadventures, and in the history books they will go down as envoys of the devil and barbarism sent to ruin civilized lands.

THE DEVIL IS HOMOSEXUAL

*

In Renaissance Europe, fire was the fate reserved for the children of hell, since from fire they had come. England punished with "horrendous death those who had had sexual relations with animals, Jews, or persons of the same sex."

Before the Spanish Conquest, homosexuals were free in America, except in the kingdoms of the Aztecs and the Incas. Conquistador Vasco Núñez de Balboa took Indians who practiced that abnormality with utter normality and threw them to hungry dogs. He believed homosexuality was contagious. Five centuries later, I heard the same story from the archbishop of Montevideo.

Historian Richard Nixon knew the vice could be fatal for civilization:

"You know what happened to the Greeks? Homosexuality destroyed them. Sure, Aristotle was a homo, we all know that, so was Socrates. Do you know what happened to the Romans? The last six emperors were fags."

Civilizer Adolf Hitler took drastic measures to save Germany from the peril. "Degenerates guilty of aberrant crimes against nature" were obliged to wear a pink triangle. How many of them died in the concentration camps? No one knows.

In the year 2001, the German government decided "to rectify the exclusion of homosexuals from being counted among the victims of the Holocaust." It took them more than half a century to correct the omission.

THE DEVIL IS GYPSY

❀

Hitler believed "the Gypsy plague" was a threat, and he was not alone.

Centuries ago many people became convinced that this race of dark color carries crime in its veins, and they believe it still: always unwelcome, drifters with no home but the road, defilers of lasses and latches, charmed fingers for cards and the knife.

In a single night in August 1944, 2,897 Gypsies, women, children, men, perished in the gas chambers of Auschwitz.

Of all the Gypsies of Europe, one in four was annihilated during the war.

About them, who even asked?

THE DEVIL IS INDIAN

The conquistadors confirmed that Satan, expelled from Europe, had found refuge on the islands and coasts of the Caribbean kissed by his fiery mouth.

There lived beastly beings who called carnal sin "play," and who practiced it at all hours and with all comers, who knew nothing of the Ten Commandments or the Seven Sacraments or the Seven Deadly Sins, who went about naked, and who had the habit of eating each other.

The conquest of America was a long and thorny exorcism. The evil one was so deeply rooted in this land that when the Indians seemed to be devotedly kneeling before the Virgin, they were really praying to the serpent crushed beneath her foot. And when they kissed the cross they were celebrating the encounter between the rain and the earth.

The conquistadors fulfilled the mission of returning to God the gold, silver, and numerous other riches that the devil had usurped. Recovering the booty was no easy task. Now and again, however, they got a little help from above. When the lord of hell laid an ambush in a narrow canyon to keep the Spaniards from reaching the mountain of silver in Potosí, an archangel came down from the heights and gave him a tremendous thrashing.

ORIGIN OF AMERICA

In Cuba, according to Christopher Columbus, there were mermaids with men's faces and roosters' feathers.

In Guyana, according to Sir Walter Raleigh, there were people with eyes on their shoulders and mouths in their chests.

In Venezuela, according to Father Pedro Simon, there were Indians with ears so big they dragged along the ground.

In the Amazon, according to Cristóbal de Acuña, there were natives who had their feet on backward, heels in front and toes in the rear.

According to Pedro Martín de Anglería, who wrote the first history of America but never visited it, in the New World there were men and women with tails so long they could only sit on seats with holes.

DRAGON OF EVIL

❦

In America, Europe encountered the iguana.

This diabolical beast had been foreseen in depictions of dragons. The iguana has a dragon's head, a dragon's snout, a dragon's crest and armor, and a dragon's claws and tail.

But if the dragon was like the iguana is, then Saint George's lance missed the mark.

It only acts strangely when in love. Then, it changes color and mood, grows nervous, loses its appetite and its way, and becomes skittish. When not tormented by love, the iguana makes friends with everyone, climbs trees in search of tasty leaves, swims in rivers just for fun, and naps in the sun on flat rocks, hugging other iguanas. It threatens no one, knows not how to defend itself, and is not even capable of giving a stomachache to humans who eat it.

AMERICANS

❦

Official history has it that Vasco Núñez de Balboa was the first man to see, from a summit in Panama, two oceans at once. Were the natives blind?

Who first gave names to corn and potatoes and tomatoes and chocolate and the mountains and rivers of America? Hernán Cortés? Francisco Pizarro? Were the natives mute?

The Pilgrims on the *Mayflower* heard Him: God said America was the promised land. Were the natives deaf?

Later on, the grandchildren of the Pilgrims seized the name and everything else. Now they are the Americans. And those of us who live in the other Americas, who are we?

FACES AND MASKS

❧

On the eve of every assault on a village, the Requerimiento of Obedience explained to the Indians that God had come into the world and left Saint Peter in his place and that Saint Peter named the pope as his successor and the pope had bestowed all these lands on the queen of Castile and for that reason they must either leave or pay tribute in gold and in case of refusal or delay they would be attacked and they and their women and their children would be enslaved.

This Requerimiento was read at night in the wild, in the language of Castile without interpretation, in the presence of a notary and not a single Indian.

THE FIRST WATER WAR

❧

The great city of Tenochtitlán was of water born and of water built.

Dikes, bridges, sewers, canals: along streets of water two hundred thousand canoes traveled back and forth between houses and squares, temples, palaces, markets, floating gardens, planted fields.

The conquest of Mexico began as a water war, and the defeat of water decreed the defeat of everything else.

In 1521, Hernán Cortés laid siege to Tenochtitlán, and the first thing he did was take an ax to the wooden aqueduct that carried drinking water from the Forest of Chapultepec. Following many massacres, when the city fell, Cortés ordered the temples and palaces demolished and the rubble thrown into the liquid streets.

Spain did not like water, the devil's toy, a Muslim heresy.

Vanquished water gave birth to Mexico City, raised on the ruins of Tenochtitlán. Engineers picked up where the warriors left off and, over many years, they blocked up with stone and earth the entire circulatory system of the region's lakes and rivers.

Then water took revenge, flooding the colonial city repeatedly, which only confirmed that it was an ally of the pagan Indians and the enemy of all good Christians.

Century after century, the dry world waged war on the wet world. Now Mexico City is dying of thirst. In search of water, it digs. The deeper it digs, the further it sinks. Where once there was air, now there is dust. Where once there were rivers, now there are avenues. Where once water flowed, now traffic streams by.

ALLIES

❧

Hernán Cortés conquered Tenochtitlán with a force of six hundred Spaniards and innumerable Indians from Tlaxcala, Chalco, Mixquic, Chimalhuacan, Amecameca, Tlalmanalco, and other peoples humiliated by the Aztec Empire and tired of bathing the steps of the Templo Mayor in their blood.

They thought the bearded warriors had come to liberate them.

BALL GAME

❧

Hernán Cortés threw the ball to the ground. And Emperor Charles and his numerous courtiers witnessed an unprecedented marvel: the ball bounced and flew skyward.

Europe knew nothing of that magic ball, but in Mexico and Central America rubber had been in use forever and the ball game had been around for three thousand years.

In the game, a sacred ceremony, the thirteen heavens above battled the nine underworlds below, and the bouncing ball flew back and forth between darkness and light.

Death was the prize. He who triumphed offered himself to the gods so that the sun in the sky would not go out, and rain would continue to water the earth.

OTHER WEAPONS

❦

How did Francisco Pizarro, with sixty-eight soldiers, manage to defeat the eighty thousand men of Atahualpa's army in Peru without a single casualty?

The invaders, Cortés, Pizarro, astutely exploited divisions among the invaded, torn by hatred and war, and with empty promises they managed to multiply their forces against the centers of Aztec and Incan power.

Besides, the conquistadors used weapons unknown in America.

Gunpowder, steel, and horses were incomprehensible novelties. Clubs were useless against cannon and harquebuses, lances and swords, as was cloth armor against steel, or fighters on foot against those six-legged warriors of horseman and horse. No less unknown were small-pox, measles, influenza, typhus, bubonic plague, and other involuntary allies of the invading troops.

And as if all that weren't enough, the Indians knew nothing of the customs of civilized life.

When Atahualpa, king of the Incas, approached to welcome his strange visitors, Pizarro took him prisoner and promised to free him in exchange for the largest ransom ever demanded. Pizarro got his ransom and chopped off his hostage's head.

ORIGIN OF BACTERIOLOGICAL WARFARE

❦

For America, Europe's embrace was deadly. Nine out of every ten natives died.

The smallest warriors were the most ferocious. Viruses and bacteria, like the conquistadors, came from other lands, other waters, other air.

And the Indians had no defenses against that invisible army advancing with the troops.

The numerous inhabitants of the Caribbean islands disappeared from this world, leaving not even the memory of their names. Plagues killed many more than the many killed by slavery and suicide.

Smallpox killed the Aztec king Cuitláhuac and the Incan king Huayna Cápac, and in Mexico City its victims were so numerous that entire families were buried by bringing their homes down on top of them.

The first governor of Massachusetts, John Winthrop, said smallpox had been sent by God to clear the way for His chosen people. Clearly, the Indians had settled at the wrong address. The colonists of North America lent a hand to His Holiest on more than one occasion by giving the Indians blankets infected with smallpox.

"To extirpate this execrable race," explained the commander, Lord Jeffrey Amherst, in 1763.

OTHER MAPS, SAME STORY

Nearly three centuries after Columbus disembarked in America, Captain James Cook navigated the mysterious seas of the southeast, planted the British flag in Australia and New Zealand, and opened the way for the conquest of the infinite islands of Oceania.

Due to their white skin, the natives believed those seamen were the dead returned to the world of the living. And due to their acts, the natives learned that they had come to take revenge.

And history repeated itself.

As in America, the recent arrivals took over the fertile fields and the sources of water and pushed those who lived there into the desert.

As in America, they subjected the natives to forced labor and outlawed their memory and their customs.

As in America, Christian missionaries crushed or burned pagan effigies of stone or wood. A few escaped that fate and, minus their penises, were shipped to Europe to give testimony to the war against idolatry. The god Rao, who now sits on exhibition in the Louvre, arrived in Paris with a label that defined him thusly: "Idol of impurity, vice, and unabashed passion."

As in America, few natives survived. Those not killed by hunger or bullets were annihilated by unknown plagues against which they had no defense.

BEDEVILED

*

They will come to teach fear.
They will come to castrate the sun.

Mayan prophets in Yucatan had announced this time of humiliation.

And it was in Yucatan in 1562 that Father Diego de Landa, in a lengthy ceremony, built a bonfire of books.

And the exorcist wrote:

"We found a great number of books written in these letters of theirs and, since they contained nothing but the Devil's superstition and falsehoods, we burned them all."

The scent of sulfur could be detected from afar. The Mayans deserved the stake for being curious, for tracking the course of the days through time and the route of the stars across the thirteen heavens.

Among many other devilish things, they invented the most precise of all the calendars that have ever existed, they knew better than anyone how to predict eclipses of the sun and moon, and they discovered the number zero long before the Arabs kindly brought that novelty to Europe.

PALACE ART IN THE MAYAN KINGDOMS

*

The Spanish Conquest occurred long after the fall of the Mayan kingdoms.

Only ruins remained of their immense plazas and of the palaces and temples where kings, squatting before the high priests and warrior chiefs, decided the fate and misfortune of everyone else.

In those sanctuaries of power, painters and sculptors dedicated themselves to exalting the gods and venerating the exploits of monarchs past and present.

Palace art left no room for the many who worked and remained silent.

Neither did the defeat of any kings figure in the codices or murals or bas-reliefs.

A king of Copán, for example, known as 18 Rabbit, raised Cauac Sky as a son and gave him the throne of the neighboring kingdom of Quiriguá. In the year 737, Cauac Sky returned the favor: he invaded Copán, humiliated its warriors, captured his protector, and cut off his head.

Art never found out. No bark book was written, no stone was chiseled to illustrate the sad end of the decapitated king, who in his days of splendor had been portrayed several times with his courtiers and his robes of feathers, jade, and jaguar skin.

KILLING FORESTS, THEY DIED

❧

Ever more mouths and ever less food. Ever less forest and ever more desert. Too much rain or no rain at all.

Held on by ropes, peasants scratched in vain at the steep flayed slopes. The corn found no water or earth on which to raise its stalk. The soil, without trees to retain it, stained the rivers red and was lost to the wind.

After three thousand years of history, night fell on the Mayan kingdoms.

But the days of the Mayans walked on in the lives of the peasants. Communities moved and survived, practically in secret, without pyramids of stone or pyramids of power: with no king but the sun rising every day.

THE LOST ISLE

❋

Far from the Mayan kingdoms and centuries later, Easter Island was devoured by its children.

The European navigators who arrived there in the eighteenth century found it empty of trees and of everything else.

It was terrifying. Never had they seen a solitude so lonely. No birds in the sky, no grass on the ground, no animals but rats.

Of the verdant past of long ago, no memory remained. The island was a stone inhabited by five hundred stone giants staring at the horizon, nowhere near anything or anyone.

Perhaps those statues were asking the gods to rescue them. But not even the gods could hear their mute voices, as lost in the middle of the ocean as the earth in the infinite sky.

KINGLESS KINGDOMS

❋

According to historians and practically everyone else, Mayan civilization disappeared centuries ago.

Afterward, nothing.

Nothing: community life, born in silence and in silence borne, awakened neither admiration nor curiosity.

It did evoke astonishment, however, at least at the time of the Spanish Conquest. The new lords were worried: these kingless Indians had lost the habit of obeying.

Father Tomás de la Torre recounted in 1545 that the Tzotziles from Zinacantán chose someone to run the war and "when he did not do it well, they got rid of him and chose another." In war, and also in peace, communities elected their leaders, and they chose the best listeners.

Colonial authorities used lash and noose aplenty to oblige the Maya to pay tribute and perform forced labor. In Chiapas in 1551, Magistrate Tomás López saw that they rejected servitude and he admonished:

"These are people who work enough to get by and no more."

A century and a half later, in Totonicapán, Governor Fuentes y Guzmán had to admit that the new despotism had not made much headway. The Indians continued living "without any superior leader to obey, and among themselves it is all meetings, conversation, advice, and mystery, and for ourselves nothing."

DOOMED BY YOUR PAST

❧

Corn, sacred plant of the Maya, was given several names in Europe. The names recast geography: they called it Turkish grain, Arab grain, grain of Egypt, or grain of India. These errors did nothing to rescue corn from mistrust and scorn. When people learned where it came from, they fed it to the pigs. Corn had a higher yield than wheat and it grew faster, resisted drought, and produced good food. But it was not proper for Christian mouths.

The potato was also a forbidden fruit in Europe. Like corn, its American origins condemned it. Worse, the potato was a root grown in the depths of the earth, where hell has its caves. Doctors knew it caused leprosy and syphilis. In Ireland, if a pregnant woman ate a potato at night, in the morning she would give birth to a monster. Until the end of the eighteenth century, the potato was fed only to prisoners, lunatics, and the dying.

Later on, this cursed root rescued Europe from hunger. But not even then did people stop wondering: if not food of the devil, then why are potatoes and corn not mentioned in the Bible?

DOOMED BY YOUR FUTURE

❧

Centuries before the advent of cocaine, coca was "the Devil's leaf."

Since the Indians of the Andes chewed it in their pagan ceremonies, the Church included coca among the idolatries to be extirpated. But far from disappearing, coca plantations grew fiftyfold. The Spaniards realized the plant was indispensable to mask hunger and exhaustion among the multitudes digging silver out of the bowels of Cerro Rico in Potosí.

In time, the colonial lords also embraced coca. As a tea, it cured indigestion and colds, relieved pain, renewed vigor, and eased altitude sickness.

Nowadays, coca is still sacred to the indigenous peoples of the Andes and it remains good medicine for anyone. But airplanes destroy the fields to keep coca from becoming cocaine.

Of course, cars kill many more people than cocaine and nobody talks about outlawing the wheel.

ANANAS

❦

The *ananas*, or *abacaxi*, which the Spaniards called *piña* and the English *pineapple*, had better luck.

Although it came from America, this exquisite delight was cultivated in the greenhouses of the kings of England and France, and was celebrated by every mouth that had the privilege of tasting it.

And centuries later, when machines hacked off its headdress and stripped it nude and gouged out its eyes and heart and sliced and canned it at a hundred fruits a minute, in Brazil architect Oscar Niemeyer offered it the homage it deserved: the *ananas* became a cathedral.

DON QUIJOTE

❦

Marco Polo dictated his book of marvels in the Genoa jail.

Exactly three centuries later, Miguel de Cervantes sired *Don Quijote de La Mancha* in the Seville jail, where he had been imprisoned for unpaid debts. And it was another flight of freedom launched from behind bars.

Stuffed into his tin-can armor, atop his skeletal mount, Don Quijote seemed fated for eternal ridicule. A madman who believed he was a character out of a chivalric novel and that chivalric novels were history books.

But we readers who for centuries laughed at him also laughed with him. A broom is a horse for a playful child, and while we read we share in his harebrained misadventures and make them our own. So much our own that the antihero becomes a hero, and we even attribute to him things he never said. "They bark, Sancho, the signal for us to ride," is the quotation most often cited by Spanish-speaking politicians. Only Don Quijote never said it.

The sad-faced knight had spent over three and a half centuries stumbling along the roads of the world when Che Guevara wrote his last letter to his parents. To say goodbye the revolutionary did not choose a quote from Marx. He wrote: "Once again beneath my heels I feel Rocinante's ribs. I take to the road again with my shield held high."

The sailor sails on, though he knows he will never touch the stars that guide him.

LABOR RELATIONS

❧

Rocinante, Don Quijote's stallion, was nothing but skin and bones.

"Metaphysical you are."

"Because I don't eat."

Rocinante merely ruminated on his complaints, but Sancho Panza railed against the exploitation of the squire by the knight. He complained about the pay he received for his labor, nothing but blows, hunger, bad weather, and promises, and he demanded a decent wage in cold, hard cash.

Don Quijote found such expressions of crass materialism despicable. Invoking his fellows of the errant knighthood, the noble gentleman concluded:

"Squires never ever worked for wages, rather for the good will of their masters."

And he promised Sancho Panza he would be made governor of the first kingdom his master conquered, and he would receive the title of count or marquis.

But the plebeian wanted a steady job with a regular paycheck. Four centuries have passed. We're no farther along.

HEMOPHOBIA

❧

Beginning in the fifteenth century, and for the longest time, Spain required proof of clean blood.

"Clean" meant pure Christian blood, by lineage inherited or purchased. Those who were Jews, Moors, heretics, or descendants of Jews, Moors, or heretics up to the seventh generation, could not hold public office, be it civil, military, or ecclesiastical.

From the sixteenth century on, clean blood was a prerequisite for travel to America. It seems that was the reason why Cervantes could not take off for the New World. Twice, he was rejected: "Look here for what may please you," was the terse official response.

Some Jewish blood cell was suspected of navigating the veins of the father of Don Quijote. Dishonorable races were given to literature.

DEATH BY DOCTOR

❧

At the beginning of the nineteenth century, the French bought more than thirty million leeches a year.

For many centuries, doctors had been bleeding patients by leech or by cuts to free the body of bad blood. Bleeding was the preferred remedy for pneumonia, depression, rheumatism, apoplexy, broken bones, nervous exhaustion, and headaches.

Bleeding debilitated the sick. No evidence that it worked was ever recorded, but science continued using it as a cure-all for twenty-five hundred years, until well into the twentieth century.

That infallible remedy caused more devastation than all the plagues combined.

MOLIÈRE

❦

As if the bite of the plague were not bad enough, fear of disease became a new disease.

In England, doctors looked after patients who believed they were fragile clay figurines, and who stayed away from people for fear they would bump into them and shatter. In France, Molière dedicated the last of the plays he wrote, directed, and acted in to the imaginary invalid.

Mocking his own obsessions, Molière poked fun at himself. He played the lead role: buried in the pillows of his easy chair, wrapped in furs, cap pulled down over his ears, he underwent continual bleedings, purges, and cleanses, prescribed by doctors who diagnosed bradyspepsia, dyspepsia, apepsia, lientery, dysentery, hydropsy, hypochondria, hypocrisy . . .

One afternoon, not long into a successful run, the entire cast pleaded with him to cancel the performance. Molière was very ill, truly ill and not only with a fevered imagination. He coughed more than he breathed and could barely speak or walk.

Cancel the performance? He never bothered to answer. His fellow actors were asking him to betray the kingdom where he had lived ever since that fine day when he was reborn as Molière, for the pleasure of all good people.

And that night, the imaginary invalid made the full house laugh as never before. Comedy, written and acted by Molière, took him out of his suffering and his fear of death, and he pulled off the greatest performance of his life. He coughed hard enough to break a rib, but forgot not a word of his long monologues, and when he vomited blood and fell to the floor the audience believed, or knew, that death was part of the play, and they gave him a standing ovation as the curtain fell with him.

ORIGIN OF ANESTHESIA

❦

The carnival of Venice lasted four months, except when it lasted longer.

From everywhere came acrobats, musicians, thespians, puppeteers, prostitutes, magicians, fortune-tellers, and vendors offering love potions, good-luck tonics, and elixirs for a long life.

And from everywhere came the tooth pullers and the aching mouths that Saint Apollonius had been unable to cure. In agony, the latter approached the gates of Saint Mark, where, pliers in hand, the extractors awaited, anesthetists at their side.

The anesthetists did not put patients to sleep: they entertained them. They gave them not poppy or mandrake, but jokes and pirouettes. And their humor and grace were so miraculous that pain forgot to hurt.

The anesthetists were monkeys and dwarfs, dressed for carnival.

ORIGIN OF THE VACCINATION

❧

At the beginning of the eighteenth century, smallpox killed half a million Europeans a year.

That was when Lady Mary Wortley Montagu, wife of the British ambassador in Istanbul, tried to get Europe to adopt Turkey's tried and true method of prevention: a drop of variolic pus immunized against the murderous plague. But people mocked a woman masquerading as a scientist and preaching chicanery from pagan lands.

Seventy years later, an English doctor, Edward Jenner, inoculated the son of his gardener, an eight-year-old, with the so-called cowpox, which devastated the herds but did humans little harm. And then he gave him the deadly smallpox. The child did not fall ill.

Thus the vaccination was born, owing its existence to a child of servants used as a laboratory guinea pig, and owing its name to the Latin word for cow, *vacca*.

ORIGIN OF THE PROCESSION

❧

In 1576 a plague caused a conflict between Archbishop Carlo Borromeo, a sinner on his way to sainthood, and the governor of Milan. The archbishop ordered his followers to gather in the churches and beg God to pardon the sins that had brought the plague upon them. But the governor prohibited any gathering in closed buildings to avoid contagion.

So Archbishop Borromeo invented the procession. He ordered the saints and all their relics taken from the churches and carried through the city streets on the shoulders of the crowd.

A sea of lilies, tapers, and angels' wings stopped at the door of every church to sing hymns of praise to the virtuous of Christendom, and to perform scenes from their lives and miracles.

Thespians died of envy.

MASKS

In Milan, Archbishop Borromeo deplored that "this adulterous, ungrateful world, enemy of God, this blind and crazy, ugly and pestiferous world," had submitted to the masked lasciviousness of pagan festivals.

And he passed sentence on masks:

"Masks deform the human face and thus profane our divine likeness to God."

In the name of God, the Church outlawed them. In the name of freedom, some time later, Napoleon did the same.

The masks of commedia dell'arte found refuge among the puppets.

With four sticks and a rag, puppeteers put on their tiny shows in public squares shared with acrobats, drifters, wandering minstrels, storytellers, and carnival magicians.

And when the masked puppets' mockery of the lords and ladies got out of hand, the police whacked the puppeteers with their nightsticks and hauled them off to jail. And the puppets were left abandoned, gloves without hands, in the dark and empty square.

OTHER MASKS

❧

African masks will not make you invisible. They neither hide, nor disguise, nor mask.

The gods that founded our earthly life in Africa send masks to transmit energy to their children. The mask with bull's horns gives strength, the one featuring antelope antlers offers speed, the one with an elephant's trunk teaches resistance, the one that has wings makes you fly.

Whenever a mask breaks, the mask-maker carves a new one. The mask's spirit will not be left homeless, and the people will not be left helpless.

PASQUINADES

❧

The word "pasquinade," meaning a libelous lampoon, comes from a statue in Rome. On the breast or back of that marble personage named Pasquino, anonymous hands wrote homages to the popes.

- On Alexander VI:
  Alexander sells the nails and he sells Jesus crucified.
  There'll be no challenge to those sales: Al bought the goods before He
  died.

- On Leo X:
  Dead is the tenth of the Pope Leos,
  well-known for the affection he had
  for knaves and false impresarios
  for tyrants rotten, dishonest, and bad.

- On Paul IV:
  More faith, my children, and much less thought,
  the Holy Office says a lot.
  And there's no reason they need name,

since to extinguish reason they have flame.
And keep your tongues hidden, don't let them be viewed,
'cause Pope Paul likes them barbecued.

- And this is what the statue of Pasquino said to Pope Pius V, who sent quite a few suspected writers of pasquinades to the stake:
The gallows, oh, and the slow fire,
all the torments you desire,
frighten me not, Pius my dear.
You can send me to the stake
but shut me up you cannot make.
Of stone I'm made. I laugh, I sneer.
For you I am a threat to fear.

RECORD OF THE DEVIL'S CONFESSION

❧

He had been decrepit since childhood.

Charles II, king of Spain and of America, was over thirty yet he had to be spoon-fed and he could not walk without falling down.

Useless were the dead pigeons the doctors placed on his head, and equally useless the capons raised on snake meat that his servants put down his throat, the cow's piss they gave him to drink, and the scapularies stuffed with fingernails and eggshells slipped under his pillow by the friars who watched over his sleep.

Twice they married him off and no prince was born to either queen, even though both breakfasted on donkey's milk with extract of agaric mushroom.

At that time the devil lived in Asturias, inside the body of a nun in the convent at Cangas. The exorcist, Father Antonio Álvarez Argüelles, extracted this confession:

"It is true that the king has been cursed," the exorcist said the nun said the devil said. And the hex had been carried out with the remains of a cadaver.

"Using brains to disarm his ability to lead. Using entrails to destroy his health. Using kidneys to keep him from siring."

And the exorcist said the nun said the devil said the author of the evil deed was a woman. The king's mom, to be precise.

TERESA

&

Teresa of Ávila entered the convent to save herself from hell, the conjugal hell. Better to be a slave to God than servant to a brute.

But Saint Paul gave women three rights: "to obey, to serve, and to remain silent." So the representative of His Holiness the pope found Teresa guilty "of being an apprehensive and unsettled female, disobedient and contumacious, who under the guise of devotion invents evil doctrines against Saint Paul, who commanded women not to teach."

In Spain, Teresa founded several convents where the nuns not only gave classes but were in charge, where virtue was prized and lineage worthless, where no one had to submit proof of clean blood.

In 1576 she was accused before the Inquisition, because her grandfather claimed to be a true Christian but was a converted Jew, and because her mystical trances were the work of the devil ensconced in her body.

Four centuries later, on his deathbed, Francisco Franco wielded Teresa's right arm to defend himself from the devil. By one of those strange turns life takes, Teresa had become a saint and a role model for Iberian women and, except for one foot which ended up in Rome, her remains were housed in several churches around Spain.

JUANA

&

Like Teresa of Ávila, Juana Inés de la Cruz became a nun to remain free of the matrimonial cage.

Like Teresa, in the convent her talent caused offense. Did this head of a woman contain the brain of a man? Why did she have a man's handwriting? Since she was such a good cook, why would she want to think? Deriding her questioners, she answered:

"What could we women know, but kitchen philosophy?"

Like Teresa, Juana wrote, although the priest Gaspar de Astete warned her that "Christian maidens need not know how to write, and it may cause them harm."

Like Teresa, Juana not only wrote, but, scandal of scandals, she wrote undeniably well.

In different centuries, on different shores of the same sea, Juana the Mexican and Teresa the Spaniard defended, aloud and on paper, the despised half of the world.

Like Teresa, Juana was threatened by the Inquisition. And the Church, her Church, persecuted her for extolling human concerns as much or more than divine ones, for seldom obeying, and for questioning far too much.

With blood, not ink, Juana signed her confession. She vowed eternal silence. And mute she died.

GOODBYE

&

The best paintings by Ferrer Bassa, the Giotto of Catalunia, are on the walls of the convent of Pedralbes, place of bleached stones, in the heights of Barcelona.

There, detached from the world, lived the cloistered nuns.

It was a one-way street: the gate closed behind them and it closed for good. Their families paid large dowries so they would merit the glory of being forever married to Christ.

Within the convent, at the foot of one of the Ferrer Bassa frescoes in the chapel of Saint Michael, there are words that have survived, as if in hiding, the passing of the centuries.

No one knows who wrote them.

But we do know when. There is a date in Roman numerals, 1426.

The words are barely decipherable. In gothic letters, in Catalan, they pled and plead still:

Tell Juan
not to forget me.

TITUBA

❧

She was captured in South America as a child, and was sold and sold again and then once more, passed from owner to owner until she ended up in the town of Salem in North America.

There, in that Puritan sanctuary, the slave Tituba served in the home of Reverend Samuel Parris.

The daughters of the reverend adored her. They were in heaven when Tituba told them stories of apparitions or read their fortunes in the whites of an egg. And in the winter of 1692, when the girls were possessed by Satan and writhed shrieking on the floor, only Tituba could calm them. She caressed them and whispered stories until they fell asleep in her lap.

That sealed her fate: she was the one who had brought hell into the virtuous kingdom of God's chosen people.

The storytelling magician was put in the stocks in the public square, and she confessed.

They accused her of baking pies from the devil's recipe book, and they whipped her until she said yes.

They accused her of dancing naked at the witches' Sabbath, and they whipped her until she said yes.

They accused her of sleeping with Satan, and they whipped her until she said yes.

And when they told her that her accomplices were two old ladies who never went to church, the accused became the accuser and she pointed her finger at the possessed pair. And they stopped whipping her.

Then other accused also accused.

And the gallows were never empty.

WOMEN POSSESSED

❧

Theologian and friar Martín de Castañega confirmed that the devil preferred women to men, because "they are pusillanimous and have less robust hearts and more humid brains."

Satan seduced them by caressing them with his goat's hoof and his wooden claw, or by disguising himself as a toad dressed as a prince.

Exorcisms of possessed women brought overflow crowds to the churches.

Protecting the breast of the exorcist were scapularies filled with consecrated salt, blessed rue, and the hair and nails of saints. Crucifix held high, he did battle with witchcraft. The bedeviled woman swore, howled, bit, shrieked insults in the tongues of hell, and with loud laughter tore off her clothes and proffered her naughty parts. The climax came when the exorcist rolled on the floor hugging the body where the devil had made himself at home, until the convulsions and wailing ceased.

Afterward, some searched the floor for the nails and bits of glass vomited by the possessed.

HENDRICKJE

&

In the year 1654, a young and flagrantly pregnant woman named Hendrickje Stoffels was judged and found guilty by the council of the Reformed Church in Amsterdam.

She confessed to "having fornicated with the painter Rembrandt," and admitted to sharing his bed without being married, "like a whore," or in a more literal translation, "committing whoredom."

The council punished her by obliging her to repent and do penance and by permanently excluding her from the table of Our Lord Jesus Christ.

Rembrandt was not found guilty, perhaps because the jury had in mind the episode of Eve and the apple. But the scandal caused the price of his work to tumble and he had to declare bankruptcy.

The master of chiaroscuro, who revealed light born of darkness, spent his final years in the shadows. He lost his house and his paintings. He was buried in a rented grave.

RESURRECTION OF VERMEER

*

His works were worthless when he died. In 1676 his widow paid the baker with two paintings.

Vermeer van Delft was sentenced to oblivion.

Two centuries passed before he returned to the world, rescued by the impressionists, hunters of light. Renoir said his portrait of a woman making lace was the most beautiful painting he had ever seen.

Vermeer, chronicler of triflings, painted only his home and a bit of the neighborhood. His wife and daughters were his models, and domestic chores were his subjects. Always the same, never the same: in the household routine, Vermeer, like Rembrandt, knew how to unveil the suns that the dark northern sky denied him.

In his paintings there are no hierarchies. Nothing and no one is more or less luminous. The light of the universe vibrates, secretly, as much in the glass of wine as in the hand that offers it, in the letter as much as in the eyes that read it, in a worn tapestry as much as in the unworn face of the girl watching.

RESURRECTION OF ARCIMBOLDO

*

Each person was a source of flavor, odor and color:
the ear, a tulip
the eyebrows, two crayfish
the eyes, two grapes
the eyelids, ducks' bills
the nose, a pear
the cheek, an apple
the chin, a pomegranate
and the hair, a forest of branches.

Giuseppe Arcimboldo, court painter, kept three emperors in stitches.

They celebrated him because they did not understand him. His paintings looked like amusement parks. And that was how the pagan artist managed to survive and live in luxury.

Arcimboldo indulged in the mortal sin of idolatry, exalting human communion with wild exuberant nature. His portraits, said to be inoffensive and playful, in actual fact were ferocious mockery.

When he died, art's memory suppressed him like a nightmare.

Four centuries later, he was resuscitated by the surrealists, his belated children.

THOMAS MORE

❧

Thomas More was understood all too well, and that may be what cost him his life. In 1535 Henry VIII, the glutton king, raised his head on a pike beside the Thames.

Twenty years previous, the man who would be beheaded had written a book that recounted the customs of an island called Utopia, where property was held in common, money did not exist, and there was neither poverty nor wealth.

In the voice of his character, a traveler returned from America, Thomas More expressed his own dangerous ideas:

- On wars:
  Robbers prove sometimes gallant soldiers, soldiers often prove brave robbers; so near an alliance there is between those two sorts of life.

- On thievery:
  No punishment, how severe soever, [is] able to restrain those from robbing who can find out no other way of livelihood. You first make thieves and then punish them.

- On the death penalty:
  It seems to me a very unjust thing to take away a man's life for a little money; for nothing in the world can be of equal value with a man's life . . . extreme justice is an extreme injury.

- On money:
  So easy a thing would it be to supply all the necessities of life, if that blessed

thing called money, which is pretended to be invented for procuring them,
was not really the only thing that obstructed their being procured!

- On private property:
  Till property is taken away, there can be no equitable or just distribu-
  tion of things, nor can the world be happily governed.

ERASMUS

❧

Erasmus of Rotterdam dedicated *In Praise of Folly* to his friend Thomas More.

In that book Folly spoke in the first person. She said all joy and happiness was due to her favors, she urged smoothing the furrowed brow, proposed an alliance of children and the elderly, and mocked "arrogant philosophers, empurpled kings, pious priests, thrice-holy pontiffs, and all that rabble of gods."

This annoying, irreverent man preached the communion of Christian teachings and pagan traditions:

"Saint Socrates, pray for us."

His insolent output was censured by the Inquisition, placed on the Catholic Index of Forbidden Books, and frowned on by the new Protestant church.

ORIGIN OF THE ELEVATOR

❧

King Henry VIII of England had six queens.

He widowed easily.

He devoured women and banquets whole.

Six hundred lackeys served at his table, overflowing with partridge pastries, peacocks in all their sublime plumage, and cuts of mutton or suckling pig on which, knife in hand, he bestowed noble titles before biting into them.

When his last queen arrived, Henry was so fat he could no longer ascend the staircase that led from the dining room to the nuptial bed.

The king had no choice but to invent a chair that by means of a complicated mechanism of pulleys carried him seated from plate to pillow.

PRECURSOR OF CAPITALISM

❧

England, Holland, France, and other countries owe him a statue.

A goodly part of the power of the powerful comes from the gold and silver he stole, from the cities he burned, from the galleons he pillaged, and from the slaves he rounded up.

Some fine sculptor ought to carve an effigy of this armed functionary of nascent capitalism: knife between the teeth, patch on one eye, peg leg, hook for a hand, parrot on the shoulder.

DANGEROUS CORNERS OF THE CARIBBEAN

❧

Pirates built America. On the islands and coasts of the Caribbean, they were more feared than hurricanes.

In his diary, Columbus mentioned God fifty-one times and gold a hundred and thirty-nine times, even though God was everywhere while there was not enough gold to fill a tooth.

But time passed and the fertile fields of America flowered with abundant gold, silver, sugar, cotton, and other marvels. Pirates specialized in purloining such fruit. And in reward for their efforts, these instruments of capital accumulation were inducted into British nobility.

Queen Elizabeth of England was a partner of the fearsome Francis Drake, who provided her with a profit of 4,600 percent on her investment. She made him Sir Francis. She also knighted Drake's uncle, John Hawkins, and she took part in the business Hawkins founded when he bought three hundred slaves in Sierra Leone, sold them in Santo Domingo, and his three ships returned to London loaded down with sugar, skins, and ginger.

From that point forward, the slave trade became England's own mountain of silver, the Cerro Rico of Potosí it had lacked.

RALEIGH

❧

In the south of America, he sought El Dorado. In the north, he found tobacco. He was a navigator, a warrior, an explorer, a poet. And he was a pirate.

Sir Walter Raleigh:

who smoked a pipe and revealed the pleasures of tobacco to British nobility;

who in court wore a doublet studded with diamonds, and in battle wore armor made of silver;

the favorite of Elizabeth, the Virgin Queen;

who for her named Virginia, the land still called by that name;

who for her assaulted Spanish ports and galleons, and who was made at the tap of her sword a noble knight;

who years later for the same deeds had his head chopped off in the Tower of London.

With Elizabeth dead, King James wanted a Spanish queen, so the pirate Raleigh, the villain of the movie, was convicted of high treason.

His widow received, as was the custom, his embalmed head.

FAMILY PORTRAIT IN ENGLAND

❧

The feud between the Yorks and the Lancasters might not have been more than a quarrel among neighbors if William Shakespeare had not set his pen to the topic.

The poet surely never imagined that by dint of his talent the dynastic war between the white rose and the red rose would acquire a universal dimension.

In England's history and in Shakespeare's play, King Richard III, patron saint of serial killers, unleashed a river of blood on his way to the throne. He killed King Henry VI and Prince Edward too. He drowned his brother Clarence in a barrel of wine and, that accomplished, he did away with his nephews. He locked up the two little princes in the Tower of London, smothered them with their pillows, and buried them in secret at the foot of a staircase. He also strangled Lord Hastings and decapitated the Duke of Buckingham, his best friend, his other self, just in case they were plotting something.

Richard III was the last English monarch to die in battle.

Shakespeare gave him the words that made him immortal: "My kingdom for a horse!"

MARE NOSTRUM

More than a century after the pope in Rome divided half the world between Spain and Portugal, the English jurist John Selden published *Mare clausum* in 1635.

This treatise proved that not only the land had an owner, but the sea as well, and His Majesty the king of England was, by natural right, the legitimate proprietor of the lands and waters of his expanding empire.

Thus the foundation of British property law was laid on the god Neptune, on Noah and his three sons, on Genesis, Deuteronomy, and the Psalms, and on the prophecies of Isaiah and Ezekiel.

Three hundred and sixty years later, the United States claimed all rights over outer space and the celestial bodies, but they did not invoke such prestigious authorities.

THANKS

Year after year, at the end of November, the United States celebrates Thanksgiving. The nation expresses its gratitude to God and to the Indians who helped God save the conquering Pilgrims.

The winter of 1620 had killed half the Europeans who arrived on the *Mayflower*. The following year God decided to save the survivors. The Indians gave them shelter, hunted and fished for them, taught them to grow corn, to avoid poisonous plants, to use medicinal plants, and to find nuts and cranberries and other wild fruits.

The saved then offered their saviors a Thanksgiving feast. It was held in the English village of Plymouth, which a short while before had been Patuxet, an Indian village devastated by smallpox, yellow fever, and other novelties brought from Europe.

That was the first and last Thanksgiving in colonial times.

When the colonists invaded Indian lands, the moment of truth arrived. The invaders, calling themselves "holy" and also "the chosen," stopped calling the Indians "natives" and started calling them "savages."

THIS EXECRABLE CREW OF BUTCHERS

❧

At the beginning of the eighteenth century, Jonathan Swift portrayed the colonial adventure in the final chapter of *Gulliver's Travels:*

A crew of pirates goes on shore to rob and plunder, they see a harmless people, are entertained with kindness; they give the country a new name; they take formal possession of it for their king; they set up a rotten plank, or a stone, for a memorial.

Here commences a new dominion, acquired with a title by divine right. Natives are driven out or destroyed; their princes tortured to discover their gold; a free license given to all acts of inhumanity and lust, the earth reeking with the blood of its inhabitants: and this execrable crew of butchers, employed in so pious an expedition, is a modern colony, sent to convert and civilize an idolatrous and barbarous people!

FATHER OF GULLIVER

❧

The first edition of *Gulliver's Travels* was published under a different title and without the author's name.

Perils obliged caution. The previous works of Jonathan Swift, a high-ranking priest, dean of Saint Patrick's Cathedral in Ireland, had earned him several charges of sedition, and landed the publisher in jail.

The runaway success of *Gulliver* allowed Swift to sign his name to later editions. He also signed his new book. *A Modest Proposal: For*

Preventing the Children of Poor People in Ireland from Being a Burden to Their Parents or Country, and for Making Them Beneficial to the Publick was the extraordinarily long title of the fiercest political pamphlet ever written.

In the icy language of economic science, the author laid out the objective advantages of sending the children of the poor to the slaughterhouse. These children could become "at a year old a most delicious, nourishing and wholesome food, whether stewed, roasted, baked or boiled," and what's more their skins could be made into ladies' gloves.

This was published in 1729, when even ghosts were wandering the streets of Dublin in search of food. It did not sit well.

Swift specialized in formulating insufferable questions:

Why did his plan to promote cannibalism provoke horror when the entire country of Ireland was being eaten alive by England and no one moved a finger?

Were the Irish dying of hunger because of the climate or because of colonial strangulation?

Why was he a free man when he was in England and a slave as soon as he set foot in Ireland?

Why didn't the Irish refuse to buy English clothing and English furniture, and learn to love their country?

Why didn't they burn everything that came from England, save the people?

He was declared insane.

His savings had financed Dublin's first public insane asylum, but he was not sent there. He died before it was finished.

CELESTIAL AND TERRESTRIAL

❦

England, eighteenth century: everything was on the rise.

Smoke rose from factory chimneys,

smoke rose from victorious cannons,

waves rose from the seven seas ruled by the hundred thousand sailors of the king of England,

profits rose on all the goods England sold,

and earnings rose on all the money England loaned.

Every Englishman, no matter how uninformed, knew that the world and the sun and the stars revolved around London.

But William Hogarth, the greatest English artist of the century, was not distracted by the splendors of London at the summit of the universe. He was more attracted by lows than highs. In his paintings and etchings, everything was falling down. Across the floor rolled drunks and bottles,

broken masks,

broken swords,

broken contracts,

wigs,

corsets,

ladies' undergarments,

gentlemen's honor,

votes bought by politicians,

titles of nobility bought by the nouveaux riches,

cards that told of fortunes lost,

letters that told of loves lost,

and the rubbish of the city.

FREEDOM'S PHILOSOPHER

❧

Centuries have passed and the influence of English philosopher John Locke on universal thought continues to grow.

It is entirely appropriate. Thanks to Locke we know that God bestowed the world on its legitimate proprietors, "the industrious and rational." It was Locke who laid the philosophical groundwork for human freedom in all its dimensions: free enterprise, free trade, free competition, free hiring and firing.

And the freedom to invest. While he was writing *An Essay Concerning Human Understanding*, the philosopher did his part for human understanding by investing his savings in Royal African Company stock.

That firm, owned by the British Crown and by "the industrious and rational," hunted and captured slaves in Africa and sold them in America.

According to the Royal African Company, its efforts guaranteed "a constant and sufficient supply of Merchantable Negroes, at moderate rates."

CONTRACTS

❧

When the eighteenth century began, a Bourbon king sat on the throne in Madrid for the first time.

As soon as he donned the crown, Philip V became a slave trader.

He signed a contract with the French Compagnie de Guinée and his cousin, the king of France.

The contract gave each monarch 25 percent of the profits from the sale of forty-eight thousand slaves in the Spanish colonies of America during the following ten years, and established that the trade would be carried out on Catholic ships with Catholic captains and Catholic sailors.

Twelve years later, King Philip signed a contract with the English South Sea Company and the queen of England.

The contract gave each monarch 25 percent of the profits from the sale of one hundred and forty-four thousand slaves in the Spanish colonies of America during the following thirty years, and established that the blacks must not be old or defective, must have all their teeth, and must bear the seals of the Spanish Crown and the British company, branded in a visible spot.

The owners guaranteed a quality product.

BRIEF HISTORY OF TRADE BETWEEN AFRICA AND EUROPE

❧

Hereditary slavery had been around since the times of Greece and Rome and was nothing new. But with the Renaissance, Europe introduced certain novelties: never before had slavery been determined by skin color, and never before had the sale of human flesh been the brightest light in the world of business.

During the sixteenth, seventeenth, and eighteenth centuries, Africa sold slaves and bought rifles: it traded hands for arms.

Then during the nineteenth and twentieth centuries, Africa delivered gold, diamonds, copper, ivory, rubber, and coffee in exchange for Bibles: it traded the riches of the earth for the promise of heaven.

HOLY WATER

A map published in Paris in 1761 revealed the origins of Africa's horror. It depicted a variety of savage beasts crowded around the scarce watering holes in the desert, fighting to get at the water. Excited by the heat or by thirst, the animals mounted whatever happened to be near, paying no attention to species, and such promiscuity gave rise to the most dreadful monsters in the world.

Africans had the good fortune of being saved from this hell by the slave trade. Baptism opened the door to Paradise.

The Vatican had foreseen it. In 1454, Pope Nicholas V gave the king of Portugal authorization for the slave trade as long as he converted the Africans. A couple of years later another bull from Pope Callixtus III established that the capture of Africa was a Crusade of Christianity.

Back then, most of the African coast was still out of bounds due to fear: ship-eating serpents lay in wait in the boiling waters, and white sailors turned black as soon as they set foot on African land.

But over the following centuries, all or nearly all the European crowns built forts and outposts along the length of that ill-reputed coast. From there, they ran the most profitable business of all. And to fulfill the will of God they sprinkled holy water on the slaves.

In the contracts and in the accounts, slaves were referred to as "pieces" or "merchandise," even though baptism placed souls in those empty bodies.

CANNIBAL EUROPE

❦

The slaves trembled as they boarded the ships. They believed they were going to be eaten. They were not far off. When all was said and done, the slave trade was the mouth that devoured Africa.

Long before, African kings held slaves and fought each other, but the capture and sale of people became the axis of the economy and of everything else only after the kings of Europe devised the venture. Black Africa was then bled of young people and, thus emptied, its destiny was sealed.

Mali is now one of the poorest countries in the world. In the sixteenth century it was an opulent and cultured kingdom. The university at Timbuktu had twenty-five thousand students. When the sultan of Morocco invaded Mali, he did not find the yellow gold he sought, because little was left. But he found black gold to sell to the European traffickers, and thus profited even more: his prisoners of war, among whom were doctors, judges, writers, musicians, and sculptors, were enslaved and marched off to the plantations of America.

The slavery machine demanded hands and the hunt for hands demanded arms. The war economy of Africa's kingdoms came to depend more and more on things come from afar. A catalog published in 1655 in Holland listed the weaponry most coveted on the African coast, and also the best offerings with which to entice those stage prop kings. Gin was highly prized, and a fistful of Murano glass beads was worth seven men.

FASHION

❦

The sale of slaves unleashed a shower of imported products.

Although Africa produced good quality iron and steel, European swords were status symbols for the monarchs and courtiers of the many kingdoms and principalities that sold blacks to the white companies.

It was the same story with African fabric made of fibers ranging from cotton to tree bark. At the beginning of the sixteenth century, Portuguese navigator Duarte Pacheco reported that palm-leaf clothing from the Congo was "soft as velvet and so beautiful that Italy does not have better." But imported clothing, which cost twice as much, conferred prestige. Price dictated value. Being cheap and abundant, slaves were worth nothing, while expensive and scarce objects were coveted. And the less practical the better: the fascination with what came from abroad gave pride of place to useless novelties and changing fashions, today this, tomorrow that, the day after who knows what.

These fleeting splendors, symbols of power, separated the rulers from the ruled.

Like today.

CAGES UNDER SAIL

❧

The slave trader who loved freedom more than anything named his finest ships the *Voltaire* and the *Rousseau*.

Several traffickers christened their vessels with religious names: *Souls, Misericordia, The Prophet David, Jesus, Saint Anthony, Saint Michael, Saint James, Saint Philip, Saint Anne,* and *Our Lady of the Immaculate Conception.*

Others paraded their love for humanity, nature, or their girlfriends: *Hope, Equality, Friendship, Hero, Rainbow, Dove, Nightingale, Hummingbird, Desire, Charming Betty, Little Polly, Lovable Cecile, Prudent Hannah.*

The most forthright called their ships *Subordinator* and *Vigilante.*

These ships laden with human cargo did not announce their arrival in port with sirens or fireworks. No need. Their presence could be felt from afar, by the stench.

In the hold, their pestilent merchandise was piled high. The slaves lay together day and night without moving, packed in so tightly no space was wasted, pissing on each other, shitting on each other, chained one to another, neck to neck, wrist to wrist, ankle to ankle, and all of them shackled to long iron bars.

Many died on the ocean voyage.

Each morning the guards tossed those packages overboard.

PROGENY OF THE MIDDLE PASSAGE

❦

The leaky little tubs which the sea devours are the granddaughters of those slave ships.

Today's slaves, though no longer called by that name, enjoy the same freedoms as their grandparents who were driven by the lash to the plantations of America.

They do not simply depart: they are pushed. No one emigrates by choice.

From Africa and from many other places, the desperate flee wars and droughts and exhausted lands and poisoned rivers and empty bellies.

Shipments of human flesh are nowadays the most successful export from the south of the world.

FIRST SLAVE REBELLION IN AMERICA

❦

It happens at the beginning of the sixteenth century.

A couple of days after Christmas, the slaves rise up at a sugar mill in Santo Domingo owned by the son of Christopher Columbus.

Following the victory of Divine Providence and James the Apostle, the roads are lined with black men, hanged.

STUBBORN FREEDOM

❦

It happens in the middle of the sixteenth century.

The slaves who fail in their first attempt to escape are punished by mutilation: an ear cut off, or a tendon sliced through, or a foot or hand removed, and in vain the king of Spain outlaws "cutting off parts that cannot be named."

Repeat offenders lose whatever is left and then end up on the gallows, at the stake, or on the chopping block. Their heads are exhibited on pikes in town squares.

But all over the Americas bastions of freedom proliferate, in the depths of the jungle or in mountain hideaways, surrounded by quicksand that looks like firm ground and by false paths sowed with sharpened stakes.

The runaway slaves come from different African nations and become compatriots through the humiliations they share.

KINGDOM OF THE FREE

*

It happens throughout the seventeenth century.

The havens of escaped slaves sprout like mushrooms. In Brazil they are called *quilombos*, an African word that means community, although racism translates it as disorder, revelry, or whorehouse.

In the *quilombo* of Palmares, former slaves live free of their owners and also free of the tyranny of sugar, which allows nothing else to grow. They plant all sorts of seeds and eat everything. The diet of their former owners arrives by ship. Theirs comes from the earth. Their smithies, built in the African way, give them hoes, picks, and shovels to work the land, and knives, axes, and lances to defend it.

QUEEN OF THE FREE

*

It happens in the first half of the eighteenth century.

The international division of labor decides that Jamaica exists to sweeten Europe's table. The land produces sugar, sugar, and more sugar.

In Jamaica, as in Brazil, diversity of diet is a privilege of those who escape. Although fertile land is hard to find high in the mountains, the maroons figure out how to grow everything, and even raise pigs and chickens.

Hidden here, they see without being seen, they sting, and then they vanish.

In these windward Blue Mountains, Nanny has her temple and her throne. She is queen of the free. Once a machine for birthing slaves, now she wears necklaces made of the teeth of English soldiers.

ART OF THE FREE

❧

It happens in the middle of the eighteenth century.

The sanctuaries of freedom in Suriname resist by staying on the move. When Dutch troops discover their villages, after much pain and anguish, they find nothing but ashes.

What things do they need most? Sewing needles, colored thread, the maroons ask of the occasional peddler, who by mistake or madness runs across them. What would become of their lives without brightly colored clothes made from bits of scrap cloth expertly arranged and sewn?

From the sails of plantation windmills, broken in pieces, they make rings, bracelets, and ornaments that lend a warrior dignity. And with what the forest offers, they invent musical instruments to give rhythm to their bodies yearning to dance.

KING OF THE FREE

❧

It happens at the end of the eighteenth century.

The colonial powers hang Domingo Bioho yet again, but he still reigns.

Here in Palenque, not far from the port of Cartagena de Indias, the maroons choose the bravest among them to inherit the name passed down from king to king. Domingo Bioho is one and many.

IN SEARCH OF ESCAPED PROPERTY

❧

It happens at the beginning of the nineteenth century.

At the dinner table, the aristocracy talks of weddings, inheritance, and nigger dogs.

The newspapers of Mississippi, Tennessee, and South Carolina advertise the services of such dogs at five dollars a day. The ads praise the virtues of the mastiffs, which hunt down escaped slaves, capture them, and return them intact to their owners.

Their noses are crucial. A good hunting dog can follow a scent many hours after the prey has passed by. Also highly prized is speed and tenacity, because to erase their scent the slaves swim rivers and streams or spread pepper in their wake, and the hound that deserves its bone never gives up, never stops scouring the ground until it picks up the trail.

But most important of all is the extensive training that teaches the dog not to make hamburger of black flesh. Only the legitimate owner has the right to punish the bad behavior of his animals.

HARRIET

❧

It happens in the middle of the nineteenth century.

She escapes. Harriet Tubman carries with her as souvenirs the scars on her back and a crack in her skull.

She leaves her husband behind. He tells her:

"You're crazy. You can get away, but you won't live to tell the tale."

She escapes, tells the tale, returns to Maryland, and rescues her parents, Ashantis captured in Africa. She returns again and rescues her brothers. Nineteen trips she makes from the plantations of the South to the lands of the North, traveling at night, night after night, freeing more than three hundred blacks over ten years.

None of her fugitives is captured. People say Harriet cures exhaustion and regret with a gunshot. And people say she says with pride:

"I have never lost a single passenger."

She has the highest priced head of her generation. Forty thousand dollars cold cash is the reward they offer.

No one collects it.

Her theatrical disguises make her unrecognizable, and she throws the bounty hunters off with false trails and routes never imagined.

DON'T MISS IT!

❧

No lawyer will defend them. Neither can they defend themselves, for the law does not believe in the oaths of Negroes.

The judge finds them guilty in the blink of an eye.

The number of fires in New York City in the year 1741 demands an iron hand against slaves ruined by too much freedom. If those found guilty are indeed the ones who set the fires, the punishment will be just. If they are not, the punishment will be a warning.

Thirteen black men will be chained to stakes and burned alive, seventeen blacks will be hanged and will swing from the gallows until they rot, and four whites, poor but white, will march to their deaths, because someone must have been the brains behind this infernal conspiracy, and brains are white.

The spectacle is a week away and already a crowd is camping out to get the best view.

THE AGES OF ROSA MARIA

❧

In 1725, when she was six, a slave ship brought her from Africa and she was sold in Rio de Janeiro.

When she was fourteen, the master spread her thighs and taught her a trade.

When she was fifteen, she was bought by a family from Ouro Preto, who then rented her body to the gold miners.

When she was thirty, the family sold her to a priest who practiced on her his techniques for exorcism and other nocturnal exercises.

When she was thirty-two, one of the demons that lived in her body smoked through her pipe and howled through her mouth and made her writhe on the ground. For that she was sentenced to a hundred lashes in the public square of the city of Mariana, and the punishment left her arm paralyzed for life.

When she was thirty-five, she fasted and prayed and mortified her flesh with a hair shirt, and the mother of the Virgin Mary taught her to read. They say that Rosa Maria Egipcíaca da Vera Cruz was the first literate black woman in Brazil.

When she was thirty-seven, she founded a home for abandoned female slaves and whores past their prime, which she financed by selling cakes made with her own saliva, an infallible remedy for any disease.

When she was forty, many people loyally attended her trances, where, wrapped in a cloud of tobacco smoke, she would dance to a chorus of angels, and the Baby Jesus would suckle her breasts.

When she was forty-two, she was accused of witchcraft and locked up in the Rio de Janeiro jail.

When she was forty-three, theologians confirmed she was a witch, because she withstood without complaint a lit candle held for a long while under her tongue.

When she was forty-four, she was sent to Lisbon, to the prison of the Holy Inquisition. She entered the torture chambers to be interrogated and was never heard of again.

BRAZIL SLEPT ON A BED OF GOLD

❧

It sprouted from the ground like grass.

It drew crowds like a magnet.

It shined like gold.

And gold it was.

The bankers of England celebrated each new strike as if the gold were theirs.

And theirs it was.

Lisbon, which produced nothing, sent the gold of Brazil to London in exchange for loans, fancy clothing, and all the needs of a parasitic life.

At the heart of gold's splendor lay Ouro Preto, "Black Gold," so named because black were the rocks that held the gold, nights with suns deep inside, although the place could just as easily have earned its name from the black hands that dug the gold from mountains and riverbanks.

Those hands grew more and more expensive to buy. The slaves, who formed a clear majority in the mining region, were the only ones who worked.

And even more expensive was food. No one grew anything. In the early years of mining euphoria, the price of a cat was equivalent to the gold a slave could dig in two days. Chicken was cheaper, only a day's worth of gold.

After more than a century, the price of food was still beyond belief, as were the lavish celebrations of the mine owners, who lived on a perpetual spree. But the gushing spring of gold, which once seemed inexhaustible, began to dwindle. And it became harder and harder to squeeze out of the mines the taxes that financed the torpor of the Portuguese Court, worn out from so much resting in the service of the bankers of England.

In 1750, when the king of Portugal died, the royal coffers were empty. And it was they, the bankers of England, who paid for his funeral.

DIGESTIONS

✷

Potosí, Guanajuato, and Zacatecas ate Indians. Ouro Preto ate blacks.

The silver that came from forced labor hit Spanish soil in Seville and bounced. It landed some distance away, filling the bellies of Flemish, German, and Genovese bankers, and those of Florentine, English, and French merchants, to whom the Spanish Crown and all its income were mortgaged.

Without the silver from Bolivia and Mexico, a veritable silver bridge across the sea, could Europe have become Europe?

The gold that came from slave labor hit Portuguese soil in Lisbon and bounced. It landed some distance away, filling the bellies of British bankers and merchants, the kingdom's creditors, to whom the Portuguese Crown and all its income were mortgaged.

Without the gold from Brazil, a veritable golden bridge across the sea, could the Industrial Revolution have taken place in England?

And without the buying and selling of slaves, would Liverpool have become the most important port in the world, and would Lloyd's have become the king of insurance?

Without capital from the slave trade, who would have financed James Watt's steam engine? What furnaces would have forged George Washington's cannons?

FATHER OF THE MARIONETTE

❧

Antonio José da Silva, of Brazilian birth, lives in Lisbon. His puppets bring laughter to the Portuguese stage.

For nine years he has been unable to use his fingers, mangled in the torture chambers of the Holy Inquisition, but his characters carved from wood, Medea, Don Quijote, Proteus, still delight and console adoring crowds.

It ends early. It ends at the stake: for being a Jew and a buffoon, and because his marionettes fail to show due respect to the Crown or the Church or the hooded executioners who make fools of themselves chasing each other onstage.

From the box of honor, João V, the king of Portugal known as the Magnanimous, observes the auto-da-fé where the king of puppets burns.

Thus this Antonio bids farewell to the world, while on the very same day of the same year, 1730, on the other side of the sea another Antonio says hello.

Antonio Francisco Lisboa is born in Ouro Preto. He will be called Aleijadinho the Cripple. He too will lose his fingers, not from torture but from a mysterious curse.

ALEIJADINHO

*

Brazil's ugliest man creates the finest beauty in colonial art.

In stone, Aleijadinho sculpts the glory and agony of Ouro Preto, the Potosí of gold.

Son of an African slave, this mulatto has slaves who carry him, bathe him, feed him, and tie the chisel to his stump.

Assailed by leprosy, syphilis, or who knows what, Aleijadinho has lost an eye and his teeth and his fingers, but the rest of him carves stone with the hands he lacks.

Night and day he works, as if bent on revenge, and his Christs, his Virgin Marys, his saints, his prophets shine brighter than gold, while the fount of gold itself grows ever more chary in fortunes and prodigious in misfortune and unrest.

Ouro Preto and the entire region agree with the precocious appraisal offered by the Count of Assumar, who was its governor:

"It seems as if the earth exhales tumult, and water riots; the clouds vomit disobedience, and the stars disorder; this climate is the tomb of peace and the cradle of rebellion."

PALACE ART IN BRAZIL

*

The brush of Pedro Américo de Figueiredo e Melo, an artist of the epic genre, depicted the sacred moment for all eternity.

In his painting, a lively horseman unsheathes his sword and utters the earth-shattering cry that gives birth to the Brazilian nation, while the Dragoons of the Honor Guard pose for the occasion, weapons held high, plumes on war helmets and manes on horses aflutter in the breeze.

Contemporary accounts do not coincide precisely with those brush-strokes.

They say the hero, Pedro, a Portuguese prince, squatted on his haunches on the bank of a stream called Ipiranga. His supper had not sat well with him and he was "doubling over to answer the call of nature," in the words of one chronicle, when a messenger brought a letter from Lisbon. Without interrupting his efforts, the prince had him read out the letter from his royal parents, which contained certain affronts, perhaps aggravated by his bellyache. In the midst of the reading, he stood up and swore lengthily, which official history translated in abbreviated form as the famous cry:

"Independence or death!"

Thus, that morning in 1822, the prince tore the Portuguese insignia off his cassock and became emperor of Brazil.

THE AGES OF PEDRO

❧

Bearing nine years of age and eighteen names, Pedro de Alcântara Francisco Antônio João Carlos Xavier de Paula Miguel Rafael Joaquim José Gonzaga Pascoal Sipriano Serafim de Bragança e Bourbon, prince and heir to the Portuguese crown, disembarked in Brazil. The British brought him here along with all his court to keep him safe from Napoleon's assaults. At the time, Brazil was Portugal's colony and Portugal was England's colony, although the latter went unsaid.

At the age of nineteen, Pedro was married to Leopoldina, the archduchess of Austria. He paid her no heed. Like many other tourists to come, he spent his time chasing dark-skinned lovelies in Rio's blazing night.

At the age of twenty-four, he proclaimed Brazil independent and became Emperor Pedro I. Without pause, he then signed the first loan agreements with British banks. The new nation and the foreign debt were born as twins. They remain inseparable.

At the age of thirty-three, he got the crazy notion to abolish slavery. He dipped his quill in the inkpot but did not manage to sign the decree. A coup d'état left him throneless, sitting on air.

At the age of thirty-four, he returned to Lisbon and became King Pedro IV of Portugal.

At the age of thirty-six, this king of two thrones died in Lisbon and was buried there, in the land that had been his mother and his enemy.

FREEDOM BETRAYS

§

The official history of Brazil continues to call the first uprisings for national independence *inconfidencias*, acts of disloyalty.

Long before the Portuguese prince declared himself emperor of Brazil, there were several failed attempts. The most notable were the *Inconfidencia mineira* in Ouro Preto in 1789, which died stillborn, and the *Inconfidencia bahiana*, which broke out in 1794 in Salvador da Bahia and lasted four years.

The only leader of the former to be hanged and quartered was a low-ranking officer, Tiradentes, the tooth puller. The other conspirators, mining barons fed up with paying colonial taxes, were pardoned.

The Bahian rebellion lasted longer and went farther. It sought not only an independent republic but also equality of rights for all, no matter the color of your skin.

After much blood was spilled and the rebellion put down, colonial authorities pardoned all but four of the leaders. Hanged and quartered were Manoel Lira, João do Nascimento, Luis Gonzaga, and Lucas Dantas. These four were black, the sons or grandsons of slaves.

And there are those who believe justice is blind.

RESURRECTION OF TÚPAC AMARU

§

Túpac Amaru, the last king of the Incas, fought the Spaniards for forty years in the mountains of Peru. In 1572, when the executioner's ax severed his neck, Indian prophets announced that one day the head would rejoin the body.

And it did. Two centuries later, José Gabriel Condorcanqui claimed the name waiting for him. Transformed into Túpac Amaru, he led the largest and longest indigenous rebellion in the entire history of the Americas.

The Andes were on fire. From the summits to the sea, up rose the victims of forced labor in the mines, plantations, and workshops. The rebels threatened the colonial dinner plate with victory after victory as they advanced at an unstoppable pace, fording rivers, climbing mountains, crossing valleys, taking town after town. They were on the verge of conquering Cuzco.

The sacred city, the heart of power, lay before them: from the heights they could see it, they could taste it.

Eighteen centuries had passed since Spartacus had Rome within his grasp, and history repeated itself. Túpac Amaru decided not to attack. Indian troops, led by a chief who had sold out, defended the besieged city, and Túpac did not kill Indians. Not that, never. He knew it was necessary, there was no other way, but . . .

While he vacillated from yes to no to who knows, days and nights passed and Spanish soldiers, lots of them and well armed, were making their way from Lima.

In vain his wife, Micaela Bastidas, who commanded the rearguard, sent him messages:

"You have to bring these sorrows to an end . . . "

"I have not the patience to put up with all this . . . "

"Many times I have told you not to waste time in those towns . . . "

"I have sent you plenty of warnings . . . "

"If it is our ruin you want, just lie down and go to sleep."

In 1781, the rebel leader entered Cuzco. He entered in chains, under a hail of stones and insults.

RAIN

❧

In the torture chamber, the king's envoy interrogated him.

"Who are your accomplices?" he asked.

And Túpac Amaru answered:

"Here there are no accomplices but you and I. You the oppressor and I the liberator, we both deserve death."

He was sentenced to die by being quartered. They tied him to four horses, his arms and legs forming a cross, and his body did not break. Spurs dug into the bellies of the horses, which lurched in vain, and his body did not break.

They turned to the executioner's ax.

It was a time of long drought in the Valley of Cuzco and the noon was ferociously bright, but the sky suddenly grew black and cracked and unleashed one of those downpours that drown the world.

The other rebel leaders, male and female, Micaela Bastidas, Túpac Catari, Bartolina Sisa, Gregoria Apaza . . . were quartered. And through the towns that had rebelled, their remains were paraded, then burned, and the ashes thrown to the wind, "so that no memory of them shall remain."

HAVES AND HAVE-NOTS

In 1776, the independence of the United States foreshadowed what would occur later on from Mexico south.

To remove any doubts about the place of the Indians in the new nation, George Washington proposed "the total destruction and devastation of their settlements." Thomas Jefferson voiced the opinion that "this unfortunate race has justified its extermination." And Benjamin Franklin suggested that rum could be the "appointed means" to get rid of the savages.

To remove any doubts about the place of women, the Constitution of the State of New York added the adjective "masculine" to the right to vote.

To remove any doubts about the place of poor whites, the signatories to the Declaration of Independence were all rich whites.

And to remove any doubts about the place of blacks in the newborn nation, six hundred and fifty thousand slaves remained enslaved. Black hands built the White House.

MISSING FATHER

The Declaration of Independence affirmed that all men are created equal.

Shortly thereafter, the Constitution of the United States clarified the concept: it established that each slave was worth three-fifths of a person.

One drafter of the Constitution, Gouverneur Morris, opposed this provision, but in vain. Not long before he had tried, also in vain, to get the State of New York to abolish slavery, and managed to extract a constitutional promise that in the future "every being who breathes the air of this State shall enjoy the privileges of a freeman."

Morris, a central figure at the moment the United States acquired a face and a soul, was a founding father that history forgot.

In the year 2006, Spanish journalist Vicente Romero looked for his grave. He found it behind a church in the South Bronx. The gravestone, erased by rain and sun, provided a platform for two large garbage cans.

ANOTHER MISSING FATHER

❧

Robert Carter was buried in the garden.

In his will he asked "to be laid under a shady tree, where he might be undisturbed, and sleep in peace and obscurity. No stone, nor inscription."

This Virginia patrician was one of the richest, if not the richest, of all the prosperous landowners who broke ties with England.

Although several other founding fathers looked askance at slavery, none of them freed their slaves. Carter was the only one to unchain the four hundred and fifty blacks he owned "to allow them to live and work according to their own will and pleasure." He freed them seventy years before Abraham Lincoln abolished slavery, and he did so gradually, taking care that none was simply turned out and deserted.

Such folly condemned him to solitude and oblivion.

He was cut off by his friends, his neighbors, and his family, all of whom were convinced that free blacks were a threat to personal and national security.

Later on, his acts were rewarded with collective amnesia.

SALLY

❧

When Jefferson lost his wife, her property became his. Among other goods, he inherited Sally.

There is testimony of her beauty in her early years.

Later on, nothing.

Sally never spoke, or if she did either no one listened or no one bothered to write it down.

Of President Jefferson, in contrast, we have several portraits and many words. We know that he harbored well-founded suspicions that "the blacks are inferior to the whites in the endowments both of the body and the mind," and that he always expressed "great aversion" to the mixing of white blood and black blood, which to him was morally repugnant. He believed that if the slaves were one day to be freed, the peril of contamination would have to be avoided by removing them "beyond the reach of mixture."

In 1802, journalist James Callender published an article in the Richmond *Recorder* which made public what everyone knew: President Jefferson was the father of Sally's children.

DEATH TO TEA, LONG LIVE COFFEE

❧

The British Crown decreed that its colonies had to pay an unpayable tax. In 1773, furious colonists in North America sent forty tons of London tea to the bottom of the harbor. The operation was dubbed the Boston Tea Party. And the American Revolution began.

Coffee became a symbol of patriotism, though there was nothing patriotic about it. It had been discovered who knows when in the hinterland of Ethiopia, when goats ate the red fruit of a bush and danced all night, and after a voyage of centuries it reached the Caribbean.

In 1776, Boston's cafés were dens of conspiracy against the British Crown. And years later, President George Washington held court in a café that sold slaves and coffee cultivated by slaves in the Caribbean.

A century later, the men who won the West drank coffee by the light of their campfires, not tea.

IN GOD WE TRUST?

❧

Presidents of the United States tend to speak in God's name, although none of them has let on if He communicates by letter, fax, telephone, or telepathy. With or without His approval, in 2006 God was proclaimed chairman of the Republican Party of Texas.

That said, the All Powerful, who is even on the dollar bill, was a shining absence at the time of independence. The constitution did not mention Him. At the Constitutional Convention, when a prayer was suggested, Alexander Hamilton responded:

"We don't need foreign aid."

On his deathbed, George Washington wanted no prayers or priest or minister or anything.

Benjamin Franklin said divine revelation was nothing but poppycock.

"My mind is my own church," affirmed Thomas Paine, and President John Adams believed that "this world would be the best of all possible worlds, if there were no religion in it."

According to Thomas Jefferson, Catholic priests and Protestant ministers were "soothsayers and necromancers" who divided humanity, making "one half the world fools and the other half hypocrites."

A PROLOGUE TO THE FRENCH REVOLUTION

❧

Down the main street of Abbeville marched the procession.

Everyone on the sidewalks doffed their hats when the host, raised high above the crosses and saints, passed by. Everyone, that is, except for three young men who had their eyes on the girls in the crowd and did not notice.

They were charged. Not only had they refused to bare their heads before the white flesh of Jesus, they had smirked at it. Witnesses brought additional grave evidence: the host had been broken, causing it to bleed, and a wooden cross had been found mutilated in a ditch.

The tribunal focused its bolts of ire on one of the three, Jean-François de La Barre. Although he had just turned twenty, that insolent young man bragged that he had read Voltaire, and he defied the judges with his stupid arrogance.

The day of the execution, a fine morning in the year 1766, no one was missing from the market square. Jean-François climbed the scaffold with a sign hanging from his neck:

"Impious, blasphemer, sacrilegious, execrable, abominable."

The executioner tore out the tongue of the condemned man and cut off his head. He chopped up the body and threw the pieces into a bonfire. Along with the body parts, he tossed in a few of Voltaire's books, so that author and reader could burn together.

ADVENTURES OF THE MIND IN DARK TIMES

❧

Twenty-seven volumes.

The figure is not so impressive considering the seven hundred and forty-five volumes of the Chinese encyclopedia, published a few years previous.

But the French *L'Encyclopédie* put its seal on the Enlightenment and in a way offered the light that gave it its name. The pope in Rome ordered that blasphemous book burned and he excommunicated anyone found in possession of it. The authors, Diderot, D'Alembert, Jaucourt, Rousseau, Voltaire, and several more, risked or suffered jail and exile, but the influence of their great collective work was felt all over Europe.

Two and a half centuries later, their invitation to think is still astonishing. A few definitions, plucked from its pages:

Authority: "Nature gives no man the right to rule over others."

Censure: "Nothing is more dangerous to faith than having it subject to human opinion."

Clitoris: "A woman's center of sexual pleasure."

Courtier: "Applied to those who have been placed between kings and the truth, with the objective of keeping truth from reaching the kings."

Man: "Man is worthless without land. Land is worthless without man."

Inquisition: "Moctezuma was condemned for sacrificing prisoners to his gods. What would he say if he laid eyes on an auto-da-fé?"

Slavery: "Hateful commerce, against the law of nature, in which certain men buy and sell other men as if they were animals."

Orgasm: "Is there anything else so worth achieving?"

Usury: "Jews did not practice usury. It was Christian oppression that forced the Jews to become money-lenders."

MOZART

❧

The man who was music wrote music all day and all night and beyond all day and night, as if he were racing against death, as if he knew death would come soon.

He composed at a feverish pace, one piece after another, and in his scores he left some measures blank for improvising adventures in freedom.

No one knows how he found the time, but in his fleeting life he spent long hours with his nose in the books of his vast library, or enmeshed in animated discussion with people despised by the imperial police, like Joseph von Sonnenfels, the jurist who managed to get Vienna to outlaw torture, a first in Europe. His friends were the enemies of despotism and stupidity. A child of the Enlightenment, reader of *L'Encyclopédie*, Mozart shared the ideas that stirred up his times.

At the age of twenty-five, he lost his job as the king's musician and never set foot in court again. From then on, he lived from his concerts and the sales of his works, which were many and highly valued, though lowly priced.

He was an independent artist when independence was a rare feat, and it cost him dearly. In punishment for his freedom, he died suffocated by debt: the world owed him for so much music, yet he died owing.

WIGS

At the court in Versailles, more than a hundred *perruquiers* worked on those contraptions, which leaped over the Channel and landed on the skulls of the king of England, the duke of York, and other slave traders who imposed French fashion on the high nobility of Britain.

Male wigs began in France as a way to show class, not to hide baldness. The ones made of natural hair showered in talcum powder were the most expensive and required the most effort every morning.

High class, high towers: the ladies, helped out by switches, now called extensions, wore complicated wire frames perched on their heads so their hair could rise floor by exuberant floor adorned with feathers and flowers. The rooftop of the hairdo might have been decorated with little sailboats or farms complete with toy animals. Putting it together was no mean feat, and just keeping it on your head was a challenge. As if that were not enough, the ladies had to navigate while wedged inside enormous crinolines that had them constantly bumping into each other.

Tresses and attire ate up nearly all the time and energy of the aristocracy. Any left over was spent at banquets. All that sacrifice was exhausting. The French Revolution did not meet much resistance when it swallowed the feast and crushed the wigs and crinolines.

THE DESPICABLE HUMAN HAND

In Spain, manual trades were dishonorable until the end of the eighteenth century.

Whoever lived or had lived from the labor of his hands, or who had a father, a mother, or grandparents of lowly, vile occupations, did not merit the courtesy of being called "sir."

Among those lowly, vile occupations were

farmers,

stone carvers,

woodworkers,

vendors,

tailors,

barbers,

grocers,

and shoemakers.

These degraded beings paid taxes.

In contrast, exempt from paying taxes were

military officers,

nobles,

and priests.

THE REVOLUTIONARY HUMAN HAND

❧

In 1789, the Bastille was attacked and taken by a furious mob.

And in all France the producers rose up against the parasites. The population refused to continue paying the tribute and tithes that had fattened the venerable and useless institutions of the monarchy, the aristocracy, and the Church.

It wasn't long before the king and queen fled. Their carriage headed north toward the border. The little princes were dressed up as girls. The governess, dressed as a baroness, carried a Russian passport. The king, Louis XVI, was her butler; the queen, Marie Antoinette, her servant.

Night had fallen when they reached Varennes.

Suddenly, a crowd emerged from the shadows, surrounded the carriage, captured the monarchs, and returned them to Paris.

MARIE ANTOINETTE

❧

The king mattered little. The queen, Marie Antoinette, was the one they despised: for being a foreigner, for yawning during royal ceremonies, for going without a corset, for taking lovers. And for her extravagance. They called her "Madame Deficit."

The spectacle drew a crowd. When the head of Marie Antoinette rolled at the feet of the executioner, the audience roared its approval. A disembodied head. And no necklace.

All France was convinced the queen had bought herself the most expensive piece of jewelry in Europe, a necklace made of six hundred and forty-seven diamonds. Everyone also believed she had said if the people had no bread, let them eat cake.

THE MARSEILLAISE

*

The most famous anthem in the world came into being at a famous moment in world history. But it was also the child of the hand that wrote it and of the mouth that first sang it: the hand and mouth of its utterly unfamous composer, Captain Claude Rouget de Lisle, who wrote it in a single night.

Cries from the street dictated the words, and the music poured forth as if it had always been waiting inside him.

It was the turbulent year 1792: Prussian troops were marching against the French Revolution. Speeches and proclamations were stirring the streets of Strasbourg:

"Citizens, to arms!"

To defend the besieged revolution, the recently recruited Armée du Rhin was headed for the front. Rouget de Lisle's anthem rallied the troops. The chorus swelled, tears flowed, and a couple of months later it reappeared, who knows how, at the other end of France. Volunteers in Marseille marched off to battle singing that powerful tune, which came to be called "The Marseillaise," and all France sang the chorus. When the people attacked the Palace of the Tuileries, that was the song on their lips.

The composer was imprisoned, accused of treason for having committed the indiscretion of disagreeing with the Revolution's sharpest ideologue, Madame Guillotine.

In the end Captain Rouget de Lisle was released. No uniform, no income.

For years he scrounged a living on the street, devoured by fleas, hounded by the police. When he said he was the father of the anthem of the Revolution, people laughed in his face.

ANTHEMS

*

The first known national anthem was born of parents unknown in England in 1745. Its verses declared the kingdom would crush the Scottish rebels, to "frustrate their knavish tricks."

Half a century later, the Marseillaise warned that the Revolution would "water the fields with the impure blood" of the invaders.

At the beginning of the nineteenth century, the anthem of the United States proclaimed its imperial vocation blessed by God: "Conquer we must, when our cause it is just." And at the end of that century, the Germans consolidated their delayed national unity by erecting three hundred and twenty-seven statues of Emperor Wilhelm and four hundred and seventy of Bismarck, while singing the anthem that put Germany *über alles*, above all.

Generally speaking, anthems reinforce the identity of each nation by means of threats, insults, self-praise, homages to war, and the honorable duty to kill and be killed.

In Latin America, these paeans to the glories of the founding fathers sound like they were written for funeral pageants:

the Uruguayan anthem invites us to choose between country and grave

and the Paraguayan between the republic and death,

the Argentine exhorts us to vow to die with glory,

the Chilean proclaims the country's land will be the grave of the free,

the Guatemalan calls for victory or death,

the Cuban insists that dying for the fatherland is living,

the Ecuadorian shows that the holocaust of heroes is a fertile seed,

the Peruvian exults in the terror its cannons inspire,

the Mexican recommends soaking the fatherland's standards in waves of blood,

and the Colombian bathes itself in the blood of heroes who with geographic enthusiasm do battle at Thermopylae.

OLYMPE

❧

The symbols of the French Revolution are female, women of marble or bronze with powerful naked breasts, Phrygian caps, flags aflutter.

But what the Revolution produced was the Declaration of the Rights of Man and the Citizen, and when revolutionary militant Olympe de Gouges proposed a Declaration of the Rights of Woman and the Female Citizen, she was hauled off to jail. The Revolutionary Tribunal found her guilty and the guillotine removed her head.

At the foot of the scaffold, Olympe asked:

"If we women have the right to face the people from the guillotine, should we not also have the right to face them from the tribune?"

Not allowed. They could not speak, they could not vote. The Convention, the revolutionary congress, closed down all women's political associations and forbade women from debating men as equals.

Olympe de Gouges' companions were sent to the lunatic asylum. And soon after her execution, it was Manon Roland's turn. Manon was the wife of the minister of the interior, but not even that could save her. She was found guilty of "an anti-natural tendency to political activism." She had betrayed her feminine nature, which was to keep house and give birth to brave sons, and she had committed the deadly offense of sticking her nose into the masculine affairs of state.

And the guillotine dropped once more.

THE GUILLOTINE

❧

A tall doorway without a door, an empty frame. At the top, poised, the deadly blade.

She went by several names: the Machine, the Widow, the Barber. When she decapitated King Louis, she became Little Louise. And in the end, one name stuck, the guillotine.

Joseph Guillotin protested in vain. A thousand and one times, the doctor and sworn enemy of the death penalty protested that the executioner who sowed terror and drew multitudes was not his daughter. No one listened. People went right on believing that he was the father of the leading lady of the most popular show in Paris.

People also believed, and still do, that Guillotin died on the guillotine. In reality, he breathed his last breath in the peace of his own bed, his head well attached to his body.

The guillotine labored on until 1977. Its last victim was a Tunisian immigrant executed in the yard of a Paris prison by a superfast model with an electronic trigger.

THE REVOLUTION LOST ITS HEAD

❧

To sabotage the Revolution, landowners set fire to their crops. The specter of hunger roamed the cities. The kingdoms of Austria, Prussia, England, Spain, and Holland prepared for war against the contagious French Revolution, which insulted tradition and threatened the holy trinity of crown, wig, and cassock.

Besieged from within and without, the Revolution reached the boiling point. The people were the audience watching a drama performed in their name. Not many attended the debates. There was no time. The lineups for food were long.

Differences of opinion led to the scaffold. All the revolutionary leaders were enemies of monarchy, but some of them had kings in their hearts, and by a new, divine revolutionary right, they were the owners of the absolute truth and absolute power. Whoever dared to disagree was a counterrevolutionary ally of the enemy, a foreign spy, a traitor to the cause.

Marat escaped the guillotine because a mad girl stabbed him in the bath.

Saint-Just, inspired by Robespierre, accused Danton.

Danton, sentenced to death, asked them not to forget to put his head on display, and as a bequest he left his balls to Robespierre. He said the man would need them.

Three months later, Saint-Just and Robespierre were decapitated.

Without wanting it or knowing it, the desperate, chaotic republic was working for the restoration of the monarchy. The Revolution, which had promised liberty, equality, and fraternity, ended up paving the way for the despotism of Napoleon Bonaparte, who founded his own dynasty.

BÜCHNER

❧

In 1835, German dailies published this notice from the authorities:

> WANTED
>
> GEORG BÜCHNER, DARMSTADT MEDICAL STUDENT,
> 21 YEARS OLD, GRAY EYES,
> PROMINENT FOREHEAD, LARGE NOSE, SMALL MOUTH,
> NEARSIGHTED.

Büchner, a social agitator, organizer of poor peasants, traitor to his class, was on the run from the police.

Soon thereafter, at the age of twenty-three, he died.

He died of fever: so much life in so few years. Between one leap and the next in his life as a fugitive, Büchner wrote, a century ahead of his time, the plays that would found modern theater: *Woyzeck, Leonce and Lena, Danton's Death.*

In *Danton's Death*, the German revolutionary had the courage to put onstage, painfully and mercilessly, the tragic fate of the French Revolution, which had begun by proclaiming "the despotism of freedom" and ended up imposing the despotism of the guillotine.

WHITE CURSE

❧

The black slaves of Haiti gave Napoleon Bonaparte's army a tremendous thrashing, and in 1804 the flag of the free fluttered over the ruins.

But Haiti was a country ruined from the first. On the altars of French sugar plantations, lands and lives had been burned alive, and then the calamities of war exterminated a third of the population.

The birth of independence and the death of slavery, feats accomplished by blacks, were unpardonable humiliations for the white owners of the world.

Eighteen of Napoleon's generals were buried on the rebel isle. The new nation, born in blood, was sentenced to blockade and solitude: no one bought from her, no one sold to her, no one recognized her. For being disloyal to the colonial master, Haiti was obliged to pay France a gigantic sum in reparations. This expiation for the sin of dignity, which she paid for nearly a century and a half, was the price France exacted for diplomatic recognition.

No one else recognized her. Not even Simón Bolívar, who owed her everything. Haiti had provided ships, weapons, and soldiers for his war of independence against Spain, on only one condition: that the slaves be freed, an idea that had never occurred to the man known as the Liberator. Later on, when Bolívar triumphed, he refused to invite Haiti to the congress of new Latin American nations.

Haiti became the leper of the Americas.

Thomas Jefferson warned from the beginning that the plague had to be confined to that island, because it provided a very bad example.

Bad example: disobedience, chaos, violence. In South Carolina, by law any black sailor could be jailed while his ship was in port, for fear he might spread the antislavery fever that threatened all the Americas. In Brazil, that fever was called *haitianismo*.

TOUSSAINT

❧

He was born a slave, the son of slaves.

He was frail and homely.

He spent his childhood chatting with horses and plants.

In time he became the master's coachman and doctor to his gardens.

He had never killed a fly when the exigencies of war placed him where he now stands. Now he is called Toussaint L'Ouverture, because the blows of his sword part the enemy's defenses. This self-made general instructs his troops, illiterate slaves, explaining the whys and hows of the Revolution through stories he learned or made up as a child.

It is 1803, and the French army is on its last legs.

General Leclerc, Napoleon's brother-in-law, proposes:

"Let's talk."

Toussaint agrees.

They capture him, place him in chains, load him onto a ship.

Imprisoned in the coldest castle in France, from the cold he dies.

SLAVERY DIED MANY DEATHS

❧

Look in any encyclopedia. Ask which was the first country to abolish slavery. The encyclopedia will answer: Britain.

It is true that one fine day the British Empire, the world champion of the slave trade, changed its mind after it totted up the numbers and realized the sale of human flesh was no longer so profitable. But London discovered slavery was evil in 1807 and the news was so unconvincing that it had to be repeated twice over in the next thirty years.

It is also true that the French Revolution had freed the slaves of the colonies, but the liberating decree, called "immortal," died a short time later, assassinated by Napoleon Bonaparte.

The first country that was free, truly free, was Haiti. It abolished slavery three years before England, on a night illuminated by the sun of bonfires, while celebrating its recently won independence and recuperating its forgotten indigenous name.

DEAD MAN SPEAKING

❧

The abolition of slavery was also repeated throughout the nineteenth century in the new Latin American nations.

Repetition was proof of impotence. In 1821, Simón Bolívar pronounced slavery dead. Thirty years later, the deceased still enjoyed good health, and new laws of abolition were decreed in Colombia and Venezuela.

The very day in 1830 that Uruguay's constitution was proclaimed, the newspapers featured advertisements like:

For sale: very cheap, a Negro shoemaker.

For sale: one maid recently given birth, good for the lady.

For sale: one young Negro, 17 years old, no vices.

For sale: one very Spanish-looking mulatta for all farm work, and one large sugar kettle.

Five years before, in 1825, the first law forbidding the sale of persons in Uruguay had been passed, and it had to be repeated in 1842, 1846, and 1853.

Brazil was last in the Americas, next to last in the world. Slavery was legal until the end of the nineteenth century. Afterward, it was illegal but still operative, and that remains the case today. In 1888, the Brazilian government ordered all existing documentation on the topic burned. Thus slave labor was officially erased from the country's history. It died without having existed, and it exists despite having died.

THE AGES OF IQBAL

❧

In Pakistan, as in other countries, slavery survives.

Children of the poor are disposable goods.

When Iqbal Masih was four, his parents sold him for fifteen dollars.

He was bought by a rug maker. He worked chained to the loom fourteen hours a day. At the age of ten, Iqbal was a hunchback with the lungs of an old man.

Then he escaped and became the spokesman for Pakistan's child slaves.

In 1995, when he was twelve years old, a fatal bullet knocked him from his bicycle.

FORBIDDEN TO BE A WOMAN

❧

In 1804, Napoleon Bonaparte crowned himself emperor and decreed a civil code known as the Napoleonic Code, which still serves as the legal foundation for nearly the entire world.

This masterpiece of the bourgeoisie in power consecrated double standards and elevated property rights to the highest perch on the altar of justice.

Married women were deprived of rights, as were children, criminals, and the mentally deficient. A woman had to obey her husband. She had to follow him wherever he led, and she needed his permission for practically everything but breathing.

Divorce, which the French Revolution had made into a simple transaction, was restricted by Napoleon to cases of serious misconduct. The husband could divorce his wife for adultery. The wife could only get a divorce if enthusiasm led the husband to bed his lover on the matrimonial mattress.

In the worst of cases, the adulterous husband paid a fine. In every case, the adulterous wife went to prison.

The code did not authorize murdering an unfaithful wife caught in flagrante. But when a cuckolded husband killed, the judges, always men, whistled and looked the other way.

These dispositions, these customs, held sway in France for more than a century and a half.

PALACE ART IN FRANCE

❧

In the midst of conquering Europe, Napoleon crossed the Alps at the head of his immense army.

Jacques-Louis David painted the scene.

In the painting Napoleon wears the handsome dress uniform of the commanding general of the French army. The golden cape flutters with timely elegance in the breeze. His hand, held high, points to the heavens. His brisk white steed, mane and tail curled in the beauty shop, echoes his gesture by rearing up on two legs. The rocks on the ground are engraved with the names of Bonaparte and his two comrades, Hannibal and Charlemagne.

In reality, Napoleon did not wear a uniform. He crossed the freezing heights shivering with cold, wrapped in a heavy gray overcoat that covered his face, and on the back of an equally gray mule that struggled to keep its foothold on the slippery anonymous rocks.

BEETHOVEN

❧

He had a prisonlike childhood and he believed in freedom as a religion.

That is why he dedicated his Third Symphony to Napoleon and then erased the dedication,

he invented music with no thought to what people might say,

he mocked the princes,

he lived in perpetual disagreement with everyone,

he was alone and he was poor, and he had to move house seventy times.

And he hated censorship.

In the Ninth Symphony, the censors changed the title "Ode to Freedom," taken from the poet Friedrich von Schiller, to "Ode to Joy."

At the debut of the Ninth in Vienna, Beethoven took revenge. He conducted the orchestra and the chorus with such unbridled energy that the censored "Ode" became a hymn to the joy of freedom.

After the piece ended, he stood with his back to the audience, until someone turned him around and he could see the ovation that he could not hear.

ORIGIN OF NEWS AGENCIES

❦

Napoleon was crushed by the British at the Battle of Waterloo, south of Brussels.

Field Marshall Arthur Wellesley, the Duke of Wellington, took credit for the victory, but the true winner was the banker Nathan Rothschild, who did not fire a shot and was far from the scene.

Rothschild was the commander in chief of a platoon of carrier pigeons. Quick and well trained, they brought him the news in London. Before anyone else, he knew that Napoleon had lost, but he spread word that the French victory had been overwhelming, and he fooled the market by selling off everything British: bonds, stocks, pounds. Before you could say amen, everyone followed the lead of the man who always knew what he was doing. The assets of the nation they believed had been defeated got sold off as junk. Then Rothschild bought. He bought everything for nothing.

Thus was England victorious on the battlefield and vanquished on the stock exchange.

The banker Rothschild multiplied his fortune twenty times over and became the richest man in the world.

Several years later, toward the middle of the nineteenth century, the first international news agencies were born: Havas, now called France Presse, Reuters, Associated Press . . .

They all used carrier pigeons.

ORIGIN OF THE CROISSANT

❦

Napoleon, a symbol of France, was born in Corsica. His father, an enemy of France, gave him an Italian name.

The croissant, another symbol of France, was born in Vienna. Not for nothing does it bear the name and form of a crescent moon, which was and remains the symbol of Turkey. Turkish troops had laid siege to Vienna. One day in 1683, the city broke the siege and that same night, in a pastry shop, Peter Wender invented the croissant. And Vienna ate the vanquished.

Then Georg Franz Kolschitzky, a Cossack who had fought for Vienna, asked to be paid in coffee beans, which the Turks had left behind in their retreat, and he opened the city's first café. And Vienna drank the vanquished.

ORIGIN OF FRENCH COOKING

❦

The cuisine that is the pride of France was founded by Jean Anthelme Brillat-Savarin, a disillusioned revolutionary, and Alexandre Balthazar Laurent Grimod de La Reynière, a nostalgic monarchist.

The Revolution was over, the serfs had changed lords. A new order was emerging, a new class was in charge, and these two set out to tutor the palates of the victorious bourgeoisie.

Brillat-Savarin, author of the first treatise on gastronomy, is said to have uttered the words later repeated by so many others: "Tell me what you eat and I will tell you who you are." And also: "The discovery of a new dish contributes more to human happiness than that of a new star." His knowledge came from his mother, Aurora, a specialist who died at the dinner table at the age of ninety-nine: she felt ill, drained her wineglass, and begged them to hurry the dessert.

Grimod de La Reynière was the founder of culinary journalism. His articles in newspapers and yearbooks fed restaurants with new ideas. No more was the art of good eating a luxury reserved for the banquet halls of nobility. The one whose fingers were all over this had none: Grimod de La Reynière, grand master of pen and spoon, was born with no hands, and he wrote, cooked, and ate with hooks.

GOYA

*

In 1814 Ferdinand VII posed for Francisco de Goya. There was nothing unusual in that. Goya, court painter for the Spanish Crown, was doing a portrait of the new monarch. But artist and king detested each other.

The king suspected, and with good reason, that Goya's court paintings were disingenuously kind. The artist had no choice but to do the job that earned him his daily bread and provided an effective shield against the enmity of the Holy Inquisition. There was no lack of desire on God's tribunal to burn alive the creator of *La maja desnuda* and numerous other works that mocked the virtue of priests and the bravery of warriors.

The king had power and the artist had nothing. It was to reestablish the Inquisition and the privileges of nobility that Ferdinand came to the throne borne on the shoulders of a crowd cheering:

"Long live chains!"

Sooner rather than later, Goya lost his job as the king's painter and was replaced by Vicente López, an obedient bureaucrat with a brush.

The unemployed artist then took refuge in a country home on the banks of the Manzanares River, and on the walls he created the masterpieces known as the Black Paintings.

Goya painted them for himself, for his own pleasure or displeasure, in nights of solitude and despair. By the light of candles bristling on his hat, this utterly deaf man managed to hear the broken voices of his times and give them shape and color.

MARIANA

*

In 1814 King Ferdinand killed Pepa.

Pepa was what the people called the Constitution of Cádiz, which two years earlier had abolished the Inquisition and enshrined freedom of the press, the right to vote, and other insolent novelties.

The king decided that Pepa never was. He declared it "null and worthless and void, as if such acts, which ought to have been removed from time's way, had never occurred."

Then to remove from time's way the enemies of monarchic despotism, gallows were built all over Spain.

Early one morning in 1831, outside one of the gates of the city of Granada, the executioner twisted the tourniquet until the iron collar broke the neck of Mariana Pineda.

She was guilty. Of embroidering a flag, of not betraying freedom's conspirators, and of refusing to provide the judge who condemned her with the favor of her love.

Mariana had a brief life. She liked forbidden ideas, forbidden men, black mantillas, hot chocolate, and slow tunes.

FANS

🕯

The "lady liberals," as Cádiz police called them, conspired in code.

From their Andalusian grandmothers they had learned the secret language of fans, which worked equally well for disobeying husband or king: the slow unfoldings and rapid closings, the ripplings, the flutterings.

If a lady swept her hair off her forehead with the fan closed, it meant: "Do not forget me."

If she hid her eyes behind the open fan: "I love you."

If she opened the fan beside her lips: "Kiss me."

If she rested her lips on the closed fan: "I don't trust him."

If she drew her finger across the ribs: "We have to talk."

If she fanned herself while looking out from the balcony: "Let's meet outside."

If she closed her fan upon entering: "Today I cannot go out."

If she fanned with her left hand: "Do not believe that woman."

PALACE ART IN ARGENTINA

❧

May 25, 1810: it is raining in Buenos Aires. Under umbrellas, a crowd of top hats. White and sky-blue badges are handed around. In what today is called the Plaza de Mayo, the assembled gentlemen in frock coats bellow, "Long live the fatherland" and "Send the viceroy packing."

In real reality, not airbrushed for a grade-school lithograph, there were no top hats or frock coats, and it seems it was not even raining, so no umbrellas. There was a choir recruited to stand outside and cheer the few men inside City Hall who were discussing independence.

Those few, shopkeepers, smugglers, learned doctors, and military officers, were the founding fathers who would soon lend their names to avenues and streets.

No sooner was independence declared than they established free trade.

Thus the port of Buenos Aires murdered the nation's embryonic industry just as it was being born in the thread factories, textile mills, distilleries, saddleries, and other artisan workshops of Córdoba, Catamarca, Tucumán, Santiago del Estero, Corrientes, Salta, Mendoza, San Juan . . .

A few years later, the British foreign secretary, George Canning, offered a toast to the freedom of Spain's American colonies:

"Hispanic America is British," he declared, raising his glass.

Even the curbstones were British.

THE INDEPENDENCE THAT WAS NOT

❧

Thus the lives of the heroes of Latin America's emancipation came to an end.

Shot by firing squad: Miguel Hidalgo, José María Morelos, José Miguel Carrera, and Francisco de Morazán.

Assassinated: Antonio José de Sucre.

Hanged and quartered: Tiradentes.

Exiled: José Artigas, José de San Martín, Andrés de Santa Cruz, and Ramón Betances.

Imprisoned: Toussaint L'Ouverture and Juan José Castelli.

José Martí fell in battle.

Simón Bolívar died in solitude.

On August 10, 1809, while the city of Quito celebrated its liberation, an anonymous hand wrote on a wall:

Final day of despotism
and first day of the same.

Two years later in Bogotá, Antonio Nariño admitted: "We have changed masters."

THE LOSER

❧

He preached in the desert and died alone.

Simón Rodríguez, who had been Bolívar's teacher, spent half a century roving Latin America on the back of a mule, founding schools, and saying what no one wanted to hear.

A fire took nearly all his papers. Here are a few of the words that survived:

- On independence:
  We are independent but not free. Something must be done for these poor people, who have become less free than before. Before, they had a shepherd king who did not eat them until they were dead. Now the first to show up eats them alive.

- On colonialism of the mind:
  Europe's know-how and the prosperity of the United States are for our America two enemies of freedom of thought. The new republics are unwilling to adopt anything that does not have their stamp of approval . . . If you are going to imitate everything, imitate originality!

- On colonialist trade:
  Some think prosperity is seeing their ports filled with ships—foreign

ships, and their homes turned into storerooms for goods—foreign goods. Every day brings another load of manufactured clothes, down to the caps the Indians wear. Soon we shall see little golden packages bearing the royal coat of arms containing 'newly processed' clay for children accustomed to eating dirt.

- On popular education:
  To make students recite by rote what they do not understand is like training parrots. Teach children to be curious so they learn to obey their own minds rather than obeying authorities the way the narrow-minded do, or obeying custom the way the stupid do. He who knows nothing, anyone can fool. He who has nothing, anyone can buy.

ARTIGAS

❧

The architecture of death is a specialty of the military.

In 1977 the Uruguayan dictatorship erected a gravestone in memory of José Artigas.

This enormous structure was a high-class prison: word had it that the hero might escape, a century and a half after his death.

To decorate the mausoleum and dissemble the intention, the dictatorship wanted to cover it with sayings from the founding father. But the man who had led the first agrarian reform in the Americas, the general who liked to be called "Citizen Artigas," said that the most downtrodden should become the most privileged. He insisted that our rich patrimony should never be sold off at the low price imposed by need. And he repeated again and again that his authority emanated from the people and did not extend beyond them.

The military found not a single quotation that would not prove dangerous.

They decided Artigas had been mute.

The walls of black marble feature nothing but dates and names.

TWO TRAITORS

❧

Domingo Faustino Sarmiento despised José Artigas. No one else did he hate so much. "Traitor to his race," he called him, and it was true. Artigas, though white and blue-eyed, fought alongside mestizo gauchos and blacks and Indians. And he was defeated and went into exile, and he died in solitude and oblivion.

Sarmiento was also a traitor to his race. Just look at his portraits. At war with what he saw in the mirror, he preached and practiced the extermination of dark-skinned Argentineans and their replacement by blue-eyed Europeans. And he was president of his country, a torch-bearer of civilization, covered in glory and accolades, immortal hero.

CONSTITUTIONS

❧

The main avenue in Montevideo is called "18 de julio" to honor the day the constitution of Uruguay was born. And the stadium where the very first soccer World Cup was played was built to commemorate the centenary of that foundational document.

The Magna Carta of 1830, identical to the constitution planned for Argentina, denied citizenship to women, the illiterate, slaves, and anyone who was "a paid servant, a day laborer, or a rank and file soldier." Only one out of ten Uruguayans had the right to be a citizen of the new country, and 95 percent of the population did not vote in the first elections.

So it was throughout the Americas, from north to south. All our countries were born of a lie. Independence disowned those who had risked their lives fighting for her, and women, poor people, Indians, and blacks were not invited to the party. The constitutions draped that travesty in the prestige of legality.

Bolivia took a hundred and eighty-one years to discover that it was a country made up mostly of Indians. The revelation occurred in 2006 when Evo Morales, an Aymara Indian, was elected president by an avalanche of votes.

That same year Chile found out that half of all Chileans are female, and Michelle Bachelet became president.

AMERICA ACCORDING TO HUMBOLDT

❧

When the nineteenth century was taking its first baby steps, Alexander von Humboldt entered America and revealed its innards. Years later, he wrote:

- On social classes:
  Mexico is the country of inequality. The monstrous inequality in rights and riches is striking. The greater or lesser degree of whiteness of skin decides the rank which man occupies in society.

- On slaves:
  In no place does one feel so ashamed to be European as in the Antilles, be it the French, British, Dutch, or Spanish ones. To discuss which country treats the blacks better is like choosing between being stabbed and being skinned alive.

- On Indians:
  Among all religions, none masks human unhappiness like the Christian religion. Whoever visits the ill-fated Americans living under the priests' lash will never again want to learn anything about Europeans and their theocracy.

- On the expansion of the United States:
  The North Americans' conquests disgust me. I wish them the worst in tropical Mexico. Much better would it be if they stayed home instead of spreading their insane slavery.

ORIGIN OF ECOLOGY

❧

That strange and valiant German was concerned about sustainable development long before it came to be called that. Everywhere he went he was astounded by the diversity of the natural world and horrified by how little respect it commanded.

On the island of Uruana in the Orinoco River, Humboldt noticed that the Indians left behind a good part of the eggs the turtles laid on the beach so that reproduction would continue. But he saw that the Europeans did not follow that wise custom, and warned their greed would endanger a rich resource that nature had placed within reach.

Why was the level of Venezuela's Lake Valencia falling? Because the native forest had been leveled to make way for colonial plantations. Humboldt said the old trees had delayed the evaporation of rainwater, prevented soil erosion, and kept the rivers and lakes in harmonious balance. The murder of those trees was the cause of the merciless droughts and relentless floods:

"It is not just Lake Valencia," he said. "All the region's rivers are drying up. The mountains are deforested because the European colonists cut down the trees. The rivers are dry for much of the year, and when it rains in the mountains they become torrents that destroy the fields."

MAP ERASED

❧

One evening in 1867 the Brazilian ambassador pinned the Grand Crucifix of the Imperial Order of the Cross on the chest of Bolivia's dictator Mariano Melgarejo. Melgarejo had the habit of giving away chunks of the country in return for medals or horses. That evening his eyes welled up with tears and, then and there, he gave the ambassador sixty-five thousand square kilometers of rubber-rich Bolivian jungle. With that gift, plus another two hundred thousand square kilometers seized by force, Brazil got all Bolivia's trees that cried tears of rubber for the world market.

In 1884 Bolivia lost another war, this time against Chile. They called it the War of the Pacific, but it was the Saltpeter War. Saltpeter, a vast carpet of brilliant whiteness, was the fertilizer most coveted by Europe's farmers and a key input for the military industry. John Thomas North, a British businessman who at parties liked to dress up as Henry VIII, polished off all the saltpeter that had belonged to Peru and Bolivia. Chile won the war, and he picked up the spoils. Peru lost a great deal, as did Bolivia, deprived of an outlet to the sea, four hundred kilometers of coastline, four ports, seven bays, and one hundred and twenty thousand square kilometers of desert rich in saltpeter.

But this many-times-mutilated country was not formally erased from the map until a diplomatic incident occurred in La Paz.

Maybe it happened or maybe not. I've been told the story many times and this is how it goes: Melgarejo, the drunken dictator, welcomed the representative of England by offering him a glass of *chicha*, a fermented corn liquor that was and remains the national drink. The diplomat thanked him and praised *chicha*'s virtues, but said he would prefer hot chocolate. So the president kindly served him an immense jug of hot chocolate filled to the brim. He held the ambassador prisoner throughout the night until he finished the last drop of that punishment, and at dawn he was paraded about town sitting backward on a mule.

When Queen Victoria heard the story in Buckingham Palace, she asked for a map of the world. She then asked where the hell Bolivia was, crossed the country out with a piece of chalk, and passed sentence:

"Bolivia does not exist."

MAP GOBBLED

❡

Between 1833 and 1855 Antonio López de Santa Anna was president of Mexico eleven times.

During that period Mexico lost Texas, California, New Mexico, Arizona, Nevada, Utah, and a good chunk of Colorado and Wyoming.

For the modest sum of fifteen million dollars, and a number never counted of Indian and mestizo soldiers killed, Mexico was reduced by half.

The dismemberment began in Texas, called Tejas back then. There, slavery had been outlawed. Sam Houston led the invasion that reestablished it.

Houston and Stephen Austin and other slave-owning land-grabbers are now freedom's heroes and founding fathers of the state. Their names speak of health and culture. The city of Houston offers cures or solace to the seriously ill, and Austin gives luster to academics.

MAP BROKEN

❧

The first volley did not kill Francisco Morazán. He got up as best he could and ordered the firing squad to take better aim.

After, the coup de grâce shattered his skull.

Central America was shattered too, into five pieces that today have become six. Those six countries, which alternately ignore and mistreat one another, were at the time of Morazán a single republic.

He led Central America from 1830 to 1838. He wanted it united and to that end he fought.

In his final battle he led eighty men against five thousand.

When he entered San José de Costa Rica, bound to his saddle, a crowd watched in silence.

A short while later he was sentenced and shot and the rain continued pelting him for hours.

When Morazán was born in Honduras, there was not a single public school or hospital where the poor could go before heading for the cemetery.

In Honduras and throughout Central America, Morazán turned convents into schools and hospitals, and the high priests declared that this Satan expelled from heaven was responsible for smallpox and drought and even the war the Church waged against him.

Thirteen years after Morazán's downfall, William Walker invaded these lands.

THE PREDESTINED

❧

In 1856, William Walker proclaims himself president of Nicaragua.

The ceremony includes speeches, a military parade, a mass, and a banquet featuring fifty-three toasts of European wines.

A week later, United States Ambassador John H. Wheeler officially recognizes the new president, and his speech compares him to Christopher Columbus.

Walker imposes Louisiana's constitution on Nicaragua, reestablishing slavery, abolished in all Central America thirty years previous. He does so for the good of the blacks, because "inferior races cannot compete with the white race, unless they are given a white master to channel their energies."

This Tennessee gentleman known as "the Predestined" receives orders directly from God. Gruff, grim, always dressed in mourning, he leads a band of mercenaries recruited on the docks who claim to be the Knights of the Golden Circle and like to be called, modestly, the Phalange of Immortals.

"Five or none," Walker proclaims, as he sets out to conquer all Central America.

And the five Central American countries, divorced, poisoned by mutual rancor, recover their lost unity, at least for a while: they unite against the invaders.

And the Immortals die.

MAP CHANGED

❧

In 1821, the American Colonization Society bought a piece of Africa.

In Washington the new country was christened Liberia and its capital was called Monrovia, in honor of James Monroe, who at the time was president of the United States. Also in Washington, they designed the flag to be just like their own, except with a single star, and they elected the country's government. Harvard drew up the constitution.

The citizens of the newborn nation were freed slaves, or rather slaves expelled from the plantations of the southern United States.

No sooner did they set foot in Africa than those who had been slaves became masters. The native population, "those jungle savages," owed obedience to the newcomers, who had suddenly risen from the bottom to the top.

Backed by cannon, they took over the best lands and claimed the exclusive right to vote.

Later on, with the passing of the years, they granted rubber concessions to Firestone and Goodrich, and gave away the oil, iron, and diamonds to other U.S. companies.

Their descendants, 5 percent of the population, continue running this foreign military base in Africa. Every so often, when the poor masses get rowdy, they call in the Marines to restore order.

NAME CHANGED

❦

She learned to read by reading numbers. Playing with numbers was her favorite pastime and at night she dreamed of Archimedes.

Her father forbade it:

"Such things are not for women," he said.

When the French Revolution set up the Polytechnic School, Sophie Germain was eighteen. She wanted to go. They shut the door in her face:

"Such things are not for women," they said.

By herself, she studied, researched, invented.

She sent her work by mail to Professor Joseph-Louis Lagrange. Sophie signed it Monsieur Antoine-August LeBlanc, and thus kept the most excellent professor from responding:

"Such things are not for women."

They had been writing back and forth, mathematician to mathematician, for ten years when the professor discovered that the he was a she.

From that point on, Sophie was the only woman allowed into Europe's masculine Olympus of science: in mathematics she probed theorems, and later on in physics she revolutionized the study of elastic surfaces.

A century later, her contributions helped make possible the Eiffel Tower, among other things.

The names of several scientists are inscribed on the tower.

Sophie's is not there.

Her death certificate from 1831 says she was a bondholder, not a scientist:

"Such things are not for women," the clerk said.

THE AGES OF ADA

❦

At eighteen, she runs away in the arms of her tutor.

At twenty, she marries, or is married, despite her notorious incompetence in domestic matters.

At twenty-one, she begins studying mathematical logic on her own. Not the most appropriate occupation for a lady, but her family indulges her. Maybe that way she will stay in her right mind, and stave off the insanity that her father's genes have in store for her.

At twenty-five, she invents a foolproof system based on probability theory for winning at the racetracks. She bets the family jewels. She loses everything.

At twenty-seven, she publishes a revolutionary paper. She does not put her name to it. A scientific paper by a woman? That publication makes her the first programmer in history: it lays out a new method for setting up a machine to undertake repetitive tasks and save textile workers from the drudgery of routine.

At thirty-five, she falls ill. The doctors diagnose hysteria. It is cancer.

In 1852, at the age of thirty-six, she dies. At that very age her father, the poet Lord Byron, whom she never saw, also died.

A century and a half later, in homage to her, one of the languages for programming computers is named Ada.

THE HE'S ARE SHE'S

❧

In 1847, three novels excite England's readers.

Wuthering Heights by Ellis Bell tells a devastating tale of passion and shame. *Agnes Grey* by Acton Bell strips bare the hypocrisy of the family. *Jane Eyre* by Currer Bell exalts the courage of an independent woman.

No one knows that the authors are female. The brothers Bell are actually the sisters Brontë.

These fragile girls, virgins all, Emily, Anne, Charlotte, avenge their solitude by writing poems and novels in a village lost on the Yorkshire moors. Intruders into the male world of literature, they don men's masks so the critics will forgive them for having dared. But the critics pan their works anyway, as "rude," "crude," "nasty," "savage," "brutal," "libertine" . . .

FLORA

❧

Flora Tristán, grandmother of Paul Gaugin, errant activist, revolution's pilgrim, dedicated her turbulent life to fighting against a husband's right of property over his wife, a boss's right of property over his workers, and a master's right of property over his slaves.

In 1833, she traveled to Peru. On the outskirts of Lima she visited a sugar mill. She saw the stones that ground the cane, the kettles that boiled the molasses, the refinery that made the sugar. Everywhere she looked, she saw black slaves coming and going, working in silence. They were not even aware of her presence.

The owner told her he had nine hundred. In better times, twice as many, he complained.

And he said everything he was expected to say: that blacks were lazy like Indians, that they only worked under the lash, that . . .

When they were leaving, Flora came across a lockup to one side of the plantation.

Without asking permission, she went inside.

There, in the utter darkness of a dungeon, she managed to make out the figures of two women, naked, crouching in a corner.

"They're worse than animals," the guard said scornfully. "Animals don't kill their young."

These slaves had killed their young.

The two gazed at her, who gazed back at them from the other side of the world.

CONCEPCIÓN

❧

She spent her life struggling heart and soul against the hell of jail and for the dignity of women imprisoned in jails disguised as homes.

An opponent of collective absolution, she called a spade a spade.

"When it is everyone's fault, it is no one's," she liked to say. She earned herself a few enemies this way. Over the long term her prestige became indisputable, though her country had a hard time accepting it. And not only her country, her times too.

Back in 1840-something, Concepción Arenal took courses at the law school disguised as a man, her chest flattened by a double corset.

Back in 1850-something, she continued dressing like a man to attend the Madrid soirées where unbecoming topics were debated at unbecoming hours.

And back in 1870-something, a prestigious English organization, the John Howard Association for Penal Reform, named her its representative in Spain. The document certifying her position referred to her as "Mr. Concepción Arenal."

Forty years later, another woman from Galicia, Emilia Pardo Bazán, became the first female university professor in Spain. No student bothered to attend her class. She lectured to an empty hall.

VENUS

❧

She was captured in South Africa and sold in London.

And she was mockingly named Hottentot Venus. For two shillings you could see her naked in a cage, her tits so long she could breastfeed a baby on her back. For twice as much you could touch her ass, the biggest behind in the world.

A sign described the savage as half-human, half-animal, "the epitome of all that the civilized Englishman, happily, is not."

From London she went on to Paris. Experts from the Museum of Natural History wanted to know if this Venus belonged to a species falling somewhere between man and the orangutan.

She was twenty-something when she died. Georges Cuvier, a celebrated naturalist, undertook the dissection. He reported that she had the skull of a monkey, a tiny brain, and a mandrill's ass.

Cuvier cut off the inner labia of her vagina, an enormous flap, and placed it in a jar.

Two centuries later, the jar was put on display in Paris at the Musée de l'Homme, next to the genitals of another African woman and those of a Peruvian Indian.

Nearby, in another series of jars, were the brains of several European scientists.

THE REAL AMERICA

❧

Queen Victoria received them at Buckingham Palace, they visited the courts of Europe, in Washington they were invited to the White House.

Bartola and Máximo were the tiniest beings ever. John Henry Anderson, who had purchased them, put them on display dancing in the palms of his hands.

Circus posters called them Aztecs, even though according to Anderson they came from a Mayan city hidden in the jungles of Yucatán, where cocks crowed underground and the natives wore turbans and ate human flesh.

The European scientists who studied them determined that their skulls could not hold moral principles, and that Bartola and Máximo were descended from American ancestors incapable of thinking or speaking. That is why they could only repeat a few words, like parrots, and could not understand anything but their master's orders.

DIET OF AIR

❧

In the middle of the nineteenth century, Bernard Kavanagh drew crowds in England. He announced that for seven days and seven nights he would not swallow a mouthful or drink a drop, and moreover he had been following such a diet for five and a half years.

Kavanagh did not charge to get in, but he did accept donations, which went straight into the hands of the Holy Spirit and the Most Holy Virgin.

After London, he performed his affecting spectacle in other cities, engaging in fast after fast, always inside cages or hermetically sealed rooms, always under medical control and police surveillance, and always surrounded by avid crowds.

When he died, the body disappeared and was never found. Many believed that Kavanagh had eaten himself. He was Irish, and in those years that was not at all unusual.

AN OVERPOPULATED COLONY

❧

No smoke rose from the chimneys. In 1850, after five years of hunger and disease, Ireland's countryside was depopulated, and slowly the empty houses fell in. The people had marched off either to the cemetery or to the ports of North America.

Nothing grew in that land, not even potatoes. The only thing growing was the number of crazy people. The Dublin insane asylum, paid for by Jonathan Swift, had ninety inmates when it opened its doors. A century later, it had over three thousand.

In the middle of the famine, London sent some emergency relief, but after a few months charitable feelings ran out. The empire refused to continue aiding that irksome colony. As the prime minister, Lord John Russell, put it, the ungrateful Irish repaid generosity with rebellion and slander, and that did not sit well with public opinion.

Sir Charles Edward Trevelyan, the top official in charge of the Irish crisis, attributed the famine to Divine Providence. Ireland was the most densely populated country in all Europe, and, since man could not prevent overpopulation, God was taking care of it "in all his wisdom, in an unexpected fashion, but with great efficacy."

ORIGIN OF FAIRY TALES

❧

In the first half of the seventeenth century, James I and Charles I, kings of England, Scotland, and Ireland, took a number of measures to protect Britain's embryonic industry. They outlawed the export of unprocessed wool, required the use of local textiles even in luxury clothing, and closed the doors on a good part of the manufactures coming from France and Holland.

At the beginning of the eighteenth century, Daniel Defoe, the creator of Robinson Crusoe, wrote several essays on economics and trade. In one of his most widely read works, Defoe praised the role of state protectionism in the development of the British textile industry: if it weren't for those kings, who with their customs barriers and taxes did so much to further the industry, England would have remained a provider of raw wool for foreigners. England's industrial growth led Defoe to imagine the world of the future as an immense colony dependent on its products.

Later on, as Defoe's dream came true, imperial power systematically prevented other countries, by suffocation or cannonade, from following her example.

"When it got to the top, it kicked away the ladder," said German economist Friedrich List.

Then England invented the fairy tale of free trade: nowadays, when poor countries cannot sleep at night, rich countries still tell them that story to put them to sleep.

A STUBBORN COLONY

🌶

The English government struggled to repel an invasion of fine cotton and silk cloth from India. Starting in 1685, Indian textiles were punished with heavy tariffs. The tariffs kept rising until they became prohibitive, and there were periods when the doors were simply shut.

But barriers and prohibitions did not manage to dislodge the competition. Half a century after steamships and the British industrial revolution, Indian weavers struggled on, despite their primitive technology. Their high-quality textiles and low prices kept finding customers.

Not until the beginning of the nineteenth century, when the British Empire finally conquered nearly all of India by blood and by fire, and then obliged the weavers to pay astronomical taxes, was their stubborn competitiveness routed.

Later on, in the middle of the nineteenth century, the British were kind enough to dress the survivors of that hecatomb. Once India's looms were all drowned at the bottom of the Thames, Indians became the best customers for Manchester's textiles.

At that point, Dhaka, which the legendary Clive of India had compared to London and Manchester, was empty. Four of every five inhabitants had left. Dhaka was still the center of Bengal's industry, but instead of cloth it produced opium. Clive, its conqueror, died of an overdose, but the poppy fields enjoyed good health in the midst of the ruin of everything else.

Today Dhaka is the capital of Bangladesh, a country among the poorest of the poor.

TAJ MAHAL

❧

In the seventeenth century, Indian and Chinese workshops produced half of all the world's manufactures.

In those days of splendor, Emperor Shah Jahan built the Taj Mahal on the banks of the Yamuna River, a home in death for his favorite wife.

That woman and her home were alike, in that both changed according to the time of day or night.

The Taj Mahal was designed by Ustad Ahmad Lahauri, a Persian architect and astrologer known by many other names as well. They say it was built by twenty thousand workers over twenty years, made of white marble, red sand, jade, and turquoise carried from afar by a thousand elephants.

They say. Who knows? Perhaps that weightless beauty, floating whiteness, was made of air.

At the end of the year 2000, before an awestruck multitude, India's most famous magician made it disappear for two minutes.

P. C. Sorcar Jr. said it was the art of his magic:

"I made it vanish," he said.

Did he make it vanish, or did he return it to the air?

MUSIC FOR THE HOURS

❧

Like the Taj Mahal, ragas change depending on when and for whom.

For two thousand years, India's ragas have offered music for the day's birth and for each step the day takes toward night, and they sound different according to the time of the year and the season of the soul.

The melodies rest on one note, repeated, and they rise and fall freely, always changing the way the colors of the world change, and the landscape of the spirit.

No two ragas are alike.

They are born and die and are reborn every time they are played.

Ragas do not like to be written down. The experts who tried to define them, codify them, classify them, all failed.

They are mysterious, like the silence from whence they come.

HOKUSAI

❧

Hokusai, the most famous artist in the history of Japan, said his country was a floating world. With laconic elegance, he knew how to see it and how to portray it.

He was born Kawamura Tokitaro and he died Fujiwara Iitsu. Along the way he changed his name thirty times, for his thirty rebirths in art or in life, and he moved house ninety-three times.

He never shed his poverty, even though he worked from dawn to dusk and created no less than thirty thousand paintings and etchings.

About his work, he wrote:

Of all I drew prior to the age of seventy, there is truly nothing of great note. At the age of seventy-two, I finally apprehended something of the true quality of birds, animals, insects, fish, and of the vital nature of grasses and trees. At one hundred, I shall have become truly marvelous.

He did not live beyond ninety.

ORIGIN OF MODERN JAPAN

❧

In the middle of the nineteenth century, threatened by battleships arrayed along its coasts, Japan had agreed to suffer insufferable treaties.

To counter the humiliations imposed by the Western powers, modern Japan was born.

A new emperor inaugurated the Meiji era and founded the Japanese state, incarnated in his sacred figure,

created publicly owned factories in seventy sectors of the industrial economy and provided them with protection,

hired European technicians to train the Japanese and keep them up to date,

built a system of public trains and telegraphs,

nationalized the lands of the feudal lords,

organized a new army which defeated the samurais and obliged them to change professions,

imposed free and mandatory public education,

and multiplied the number of shipyards and banks.

Fukuzawa Yukichi, who founded the most important university of the Meiji era, summed up the government's approach this way:

"A country should not fear to defend its freedom against interference even though the whole world is hostile."

And thus Japan was able to annul the harmful treaties imposed on it, and the humiliated country became a power capable of humiliating others, as China, Korea, and other neighbors soon found out.

FREE TRADE? NO THANKS

❧

When the Meiji era was taking its first steps, Ulysses S. Grant, president of the United States, paid the emperor a visit.

Grant advised him not to fall into the trap laid by British banks, for it is not generosity that leads certain countries to be so enamored of lending money, and he congratulated him on his protectionist policies.

Before being elected president, Grant had been the general victorious in the war waged by the industrial North against the plantation South, and well he knew that customs barriers had been as much a cause of the war as slavery. It took the South four years and six hundred thousand dead before it realized that the United States had broken its links of colonial servitude with England.

As president, Grant answered Britain's relentless pressure by saying:

"Within two hundred years, when America has gotten out of protectionism all that it can offer, we too will adopt free trade."

So it will be in 2075 that the most protectionist country in the world will adopt free trade.

WITH BLOOD, WORDS SINK IN

❧

While the United States and Japan pursued their independence, another country, Paraguay, was annihilated for doing the same.

Paraguay was the only country in Latin America that refused to purchase lead life jackets from the merchants and bankers of England. Its three neighbors, Argentina, Brazil, and Uruguay, had to tutor it on "the ways of civilized nations," as the English-language daily *Standard* of Buenos Aires put it.

All the combatants ended up in a bad way.

The student, exterminated.

The teachers, bankrupt.

They had claimed Paraguay would get its well-deserved lesson in three months, but the course lasted five years.

British banks financed the pedagogical mission and charged very dear. By the end, the victorious countries owed twice what they had owed five years previous, and the vanquished country, which had owed not a cent to anyone, was obliged to inaugurate its foreign debt: Paraguay received a loan of a million pounds sterling. The loan was for paying reparations to the winners. The murdered country had to pay the countries that murdered it for the high cost of its murder.

The tariffs that protected Paraguay's industry disappeared;

the state companies, public lands, steel mills, one of the first railroads in South America, all disappeared;

the national archive, incinerated with its three centuries of history, disappeared;

and people disappeared.

Argentina's president, Domingo Faustino Sarmiento, an educated educator, declared in 1870:

"The war is over. Not a single Paraguayan over ten years old is left alive."

And he celebrated:

"It was necessary to purge the earth of all that human excrescence."

TRADITIONAL DRESS

❧

South America was the market that always said yes.

Here, everything from England was welcome.

Brazil bought ice skates. Bolivia, bowler hats that now form the traditional dress of indigenous women. And in Argentina and Uruguay the traditional garb of gauchos was made in Britain for the Turkish army. At the close of the Crimean War, English merchants sent the thousands upon thousands of leftover baggy pants to the River Plate, and they became the gauchos' *bombachas*.

A decade later, England dressed the Brazilian, Argentine, and Uruguayan troops in the very same Turkish uniforms to carry out its errand to exterminate Paraguay.

HERE LAY PARAGUAY

❧

The Empire of Brazil was inhabited by a million and a half slaves and a handful of dukes, marquises, counts, viscounts, and barons.

To achieve the liberation of Paraguay, this slave state placed in charge of its troops Count d'Eu, grandson of the king of France and husband of the next in line to the throne of Brazil.

In his portraits, receding chin, nose held high, breast thick with medals, the Field Marshal of Victory was unable to hide the disgust he felt for this unpleasant matter of war.

He knew enough to always remain a prudent distance from the battlefield, where his heroic soldiers faced ferocious Paraguayan children wearing false beards and armed with sticks. And from afar he pulled off his greatest feat: when the town of Piribebuy refused to surrender, he had his troops shut the windows and doors of the hospital filled with the wounded, and burn it down with everyone inside.

He was at war for a little over a year, and upon his return confessed:

"The Paraguayan War evoked in me an invincible repugnance for any prolonged effort."

ORIGIN OF LANGUAGE

❧

Amid so much death, birth survived.

Guaraní, the original language of Paraguay, survived, and with it the certainty that words are sacred.

The oldest of traditions has it that on this earth the red cicada sang, the grasshopper sang, the partridge sang, and then the cedar sang: from the soul of the cedar burst forth the song which in Guaraní called the first Paraguayans into being.

They did not yet exist.

They were born from the word that named them.

ORIGIN OF FREEDOM OF OPPRESSION

❧

Opium was outlawed in China.

British merchants smuggled it in from India. Their diligent efforts led to a surge in the number of Chinese dependent on the mother of heroin and morphine, who charmed them with false happiness and ruined their lives.

The smugglers were fed up with the hindrances they faced at the hands of Chinese authorities. Developing the market required free trade, and free trade demanded war.

William Jardine, a generous sort, was the most powerful of the drug traffickers and vice president of the Medical Missionary Society, which offered treatment to the victims of the opium he sold.

In London, Jardine hired a few influential writers and journalists, including best-selling author Samuel Warren, to create a favorable environment for war. These communications professionals ran the cause of freedom high up the flagpole. Freedom of expression at the service of free trade: pamphlets and articles rained down upon British public opinion, exalting the sacrifice of the honest citizens who challenged Chinese despotism, risking jail, torture, and death in that kingdom of cruelty.

The proper climate established, the storm was unleashed. The Opium War lasted, with a few interruptions, from 1839 to 1860.

OUR LADY OF THE SEAS, NARCO QUEEN

❦

The sale of people had been the juiciest enterprise in the British Empire. But happiness, as everyone knows, does not last. After three prosperous centuries, the Crown had to pull out of the slave trade, and selling drugs came to be the most lucrative source of imperial glory.

Queen Victoria was obliged to break down China's closed doors. On board the ships of the Royal Navy, Christ's missionaries joined the warriors of free trade. Behind them came the merchant fleet, boats that once carried black Africans, now filled with poison.

In the first stage of the Opium War, the British Empire took over the island of Hong Kong. The colorful governor, Sir John Bowring, declared:

"Free trade is Jesus Christ, and Jesus Christ is free trade."

HERE LAY CHINA

❦

Outside its borders the Chinese traded little and were not in the habit of waging war.

Merchants and warriors were looked down upon. "Barbarians" was what they called the English and the few Europeans they met.

And so it was foretold. China had to fall, defeated by the deadliest fleet of warships in the world, and by mortars that perforated a dozen enemy soldiers in formation with a single shell.

In 1860, after razing ports and cities, the British, accompanied by the French, entered Beijing, sacked the Summer Palace, and told their colonial troops recruited in India and Senegal they could help themselves to the leftovers.

The palace, center of the Manchu Dynasty's power, was in reality many palaces, more than two hundred residences and pagodas set among lakes and gardens, not unlike paradise. The victors stole every-thing, absolutely everything: furniture and drapes, jade sculptures, silk dresses, pearl necklaces, gold clocks, diamond bracelets . . . All that survived was the library, plus a telescope and a rifle that the king of England had given China seventy years before.

Then they burned the looted buildings. Flames reddened the earth and sky for many days and nights, and all that had been became nothing.

LOOTIE

❦

Lord Elgin, who ordered the burning of the imperial palace, arrived in Beijing on a litter carried by eight scarlet-liveried porters and escorted by four hundred horsemen. This Lord Elgin, son of the Lord Elgin who sold the sculptures of the Parthenon to the British Museum, donated to that same museum the entire palace library, which had been saved from the looting and fire for that very reason. And soon in another palace, Buckingham, Queen Victoria was presented with the gold and jade scepter of the vanquished king, as well as the first Pekinese in Europe. The little dog was also part of the booty. They named it "Lootie."

China was obliged to pay an immense sum in reparations to its executioners, since incorporating it into the community of civilized nations had turned out to be so expensive. Quickly, China became the principal market for opium and the largest customer for Lancashire cloth.

At the beginning of the nineteenth century, Chinese workshops produced one-third of all the world's manufactures. At the end of the nineteenth century, they produced 6 percent.

Then China was invaded by Japan. Conquest was not difficult. The country was drugged and humiliated and ruined.

NATURAL DISASTERS

❃

An empty desert of footsteps and voices, nothing but dust stirred by the wind.

Many Chinese hang themselves, rather than killing to kill their hunger or waiting for hunger to kill them.

In London, the British merchants who triumphed in the Opium War establish the China Famine Relief Fund.

This charitable institution promises to evangelize the pagan nation via the stomach: food sent by Jesus will rain from heaven.

In 1879, after three years without rain, the Chinese number fifteen million fewer.

OTHER NATURAL DISASTERS

❃

In 1879, after three years without rain, the Indians number nine million fewer.

It is the fault of nature:

"These are natural disasters," say those who know.

But in India during these atrocious years, the market is more punishing than the drought.

Under the law of the market, freedom oppresses. Free trade, which obliges you to sell, forbids you to eat.

India is a not a poorhouse, but a colonial plantation. The market rules. Wise is the invisible hand, which makes and unmakes, and no one should dare correct it.

The British government confines itself to helping a few of the moribund die in work camps it calls "relief camps," and to demanding the taxes that the peasants cannot pay. The peasants lose their lands, sold for a pittance, and for a pittance they sell the hands that work it, while shortages send the price of grain hoarded by merchants sky-high.

Exporters do a booming trade. Mountains of wheat and rice pile up on the wharves of London and Liverpool. India, starving colony, does not eat, but it feeds. The British eat the Indians' hunger.

On the market this merchandise called hunger is highly valued, since it broadens investment opportunities, reduces the cost of production, and raises the price of goods.

NATURAL GLORIES

❦

Queen Victoria was the most enthusiastic admirer and the only reader of the verses of Lord Lytton, her viceroy in India.

Moved by literary gratitude or patriotic fervor, the viceregal poet held an enormous banquet in Victoria's honor when she was proclaimed empress. Lord Lytton invited seventy thousand guests to his palace in Delhi for seven days and seven nights.

According to the *Times*, this was "the most colossal and expensive meal in world history."

At the height of the drought, when fields baked by day and froze by night, the viceroy arose at the banquet to read out an upbeat message from Queen Victoria, who predicted for her Indian subjects "happiness, prosperity, and welfare."

English journalist William Digby, who happened to be present, calculated that about a hundred thousand Indians died of hunger during the seven days and seven nights of the great feast.

UPSTAIRS, DOWNSTAIRS

❦

In a slow and complicated ceremony marked by the back and forth of speeches, presentation of insignia, and exchange of offerings, India's princes became English gentlemen and swore loyalty to Queen Victoria. For these vassal princes, the bartering of gifts was, according to well-informed sources, a trading of bribes for tribute.

The numerous princes lived at the summit of the caste pyramid, a system reproduced and perfected by British imperial power.

The empire did not need to divide to rule. Long-sacred social, racial, and cultural divisions were history's bequest.

From 1872 on, the British census classified the population of India according to caste. Imperial rule thus not only reaffirmed the legitimacy of this national tradition, but also used it to organize an even more stratified and rigid society. No policeman could have dreamed up a better way to control the function and destiny of each person. The empire codified hierarchies and servitudes, and forbade any and all from stepping out of place.

CALLOUSED HANDS

*

The princes who served the British Crown lived in perpetual despair over the scarcity of tigers in the jungle and the abundance of jealousy in the harem.

In the twentieth century, they still consoled themselves as best they could:

the maharaja of Bharatpur bought all the Rolls-Royces on the market in London and used them for garbage collection;

the one from Junagadh had many dogs, each with his own room, servant, and telephone;

the one from Alwar set fire to the racetrack when his pony lost a race;

the one from Kapurthala built an exact replica of the Palace of Versailles;

the one from Mysore built an exact replica of Windsor Palace;

the one from Gwalior bought a miniature gold and silver train that ran about the palace dining room carrying salt and spices to his guests;

the cannons of the maharaja of Baroda were made of solid gold;

and for a paperweight the one from Hyderabad used a 184-carat diamond.

FLORENCE

❦

Florence Nightingale, the most famous nurse in the world, dedicated most of her ninety years of life to India, although she was never able to set foot in the country she loved so dearly.

Florence was a nurse who needed nursing, having contracted an incurable disease in the Crimean War. But from her London bedroom she wrote innumerable articles and letters to bring the reality of India to the attention of the British public.

- On imperial indifference to famine:
  Five times number perished as in Franco-German war. No one takes any notice. We say nothing of the famine in Orissa, when a third of its population was deliberately allowed to whiten the fields with its bones.

- On rural property:
  The very drum pays for being beat. The ryot *pays a fee for everything he does himself, and for everything the* zemindar *does not do for himself and makes the* ryot *do for him.*

- On British justice in India:
  We are told that the ryot *has the remedy of English justice. He has not. A man has not that which he can't use.*

- On the patience of the poor:
  Agrarian riots may become the normal state of things throughout India. Let us not be too sure that these patient silent millions will remain in silence and patience forever. The dumb shall speak and the deaf shall hear.

DARWIN'S VOYAGE

❦

Young Charles Darwin did not know what to do with his life. His father encouraged him thus:

"You will be a disgrace to yourself and all your family."

At the end of 1831, he left.

After five years navigating South America, the Galapagos, and other far-flung realms, he returned to London. He brought with him three giant tortoises, one of which died in the year 2007 in a zoo in Australia.

He came back a different man. Even his father noticed:

"Why the shape of his head is quite altered!"

He brought back more than tortoises. He brought questions. His head was teeming with questions.

DARWIN'S QUESTIONS

Why does the wooly mammoth have a thick coat? Could the mammoth be an elephant that found a way to stay warm when the ice age set in?

Why is the giraffe's neck so long? Could it be because over time it got stretched in order to reach fruit high in the treetops?

Were the rabbits that run in the snow always white, or did they become white to fool the foxes?

Why does the finch have a different beak depending on where it lives? Could it be that their beaks adapted bit by bit to the environment through a long evolutionary process, so they could crack open fruits, catch larvae, drink nectar?

Does the incredibly long pistil of the orchid indicate that there are butterflies nearby whose remarkably long tongues are as long as the pistil that awaits them?

No doubt it was a thousand and one questions like these which, with the passage of years and doubts and contradictions, became the pages of his explosive book on the origin of the species and the evolution of life in the world.

Blasphemous notion, intolerable lesson in humility: Darwin revealed that God did not create the world in seven days, nor did He model us in his image and likeness.

Such horrible news was not well received. Who did this fellow think he was to correct the Bible?

Samuel Wilberforce, bishop of Oxford, asked Darwin's readers:

"Are you descended from the apes on your grandfather's side or your grandmother's?"

I'LL SHOW YOU THE WORLD

❧

Darwin liked to cite James Coleman's travel notes.
No one better described the fauna of the Indian Ocean,
the sky above flaming Vesuvius,
the glow of Arabian nights,
the color of the heat in Zanzibar,
the air in Ceylon, which is made of cinnamon,
the winter shadows of Edinburgh,
and the grayness of Russian jails.
Preceded by his white cane, Coleman went around the world, from tip to toe.
This traveler, who did so much to help us see, was blind.
"I see with my feet," he said.

ONLY HUMAN

❧

Darwin told us we are cousins of the apes, not the angels. Later on, we learned we emerged from Africa's jungle and that no stork ever carried us from Paris. And not long ago we discovered that our genes are almost identical to those of mice.

Now we can't tell if we are God's masterpiece or the devil's bad joke. We puny humans:
exterminators of everything,
hunters of our own,
creators of the atom bomb, the hydrogen bomb, and the neutron

bomb, which is the healthiest of all bombs since it vaporizes people and leaves objects intact,

we, the only animals who invent machines,

the only ones who live at the service of the machines they invent,

the only ones who devour their own home,

the only ones who poison the water they drink and the earth that feeds them,

the only ones capable of renting or selling themselves, or renting or selling their fellow humans,

the only ones who kill for fun,

the only ones who torture,

the only ones who rape.

And also

the only ones who laugh,

the only ones who daydream,

the ones who make silk from the spit of a worm,

the ones who find beauty in rubbish,

the ones who discover colors beyond the rainbow,

the ones who furnish the voices of the world with new music,

and who create words so that

neither reality nor memory will be mute.

THE INSANITY OF FREEDOM

❧

It happened in Washington in 1840.

A government census measured dementia among blacks in the United States.

According to the census, there were nine times as many cases among free blacks as among slaves.

The North was a vast insane asylum, and the farther north one went the worse it got. Going from north to south, however, one went from lunacy to sanity. Among the slaves who worked the prosperous cotton, tobacco, and rice plantations, madness barely existed.

The census reaffirmed the master's convictions. The fine medicine of slavery developed moral equilibrium and good judgment. Freedom, in contrast, churned out nutcases.

In twenty-five northern cities, not a single sane black person was found, and in thirty-nine cities in the state of Ohio and twenty in New York, the number of black mental cases outnumbered the total black population.

The census might seem dubious, yet it was taken as the official truth for a quarter of a century, until Abraham Lincoln freed the slaves, won the war, and lost his life.

THE GOLD RUSH

❦

It happened in 1880.

For years John Sutter shuffled all over the Capitol and the White House wearing a threadbare colonel's uniform and hauling a bag full of documents. When by some miracle he found someone willing to listen, he pulled out his deeds to the city of San Francisco and its vast surroundings, and told the story of the millionaire undone by the gold rush.

He had founded his empire in the Sacramento Valley, where he purchased numerous Indian vassals and the title of colonel and a Pleyel piano. Then gold sprouted like wheat and his lands and homes were invaded, his cattle and sheep eaten, and his crops ruined.

He lost everything, and from then on spent his life in court. When a judge ruled in his favor, a crowd set fire to the courthouse.

He moved to Washington.

There he lived hoping, and hoping he died.

Now a street in San Francisco bears his name.

Consolation arrived late.

WHITMAN

*

It happened in Boston in 1882.

The New England Society for the Suppression of Vice blocked distribution of the second edition of *Leaves of Grass*.

A few years earlier, after the first edition came out, the author lost his job.

Public morality would not tolerate Walt Whitman's effusive praise of the pleasures of the night.

That was the case even though Whitman managed to hide what was most forbidden. In one passage, *Leaves of Grass* insinuates something, but in the remainder and even in his intimate diaries he took the trouble to change "his" to "her" and to put "she" where he had written "he."

The great poet, who celebrated resplendent nudity, had no choice but to disguise himself to survive. He invented six children he never had, lied about romances with women who never existed, and painted himself as the bearded tough guy who embodied American virility, plowing virgin fields and untouched girls.

EMILY

*

It happened in Amherst in 1886.

When Emily Dickinson died, the family discovered eighteen hundred poems hidden in her bedroom.

On tiptoe she lived, and on tiptoe she wrote. She published only eleven poems in her entire lifetime, all anonymously or under a pseudonym.

From her Puritan ancestors, she inherited boredom, a mark of distinction for her race and her class: do not touch, do not speak. Gentlemen went into politics and business; ladies perpetuated the species and lived in ill health.

Emily inhabited solitude and silence. Cloistered in her bedroom, she invented poems that broke the rules of grammar and the rules of her own isolation. And every day she wrote a letter to her sister-in-law Susan, who lived next door, and sent it by mail.

Those poems and letters formed a secret sanctuary. There, her hidden sorrows and forbidden desires could yearn freely.

UNIVERSAL TARANTULA

❧

It happened in Chicago in 1886.

On the first of May, strikes paralyzed cities across the country. The *Philadelphia Tribune* offered a diagnosis: "The labor element has been bitten by a kind of universal tarantula—it has gone dancing mad."

Dancing mad were the workers who fought for the eight-hour day and for the right to form unions.

Four labor leaders were charged with murder. The following year they were sentenced with no evidence by a kangaroo court. George Engel, Adolph Fischer, Albert Parsons, and August Spies marched to the gallows. The fifth condemned man, Louis Linng, blew himself up in his cell with a smuggled dynamite cap.

On every May first, the entire world remembers them. With the passing of time, constitutions, laws, and international accords have proved them right.

But some of the most powerful corporations have yet to find out. They outlaw unions and keep track of the workday with those melting clocks painted by Salvador Dalí.

MR. CORPORATION

❧

It happened in Washington in 1886.

Gargantuan companies won the same legal rights as regular home-grown citizens.

The Supreme Court annulled over two hundred laws that regulated or limited the activities of business, and at the same time extended human rights to private corporations. The law conferred on big companies the same rights as persons, as if they, too, breathed: the right to life, to free expression, to privacy . . .

At the beginning of the twenty-first century, corporations are still humans.

DON'T STEP ON MY FLOWERS

❧

In 1871 a revolution left Paris, for the second time, in the hands of the Communards.

Charles Baudelaire compared the police to the god Jupiter, and warned that with no aristocracy the cult of beauty would disappear.

Théophile Gautier offered an eyewitness account:

"Stinking beasts, with their savage howls, are invading us."

The short-lived government of the Commune burned the guillotine, took over the barracks, separated church from state, handed factories closed by the bosses over to the workers, outlawed night shifts, and established secular, free, and mandatory schooling.

"Secular, free, and mandatory schooling will do nothing but increase the number of imbeciles," predicted Gustave Flaubert.

The Commune did not last long. Two months and a bit. The troops that had fled to Versailles returned, attacked, and after several days of combat they crushed the workers' barricades and celebrated their victory with firing squads. For a week they killed night and day, machine guns killing by the dozen. Flaubert urged them to show no compassion for the "rabid dogs," and his first recommendation was "to do away with universal suffrage, which is shameful to the human spirit."

Anatole France also celebrated the butchery:

"The Communards are a committee of murderers, a pack of scoundrels. At long last the government of crime and lunacy is rotting before the firing squads."

Émile Zola declared:

"The people of Paris will recover from their fevers and grow in knowledge and splendor."

The winners erected the Basilica of Sacré-Coeur on Montmartre to give thanks to God for the victory He bestowed.

Today that giant cream pie is a big tourist attraction.

WOMEN OF THE COMMUNE

✺

All power to the neighborhoods. Each neighborhood became a public assembly.

And women were everywhere: workers, seamstresses, bakers, cooks, flower girls, babysitters, cleaners, ironers, barmaids. The enemy called them *pétroleuses*, incendiaries, these fiery women who demanded rights denied by the very society that demanded so many obligations.

Women's suffrage was one of those rights. In the previous revolution of 1848, the government of the Commune rejected it in a close vote, eight hundred and ninety-nine to one.

The second Commune remained deaf to the demands of women, but while it lasted, during that brief spell, women spoke up in all the debates, they raised barricades and treated wounds and took up the weapons of those who fell, and they fell fighting with red kerchiefs, the badge of their battalion, at their throats.

Afterward, in defeat, when the moment arrived for the offended powers to take revenge, more than a thousand women were tried in military court.

One of the many sentenced to deportation was Louise Michel. The anarchist teacher had joined the struggle with an old carbine and in battle had won a brand-new Remington rifle. In the confusion of the final days, she escaped death, but was sent far, far away to the island of New Caledonia.

LOUISE

❧

"I want to know what they know," she explained.

Her companions in exile warned her that the savages knew nothing, save how to devour human flesh.

"You won't get out alive."

But Louise Michel learned the language of native New Caledonians, and she went into the jungle and came out alive.

They told her their sorrows and asked her why she had been sent there:

"Did you kill your husband?"

And she told them the story of the Commune.

"Ah," they said. "You're one of the vanquished. Like us."

VICTOR HUGO

❧

He was his epoch. He was his nation.

He was a monarchist and he was a republican.

He embodied the ideals of the French Revolution, and by the art of his pen he transformed himself into the poor soul who steals out of hunger, and into the hunchback of Notre Dame. But he also believed in the redemptive mission of French military might in the world.

In 1871, he was nearly alone in condemning the repression of the Communards.

Before that, he was among the many in applauding the conquest of colonies:

"It is civilization marching against barbarism," he wrote. "It is an enlightened people setting out to meet a people living in darkness. We are the Greeks of the world, we must enlighten the world."

LESSON IN COLONIAL CULTURE

❧

In 1856, the French government hired Jean Eugène Robert-Houdin, the country's number-one master magician, to enlighten Algeria.

Algeria's sorcerers had to be taught a lesson. Tricksters who swallowed glass and cured wounds with a touch, they were sowing the seeds of rebellion against colonial rule.

Robert-Houdin showed off his talent. The big sheiks and local shamans were astonished by his supernatural powers.

At the climactic moment of the ceremony, the envoy from Europe placed a small chest on the ground and asked the strongest of Algeria's strongmen to lift it. The muscleman could not. He tried again and again and again, and he could not. With his last heave he fell to the ground, trembling violently, and he fled, terrified.

The humiliation over, Robert-Houdin was left alone in his tent. He disconnected the powerful electromagnet hidden under a floorboard, and picked up the chest as well as the little generator that triggered electric shocks.

HERE LAY INDIA

❧

Pierre Loti, a writer who sold tales of an exotic Asia to the French public, visited India in 1899.

He traveled by train.

At each station, a chorus of hunger awaited him.

More penetrating than the roar of the locomotive was the pleading of children, or rather skeletons of children, their lips purple and eyes out of orbit, peppered by flies, beseeching alms. Two or three years previous, a girl or boy cost a rupee, but now no one wanted them even for free.

The train carried more than passengers. In the back several freight cars were filled with rice and millet for export. Guards watched over them, finger on the trigger. No one came near those cars. Only the pigeons that pecked at the sacks and flew off.

CHINA DISHED UP AT EUROPE'S TABLE

❧

China produced never-ending famines, plagues, and droughts.

The so-called Boxers, who began as a secret society, wanted to restore the country's broken dignity by expelling foreigners and Christian churches.

"If it does not rain," they said, "there is a reason. The churches have bottled up the sky."

At the end of the century, they launched a rebellion from the north which set fire to China's countryside and reached all the way to Beijing.

Then eight nations, Great Britain, Germany, France, Italy, Austria, Russia, Japan, and the United States, sent shiploads of soldiers to reestablish order by decapitating all who had heads.

Next, they sliced up China as if it were a pizza, and each took ports, lands, and cities that the phantasmal Chinese dynasty bestowed upon them as concessions for periods of up to ninety-nine years.

AFRICA DISHED UP AT EUROPE'S TABLE

❧

Following in England's footsteps, Europe one fine day decided that slavery was an abominable crime. Jurists discovered that the slave trade violated people's rights and the Church revealed that it was offensive in God's eyes.

Then Europe began its colonial conquest deep inside Africa. Before, the men from cold lands went no farther than the ports where they bought slaves. Now the way to the hot lands was opened by explorers, behind whom came warriors mounted on cannons, and behind them missionaries armed with crucifixes, and behind them merchants. The highest waterfall and the largest lake in Africa were named Victoria in honor of a not-very-African queen, and the invaders baptized rivers and mountains, somehow believing the story that they were discovering everything they saw. And the blacks performing slave labor in mines and on plantations were no longer called slaves.

In 1885, in Berlin, after a year of much scuffling, the European conquistadors managed to agree on how to divvy up the loot.

Three decades later, Germany lost the First World War and with it the African colonies it had gained, thus enlarging the dominions of the British, the French, and the Belgians.

A long while had passed since Friedrich Hegel explained that Africa had no history and that it would only be of interest "for the study of barbarism and savagery," and another thinker, Herbert Spencer, judged that civilization would wipe inferior races off the map, "because every obstacle, human or brute, must be eliminated."

The three decades leading up to war in 1914 were called "an era of world peace." During those sweet years, a quarter of the planet went down the throats of a handful of countries.

CAPTAIN OF DARKNESS

❦

When Africa was carved up at the Berlin conference, King Leopold of Belgium got the Congo as his private playground.

By shooting elephants, the king turned his colony into the world's greatest source of ivory, and by whipping and mutilating blacks, he supplied abundant cheap rubber for the wheels of the automobiles that had begun to roll down the world's streets.

He never set foot in the Congo because of the bugs. Writer Joseph Conrad, however, did. And in *Heart of Darkness,* his best-known novel, Kurtz was the name he gave to Captain Léon Rom, a distinguished officer of the colonial force. The natives received his orders on all fours, and he called them "stupid beasts." At the entrance to his house, among the garden flowers, were twenty stakes that completed the decor. Each held up the head of a rebellious black. And at the entrance to his office, amid more garden flowers, hung a noose swaying in the breeze.

In his free time, when not hunting Africans or elephants, the captain painted pastoral scenes, wrote poetry, and collected butterflies.

TWO QUEENS

❧

Shortly before dying, Queen Victoria had the great pleasure of acquiring another pearl for her well-laden crown. The Ashanti kingdom, one vast gold mine, became a British colony.

The conquest had taken several wars over the course of an entire century.

The final battle began when the English demanded the Ashantis hand over the sacred throne, home of the nation's soul.

Ashanti men were ferocious, better avoided than confronted, but in the final battle a woman took the lead. The queen mother, Yaa Asantewaa, pushed the male chiefs aside:

"Where does the bravery lie? Not in you."

The fight was arduous. At the end of three months, the logic of British cannons won out.

Victoria, the triumphant queen, died in London.

Yaa Asantewaa, the vanquished queen, died far from her own land.

The victors never found the sacred throne.

Years later, the Ashanti kingdom, called Ghana, was the first colony in black Africa to win independence.

WILDE

❧

The lord chamberlain of the kingdom of Great Britain was much more than a valet. Among other things, he was in charge of censoring the theater. With help from experts, he decided which plays ought to be cut or closed in order to protect the public from the dangers of immorality.

In 1892, Sarah Bernhardt announced that Oscar Wilde's new play, *Salome*, would open in London. Two weeks before opening night, the play was shut down.

No one protested, save the playwright. Wilde reminded one and all that he was an Irishman living in a nation of Tartuffes, but the English just congratulated him on the joke. This chubby genius, who wore a white flower in his lapel and a knife blade on his tongue, was the most venerated celebrity in the theaters and salons of London.

Wilde made fun of everyone, including himself:

"I can resist everything except temptation," he said.

And one night he shared his bed with the son of the Marquis of Queensberry, tempted by his languid beauty, mysteriously youthful and jaded at once. That was the first of many nights. The marquis found out and he declared war. And he won.

After three humiliating trials, which offered daily banquets for the press and unleashed the indignation of the citizenry against this corruptor of youth, the jury found him guilty of gross indecency committed against the young men who had the pleasure of accusing him.

He spent two years in jail working with pick and shovel. His creditors auctioned off everything he owned. When he got out, his books had disappeared from the stores, his plays from the stage. No one applauded him, no one invited him.

He lived alone, and alone he drank, pronouncing his brilliant sayings for no one.

Death was kind. It came quickly.

FRIGID RIGID MORALS

❧

Dr. Watson said nothing, but Sherlock Holmes answered anyway. He answered his silences, guessing all his thoughts one after another.

This brilliant feast of deduction was repeated word for word at the beginning of two separate adventures of the English detective. And not by mistake.

The original, *The Cardboard Box*, told of a sailor who killed his wife and her lover. But when gathering his stories into a book, Arthur Conan Doyle chose to suppress this risqué tale.

In those days, good manners demanded courtesy and silence. Adultery need not be mentioned, because adultery did not exist. Not to wound the sensibilities of his readers or to displease the queen, the author censored himself. However, he rescued the opening monologue by sticking it into another adventure of the most famous detective in the world.

On boring days, when London offered only mediocre cadavers and no enigma worthy of his superior intelligence, Sherlock Holmes used to inject cocaine. Conan Doyle never felt the least compunction in mentioning his character's habit in story after story.

Drugs posed no dilemma. Victorian morals did not address the question. The queen was not about to spit in her own plate. The epoch that bears her name forbade passion, but sold consolation.

FATHER OF THE BOY SCOUTS

❧

Arthur Conan Doyle was knighted, and not for the merits of Sherlock Holmes. The writer was invited to join the ranks of the nobility as thanks for the propaganda he wrote for the imperial cause.

One of his heroes was Robert Baden-Powell, the founder of the Boy Scouts. They met while fighting savages in Africa:

"There was always something of the sportsman in his keen appreciation of war," Sir Arthur said.

Gifted in the art of following the tracks of others and erasing his own, Baden-Powell was a great success at the sport of hunting lions, boars, deer, Zulus, Ashantis, and Ndebeles.

Against the Ndebeles, he fought a rough battle in southern Africa. Two hundred and nine blacks and one Englishman died.

The colonel took as a souvenir the horn the enemy blew to sound the alarm. And that spiral-shaped horn from a kudu antelope was incorporated into Boy Scout ritual as the symbol of boys who love nature.

FATHER OF THE RED CROSS

✿

The Red Cross was born in Geneva. It grew out of an initiative by several Swiss bankers to help the wounded abandoned on the battle-fields.

Gustave Moynier led the International Committee of the Red Cross for more than forty years. He explained that the institution, inspired by evangelical values, was welcomed in civilized countries, but repudiated by the colonized.

"Compassion," he wrote, "is unknown among those savage tribes that practice cannibalism. Compassion is so foreign to them that their languages have no word to express the concept."

CHURCHILL

✿

The descendants of Lord Marlborough, perhaps best known in song as "Malbrook who went to war," had clout. And thanks to that family connection, young Winston Churchill managed to join a battalion of lancers heading off to fight in Sudan.

He was a soldier and chronicler at the Battle of Omdurman in 1898, near Khartoum on the banks of the Nile.

The British Crown was building a colonial corridor the length of Africa from Cairo in the north to Capetown in the south. The conquest of Sudan was a crucial step in the plan to expand the empire, which London explained by saying:

"We are civilizing Africa by means of trade,"

instead of confessing:

"We are trading away Africa by means of civilization."

The redemptive mission advanced by blood and by fire. Since Africans were too feeble-minded to understand, no one bothered to ask their opinion.

In the bombardment of the city of Omdurman, Churchill acknowledged that "a large number of unfortunate non-combatants were killed or wounded," victims of what a century later would come to be called "collateral damage." But in the end, the empire's weaponry achieved, in his words, "the most signal triumph ever gained by the arms of science over barbarians. Within the space of five hours the strongest and best-armed savage army yet arrayed against a modern European Power had been destroyed and dispersed."

According to the official statistics of the victors, this was the outcome of the Battle of Omdurman:

among the civilized troops, 2 percent killed or wounded,

among the savage troops, 90 percent killed or wounded.

COLOSSUS OF RHODES

❈

His objective in life was humble:

"If I could, I would annex other planets."

Boundless energy was his birthright:

"We are the first race in the world. The more of the world we inhabit the better it is for the human race."

Cecil Rhodes, the richest man in Africa, king of diamonds and owner of the only railroad with access to the gold mines, spoke clearly:

"We must obtain new lands," he explained, "where to settle the excess of population, where to find new markets for the production of our factories and mines. Empire, I have always said, is a matter of the stomach."

On Sundays, Rhodes entertained himself by tossing coins into a pool of water and having his black vassals pick them up with their teeth. But during the week he spent his time amassing land. This patriotic tycoon expanded the map of England five times over, stealing from blacks by natural right, and uprooting other whites, the Boers, from the field of colonial competition. To accomplish this he invented a rudimentary version of the concentration camp, which the Germans later perfected in Namibia before bringing it to Europe.

In homage to the feats of the English conquistador, two African countries were named Rhodesia.

Rudyard Kipling, lyre ever ready at the foot of the cannon, wrote his epitaph.

THRONE OF GOLD

❧

A number of years before Rhodes, King Midas of Phrygia wanted to turn the world into gold at the touch of his hand.

He asked the god Dionysus to give him that power. Dionysus, who believed in wine not gold, granted it to him.

Midas broke off the branch of an ash tree and it turned into a rod of gold. He touched a brick and it became an ingot. He washed his hands and a rain of gold poured from the fountain. And when he sat down to eat, his food broke his teeth and no drink could flow down his throat. He hugged his daughter and she turned into a statue of gold.

Midas was about to die of hunger, thirst, and loneliness.

Dionysus took pity on him and dunked him in the Pactolus River.

From that point on, the river had a golden bed, and Midas, who lost his magic touch but saved his life, had donkey's ears poorly hidden under a red bonnet.

ORIGIN OF CONCENTRATION CAMPS

❧

When Namibia won its independence in 1990, the main avenue of the capital city still bore the name Göring. Not for Hermann, the Nazi, but in honor of his father, Heinrich Göring, one of the perpetrators of the first genocide of the twentieth century.

That Göring, who represented the German Empire in the southwest corner of Africa, kindly approved in 1904 an annihilation order given by General Lothar von Trotta.

The Hereros, black shepherds, had risen up in rebellion. The colonial authorities expelled them all and warned that any Herero found in Namibia, man, woman, or child, armed or unarmed, would be killed.

Of every four Hereros, three were killed, by cannon fire or the desert sun.

The survivors of the butchery ended up in concentration camps set up by Göring. And Chancellor Bernhard von Bülow pronounced for the very first time the word *"Konzentrationslager."*

The camps, inspired by a British forerunner in South Africa, combined confinement, forced labor, and scientific experimentation. The prisoners, emaciated from a life in the gold and diamond mines, served as human guinea pigs for research into inferior races. In those laboratories worked Theodor Mollison and Eugen Fischer, who later became the teachers of Josef Mengele.

Mengele carried forth their work as of 1933, the year that Göring the son set up the first concentration camps in Germany, following the model his father pioneered in Africa.

ORIGIN OF THE WILD WEST

❧

While every movie revolver blasted more bullets than a machine gun, the real towns where Westerns were set were makeshift little places, where yawns drowned out any shooting on the sound track.

Cowboys, those taciturn gents on horseback riding tall through the universe rescuing damsels in distress, were starving peons with no more female company than the cattle they drove through the desert, risking their lives for a pittance. They looked nothing like Gary Cooper or John Wayne or Alan Ladd, because they were black or Mexican or toothless whites who never knew the marvels of makeup.

And the Indians, condemned to working as extras in the role of the worst of the bad guys, were nothing like those feathered, war-painted, inarticulate retards who howled as they circled the stagecoach and peppered it with arrows.

The epic of the Wild West was the invention of a handful of immigrants from Eastern Europe with a keen eye for business. In the studios of Hollywood, Carl Laemmle, William Fox, the Warner brothers, Louis B. Mayer, and Adolph Zukor cooked up the most successful universal myth of the twentieth century.

BUFFALO BILL

※

In the eighteenth century, the colony of Massachusetts paid a hundred pounds sterling for every Indian scalp.

After the United States became independent, scalps were priced in dollars.

In the nineteenth century, Buffalo Bill Cody was crowned the greatest scalper of Indians and greatest exterminator of the buffalo that gave him his name and his fame.

Not long after the sixty million buffalo had been reduced to less than a thousand, and hunger had driven the last rebellious Indians to turn themselves in, Buffalo Bill took his grand show, the Wild West Circus, on a world tour. In a new city every two days, he rescued stagecoaches harried by savages, broke indomitable colts, and shot bullets that split a fly down the middle.

The hero interrupted the tour to spend the first Christmas of the twentieth century with his family.

Surrounded by loved ones and in the warmth of his home, he raised his glass, offered a toast, took a drink, and fell to the floor, stiff as a board.

In suing for divorce, he accused his wife, Lulu, of trying to poison him.

She confessed to having put something in his drink, but claimed it was a love potion, Dragon's Blood was the brand, that a Gypsy had sold her.

THE AGES OF SITTING BULL

※

At thirty-two, baptism by fire. Sitting Bull defends his people against an enemy attack.

At thirty-six, his Indian nation elects him chief.

At forty-one, Sitting Bull sits. In the middle of a battle on the banks of the Yellowstone River, having walked toward the shooting soldiers, he sits down on the ground. He lights his pipe. Bullets zing like wasps. He remains immobile, smoking.

At forty-three, he learns that whites have found gold in the Black Hills, on lands reserved for the Indians, and their invasion has already begun.

At forty-four, during a long ritual dance, he has a vision: thousands of soldiers fall like grasshoppers from the sky. That night a dream tells him: "Your people will defeat the enemy."

At forty-five, his people defeat the enemy. The Sioux and the Cheyenne, united, give General George Custer and his troops a tremendous thrashing.

At fifty-two, following years of exile and prison, he agrees to read a speech in honor of the completion of the Northern Pacific Railroad. At the end of his speech, he sets aside the papers, faces the audience, and says:

"I hate all white people. You are thieves and liars."

The interpreter translates:

"We give thanks to civilization."

The audience applauds.

At fifty-four, he gets a job in Buffalo Bill's show. In the circus ring, Sitting Bull plays Sitting Bull. Hollywood is not yet Hollywood, but tragedy is already being repeated as farce.

At fifty-five, a dream tells him: "Your people will kill you."

At fifty-nine, his people kill him. Indians wearing police uniforms bring an arrest warrant. In the gun battle, he dies.

ORIGIN OF DISAPPEARANCES

Thousands of unburied dead wander the Argentinean pampa. They are the disappeared from the last military dictatorship.

General Jorge Videla and his henchmen used disappearance as a weapon of war on a scale never before seen. He used it, but he did not invent it. A century beforehand, against Argentina's native peoples, General Julio Argentino Roca employed the same masterpiece of cruelty, which obliges each victim to die and die again and go on dying, while his loved ones lose their minds chasing his elusive shadow.

In Argentina, as in all of the Americas, the Indians were the first disappeared. They disappeared before they even appeared. General Roca called his invasion of Indian lands the "conquest of the desert." Patagonia was "an empty space," a kingdom of nothing, inhabited by no one.

After that, Indians continued disappearing. Those who surrendered and gave up their land and everything else were called *indios reducidos:* reduced to the point of disappearing. And those who did not surrender and were defeated by gunfire and sword blows disappeared into numbers, becoming the nameless dead of military body counts. And their children disappeared too: divvied up as war booty, called by other names, emptied of memory, they became little slaves for the murderers of their parents.

TALLEST STATUE

❧

At the end of the nineteenth century, bullets from Remingtons brought the clearing of the Patagonia to a close.

As the few survivors of the killing departed, they sang a lament:

> *Land of mine do not leave me,*
> *no matter how far away I go.*

During his trip through the region, Charles Darwin had already warned that the natives were dying out not by natural selection but due to a government policy of extermination. Domingo Faustino Sarmiento believed that savage tribes constituted "a danger to society," and the architect of the final safari, General Roca, called his victims "wild animals."

The army undertook the hunt in the name of public security, but the Indians' lands were also tempting. When the Rural Society congratulated him on his mission accomplished, General Roca proclaimed:

"Forever free from Indian domination is this incredibly vast territory that now offers astonishing promise to immigrants and foreign capital."

Six million hectares passed into the hands of sixty-seven landowners. When he died in 1914, Roca left his inheritors sixty-five thousand hectares of land stolen from the Indians.

During his lifetime, not all Argentines appreciated the dedication of this warrior for the fatherland, but death enhanced his stature: now his is the country's tallest statue and thirty-five other monuments commemorate him, his figure graces the highest-denomination bill, and a city plus numerous avenues, parks, and schools bear his name.

LONGEST STREET

❧

A massacre inaugurated Uruguay's independence.

In July 1830, the constitution was approved, and a year later the new country was baptized in blood.

About five hundred Charrúa Indians, who had survived centuries of conquest, persecution, and harassment, were living north of the Negro River, exiles in their own land.

The new government summoned them to a meeting. The chiefs came accompanied by their people. They were promised peace, jobs, respect.

They ate, drank, and continued drinking until they passed out. Then, by sword and bayonet, they were executed.

This act of betrayal was termed a battle. And from then on the gulch where it occurred was called Salsipuedes—"Get out if you can."

Very few men got out. The women and children were shared around, the former as flesh for the barracks, the latter as slaves for the posh families of Montevideo.

Fructuoso Rivera, Uruguay's first president, planned and later celebrated "this civilizing mission to put an end to the raids of the savage hordes."

Foretelling the crime, he had written: "It will be grand, it will be beautiful."

The country's longest street, which cuts across the city of Montevideo, bears his name.

MARTÍ

❈

A father and son were strolling along Havana's flower-filled streets when they ran across a bald and skinny gentleman hurrying as if he were late.

And the father warned the son:

"Watch out for that one. He's white outside, but on the inside he's black."

The son, Fernando Ortiz, was fourteen.

Some time later, Fernando was to rescue, from centuries of racist denial, the hidden black roots of Cuban identity.

And that dangerous gent, the skinny bald man in a hurry, was José Martí. The most Cuban of all Cubans, a son of Spaniards, was the one who decried:

"We were but a mask, wearing underwear from England, a vest from Paris, a frock coat from America, and a cap from Spain."

He repudiated the false erudition called civilization, and he demanded:

"No more robes or epaulettes."

And he stated:

"All the glory in the world fits inside a kernel of corn."

Shortly after that sighting on Havana's streets, Martí headed for the mountains. And he was fighting for Cuba when a Spanish bullet knocked him from his horse.

MUSCLES

❈

José Martí announced it and he denounced it: the young nation in North America would become a gluttonous empire, its hunger for land insatiable. It had already devoured all of the natives' territory and half of Mexico's and it would not stop there.

"No triumph of peace is quite so great as the supreme triumph of war," proclaimed Teddy Roosevelt, who received the Nobel Peace Prize.

Mr. Teddy was president until 1909, when he gave up invading countries and went off to fight rhinoceroses in Africa.

His successor, William Howard Taft, invoked the natural order of things:

"The whole hemisphere will be ours in fact as, by virtue of our superiority of race, it already is ours morally."

MARK TWAIN

*

Some months after invading Iraq, President George W. Bush said he had taken the war to liberate the Philippines as his model.

Both wars were inspired from heaven.

Bush disclosed that God had ordered him to act as he did. And a century beforehand, President William McKinley also heard the voice from the Great Beyond:

"God told me that we could not leave the Filipinos to themselves. They were unfit for self-government. There was nothing left for us to do but to take them all, and to educate them, and uplift and civilize and Christianize them."

Thus the Philippines were liberated from the Filipino threat, and along the way the United States also saved Cuba, Puerto Rico, Honduras, Colombia, Panama, Dominican Republic, Hawaii, Guam, Samoa . . .

At the time, writer Ambrose Bierce revealed:

"War is God's way of teaching us geography."

And his colleague Mark Twain, leader of the Anti-Imperialist League, designed a new flag for the nation, featuring little skulls in place of stars.

General Frederick Funston suggested Twain ought to be hanged for treason.

Tom Sawyer and Huck Finn defended their father.

KIPLING

❧

Unlike Twain, Rudyard Kipling was enthralled by wars of conquest. His popular poem "The White Man's Burden" exhorted the invading nations to remain on invaded lands until their civilizing mission was complete:

> Take up the White Man's burden—
> Send forth the best ye breed—
> Go bind your sons to exile
> To serve your captives' need;
> To wait in heavy harness,
> On fluttered folk and wild—
> Your new-caught, sullen peoples,
> Half-devil and half-child.

The poet, born in Bombay but raised as an Englishman, saw serfs as too ignorant to know what they needed, and too ungrateful to ever appreciate the sacrifices their masters made for them:

> Take up the White Man's burden—
> And reap his old reward:
> The blame of those ye better,
> The hate of those ye guard—
> The cry of hosts ye humour
> (Ah, slowly!) toward the light . . .

SWORD OF THE EMPIRE

❧

At Wounded Knee, General Nelson A. Miles solved the Indian problem by shooting women and children.

In Chicago, General Miles solved the worker problem by sending the leaders of the Pullman strike to their graves.

In San Juan, Puerto Rico, General Miles solved the colonial problem by pulling down the Spanish flag and raising the Stars and Stripes in its place. And he nailed up posters all over town that said, "English spoken here," in case no one had noticed. He proclaimed himself governor. And he explained to the invaded that the invaders had "come not to make war, but on the contrary, to bring you protection, not only to yourselves, but to your property, and to promote your prosperity, and to . . . "

CIVILIZED RICE

From the beginning, the redemption of the Philippines enjoyed the invaluable support of the ladies of charity.

Those good souls, wives of high officials and officers of the invading forces, began by visiting the Manila jail. They noticed that the prisoners were markedly thin. When they toured the kitchen and saw what the wretches were eating, their hearts sank. It was primitive rice: grains of all sizes, opaque, dark, with the husk and germ and everything still attached.

They implored their husbands to do something, and their husbands did not pass up the chance to do good. The next ship from the United States brought a cargo of civilized rice, all the grains alike, husked and polished and shining, whitened with talcum powder.

From the end of 1901, that is what the prisoners ate. In the first ten months, 4,825 of them fell ill, and 216 died.

American doctors attributed the disaster to one of those microbes that propagate in the poor hygiene of backward countries. But just in case, they ordered the prison kitchen to go back to the old menu.

Once the prisoners were eating primitive rice again, the plague disappeared.

ORIGIN OF DEMOCRACY

*

In 1889, Brazil's monarchy died suddenly.

One morning, monarchist politicians woke up as republicans.

A couple of years later, the constitution established universal suffrage. Everyone could vote, except women and the illiterate.

Since nearly all Brazilians were either female or illiterate, practically no one voted.

In the first democratic election, ninety-eight of every one hundred Brazilians did not answer the call to the ballot box.

A powerful coffee baron, Prudente de Moraes, was elected the nation's president. He moved to Rio from São Paulo and nobody noticed. No one came out to greet him; no one even recognized him.

Now he enjoys a certain renown as the main street near the elegant beach of Ipanema.

ORIGIN OF THE UNIVERSITY

*

In colonial times, those Brazilian families who could afford the luxury sent their sons to study at the University of Coimbra in Portugal.

Later on, several schools were set up in Brazil to train lawyers and doctors: few of either, since potential clients were scarce in a country where the many had neither rights nor any medicine but death. Several schools, but no university.

Until 1922. That year Belgium's King Leopold III announced plans to visit the country, and such an august presence merited a *doctor honoris causa,* which only a university could bestow.

Thus the university was hurriedly concocted and installed in a rambling old house occupied by the Imperial Institute of the Blind. Sadly, the blind had to be evicted.

And thus Brazil, which owes the best of her music, her soccer, her food, and her joy to blacks, gave an honorary doctorate to a king whose only merit was his membership in a family that specialized in exterminating blacks in the Congo.

ORIGIN OF SADNESS

❦

Montevideo was not always gray. It was grayed.

Back around 1890, a traveler who visited Uruguay's capital could still pay homage to "the city where bright colors triumph." The houses that faced the street were red, yellow, blue . . .

Shortly thereafter, those in the know explained that such a barbaric custom was not proper for a European nation. To be European, no matter what the map said, one had to be civilized. To be civilized, one had to be serious. To be serious, one had to be sad.

And in 1911 and 1913, municipal ordinances specified that paving stones for sidewalks had to be gray and that "only paint that imitates the construction materials, like sandstone, brick, or stone in general, will be allowed" on street-facing facades.

Painter Pedro Figari mocked this example of colonial stupidity:

"Fashion insists that even the doors, window-frames, and sunshades be painted gray. Our cities aspire to be like Paris . . . Montevideo, luminous city, is sullied, crushed, castrated . . . "

And Montevideo succumbed to copyitis.

Even so, during those years Uruguay's creative energies made it the epicenter of Latin American audacity. The country had free secular education before England, women's suffrage before France, the eight-hour day before the United States, and legal divorce seventy years before it was restored in Spain. President José Battle, "Don Pepe," nationalized public services, separated church and state, and changed the names of holidays. In Uruguay, Easter is still called Tourism Week, as if Jesus had the misfortune to be tortured and killed during his week off.

OUT OF PLACE

❦

The painting made Édouard Manet famous is of a typical Sunday scene: two men and two women having a picnic on the grass on the outskirts of Paris.

Nothing out of the ordinary, save one detail. The men, impeccable gentlemen, are fully clothed and the women are completely naked. The men are discussing some serious topic, as men are wont to do, and the women are about as significant as the trees around them.

The woman in the foreground is looking at us. Perhaps she is asking, "Where am I? What am I doing here?"

Women are but decoration, and not only in the painting.

SOULLESS

❧

Aristotle knew what he was talking about:

"A woman is like a deformed man. She lacks an essential element: a soul."

Painting and sculpture were forbidden kingdoms for the beings without souls.

In sixteenth-century Bologna, there were five hundred and twenty-five painters, one of whom was a woman.

In the seventeenth century, the Académie des Beaux-Arts of Paris had four hundred and fifty members, fifteen of whom were women, all of them wives or daughters of male painters.

In the nineteenth century, Suzanne Valadon was a market vendor, a circus acrobat, and a model for Toulouse-Lautrec. She used corsets made of carrots and shared her studio with a goat. That she was the first woman who dared to paint male nudes surprised no one. She had to be nuts.

Erasmus of Rotterdam also knew what he was talking about:

"A woman is always a woman, in other words, crazy."

RESURRECTION OF CAMILLE

❧

The family declared her insane and had her committed.

Camille Claudel spent the last thirty years of her life in an asylum, held captive.

It was for her own good, they said.

In the asylum, a freezing prison, she refused to sketch or sculpt.

Her mother and her sister never visited her.

Once in a while her brother, Paul the saint, turned up.

When Camille the sinner died, no one claimed her body.

It was years before the world discovered that Camille had been more than the humiliated lover of Auguste Rodin.

Nearly half a century after her death, her works came back to life. They traveled and they astonished: bronze that dances, marble that cries, stone that loves. In Tokyo, the blind asked and were allowed to touch the sculptures. They said the figures breathed.

VAN GOGH

❧

Four uncles and a brother were art dealers, yet he managed to sell but one painting in his entire life. Out of admiration or pity, the sister of a friend paid four hundred francs for a work in oils, *The Red Vineyard*, painted in Arles.

More than a century later, his works are on the financial pages of newspapers he never read,

the priciest paintings in galleries he never set foot in,

the most viewed in museums that ignored his existence,

and the most admired in academies that advised him to take up another trade.

Today, Van Gogh decorates restaurants where no one would have served him,

the clinics of doctors who would have had him committed,

and the offices of lawyers who would have locked him away.

THAT SCREAM

❧

Edvard Munch heard the heavens scream.

Sunset had passed, but in the sun's wake tongues of fire were rising from the horizon, when the heavens screamed.

Munch painted that scream.
Now whoever sees his painting covers his ears.
The new century was born screaming.

PROPHETS OF THE TWENTIETH CENTURY

❦

Karl Marx and Friedrich Engels wrote *The Communist Manifesto* in the middle of the nineteenth century. They did not write it to understand the world, but to help change it. A century later, one-third of humanity lived in societies inspired by a pamphlet barely twenty-three pages long.

The *Manifesto* was an accurate prophecy. Capitalism is a sorcerer incapable of controlling the forces it unleashes, the authors said, and in our days anyone who has eyes in his face can see that at a glance.

But it never occurred to the authors that the sorcerer would have more lives than a cat,

or that big factories would disperse their labor force to reduce the costs of production and the threat of rebellion,

or that social revolutions would take place more frequently in countries called "barbarous" than in those called "civilized,"

or that the workers of the world would unite less often than they would divide,

or that the dictatorship of the proletariat would become the stage name for the dictatorship of the bureaucracy.

And thus, for what it said and what it did not, the *Manifesto* confirmed the most profound truth its authors had hit upon: reality is more powerful and astonishing than its interpreters. "Gray is theory and green the tree of life," Goethe said, by way of the devil's tongue. Anticipating those who would turn Marxism into an infallible science or an irrefutable religion, Marx used to caution that he was no Marxist.

ORIGIN OF ADVERTISING

❧

The Russian physician Ivan Pavlov discovered conditioned reflexes.
He called this sequence of stimulus and response "learning":
the bell rings, the dog gets fed, the dog salivates;
hours later, the bell rings, the dog gets fed, the dog salivates;
the following day, the bell rings, the dog gets fed, the dog salivates;
and the process is repeated hour after hour, day after day, until the
bell rings, the dog is not fed, but he salivates anyway.

Hours later, days later, the dog continues salivating when the bell
rings, even though his plate is empty.

POTIONS

❧

The Postum Cereal Company led you down Happiness Road to
Healthy City and on into the Sunlight. There was something religious
about those shimmering bowls in the ads, one cereal was even called
Elijah's Manna. And their Grape-Nuts prevented appendicitis, tuber-
culosis, malaria, and tooth decay.

In 1883, Professor Holloway spent fifty thousand pounds sterling
advertising a product made from soap and aloe, an infallible remedy
for the fifty diseases enumerated in the ad.

Dr. Gregory's stomach powders made your belly like new, thanks
to the exotic combination of Turkish rhubarb, calcined magnesite, and
Jamaican ginger. And Dr. Varon's liniment, "approved by members of
the Royal Academy of Medicine," cured colds, asthma, and measles.

Clark Stanley's Snake Oil, which had nothing to do with snakes, was
a mixture of kerosene, camphor, and turpentine that did away with
rheumatism. Sometimes it also did away with rheumatics, but that bit
of news was left out of the advertisements.

The ads did not mention the morphine in Mrs. Winslow's Soothing
Syrup, undoubtedly manufactured by an easygoing family. And neither
did the ads explain why the word "coca" was in the name Coca-Cola,
"the ideal brain tonic" invented by Dr. Pemberton.

MARKETING

❧

At the end of the 1920s, advertising beat the drum to spread marvelous news: "Fly, don't ride." Leaded gasoline made you go faster, and going faster meant getting ahead in life. The ads showed a car going at a snail's pace, and the embarrassed child inside: "Gee, Pop, they're all passing you!"

Gasoline with lead additives was invented in the United States, and from the United States a barrage of advertising imposed it on the world. In 1986, when the U.S. government finally decided to outlaw it, the number of victims of lead poisoning around the planet was incalculable. It was known all along that leaded gasoline was killing adults in the United States at a rate of five thousand a year, and causing irreparable damage to the nervous systems and mental development of millions of children.

The principal authors of this crime were two executives from General Motors, Charles Kettering and Alfred Sloan. They have gone down in history as generous benefactors of humanity. They founded a hospital.

MARIE

❧

She was the first woman to win the Nobel Prize, and she won it twice.

She was the first woman professor at the Sorbonne, and for many years the only one.

And later on, when it was too late to celebrate, she was the first woman accepted into the Panthéon, the portentous mausoleum reserved for "the Great Men of France," even though she was not a man and had been born and raised in Poland.

At the end of the nineteenth century, Marie Sklodowska and her husband, Pierre Curie, discovered a substance that emitted four hundred times more radiation than uranium. They called it polonium, in honor of Marie's country of birth. Next, they began experimenting with radium, three thousand times more powerful than uranium. They invented the word "radioactivity," and they received, jointly, the Nobel Prize.

Pierre had his doubts: were they the bearers of a gift from heaven or from hell? In his acceptance speech in Stockholm, he recalled the case of Alfred Nobel himself, the inventor of dynamite:

"Powerful explosives have enabled man to do wonderful work. But they are also a terrible means of destruction in the hands of the great criminals who lead people to war."

Very shortly thereafter, Pierre was killed, run over by a horse-drawn cart carrying four tons of military materiel.

Marie survived him, and lived to see her body pay the price of her success. Radiation gave her burns, open sores, and horrible pain until she finally died of pernicious anemia.

Her daughter Irene, who also won the Nobel Prize for her achievements in the new realm of radioactivity, died of leukemia.

FATHER OF THE LIGHTBULB

❧

He sold newspapers on trains. At the age of eight he started school, but he lasted only three months. The teacher sent him home, explaining, "This child is too dumb."

When Thomas Alva Edison grew up, he patented eleven hundred inventions: the incandescent lightbulb, the electric locomotive, the phonograph, the movie projector . . .

In 1878, he founded what would later become the General Electric Company and set up the first electric power plant.

Thirty-two years later, this illuminator of modern life sat down with journalist Elbert Hubbard.

He said:

"Some day some fellow will invent a way of concentrating and storing up sunshine, instead of this old, absurd Prometheus scheme of fire."

And he also said:

"Sunshine is a form of energy, and the winds and the tides are manifestations of energy. Do we use them? Oh, no! We burn up wood and coal, as renters burn up the front fence for fuel."

TESLA

❧

Nikola Tesla always claimed to have invented the radio, but Guglielmo Marconi got the Nobel for it. In 1943, after years of litigation, the U.S. Supreme Court acknowledged that Tesla's patent was first. He never heard the news. He had been in his grave for five months.

Tesla always claimed to have invented the alternating current generator, which today lights up the cities of the world, but the invention got a bad reputation because it was first tried out frying condemned men in the electric chair.

Tesla always claimed he could light a lamp from twenty-five miles away without any wires, but when he actually did so he blew up the power station in Colorado Springs and got run out of town.

Tesla always claimed he had invented little steel men guided by remote control, and rays that could photograph the inside of the body, but few took seriously this circus magician who spoke regularly with his deceased friend Mark Twain and received messages from Mars.

Tesla died in a hotel in New York with his pockets as empty as they had been sixty years before when he got off the boat from Croatia. To honor his memory, the unit of measure for magnetic flows is now called the Tesla, as is the coil that produces over a million volts of electricity.

ORIGIN OF AERIAL BOMBARDMENTS

❧

In 1911, Italian airplanes dropped grenades on several settlements in the Libyan desert.

The test proved that attacking from the air was quicker, cheaper, and more devastating than land offensives. The commander of the air force reported:

"The bombardment has been marvelously effective at demoralizing the enemy."

The experiments that followed also featured European massacres of Arab civilians. In 1912, French airplanes attacked Morocco, selecting densely populated targets so they would not miss. And the following year, the Spanish air force tested, also on Morocco, a novelty from Germany: fragmentation bombs that sprayed deadly shards of steel in all directions.

Then . . .

THE AGES OF SANTOS DUMONT

At the age of thirty-two, Brazilian argonaut Alberto Santos Dumont, inexplicably alive after multiple flying disasters, receives the title of chevalier of France's Legion of Honor. The press declares him the most elegant man in Paris.

At thirty-three, he is the father of the modern airplane. He invents a motorized bird that takes off without a catapult and climbs to an altitude of six meters. When he lands, he declares:

"I have the utmost confidence in the future of the airplane."

At forty-nine, shortly after the First World War, he warns the League of Nations:

"The feats of flying machines allow us to foresee with horror the great destructive power they could have, sowing death not only among combatants but also, lamentably, among people who are defenseless."

At fifty-three:

"I don't see why dropping explosives from airplanes could not be outlawed, when dropping poison into the water system is."

At fifty-nine, he wonders:

"Why did I invent this thing? Instead of spreading love it has become a cursed weapon of war."

And he hangs himself. Since he is so tiny, practically weightless, practically heightless, his necktie does the trick.

PHOTOGRAPH: A FACE IN THE CROWD

❧

Munich, Odeonplatz, August 1914.

The imperial flag waves overhead. Under its shelter, a multitude exults in the ecstasy of being German.

Germany has declared war. "War! War!" shout the people, crazed with joy, eager to march straight into battle.

In the photograph's lower corner, lost in the crowd, is the face of a man in a state of bliss, eyes raised toward heaven, mouth agape. Those who know him could tell us his name is Adolf, he is Austrian and rather ugly, his voice is screechy, and he is always on the verge of a nervous breakdown. He sleeps in an attic room and ekes out a living in bars, going table to table, selling his watercolors of pastoral scenes copied from calendars.

The photographer, Heinrich Hoffmann, does not know him. He has no idea that in that sea of heads his camera has recorded the presence of the Messiah, the redeemer of the race of the Nibelungs and the Valkyries, the Siegfried who will avenge the defeat and humiliation of this great Germany that will march singing from the nuthouse to the slaughterhouse.

KAFKA

❧

As the drums of the first world butchery drew near, Franz Kafka wrote *Metamorphosis*. And not long after, the war under way, he wrote *The Trial*.

They are two collective nightmares:

a man awakens as an enormous cockroach and cannot fathom why, and in the end he is swept away by a broom;

another man is arrested, charged, judged, and found guilty, and cannot fathom why, and in the end he is knifed by the executioner.

In a certain way those stories, those books, continued in the pages of the newspapers, which day after day told of the progress of the war machine.

The author, ghost with feverish eyes, shadow without a body, wrote from the ultimate depths of anguish.

He published little, practically no one read him.

He departed in silence, as he had lived. On his deathbed, bed of pain, he only spoke to ask the doctor:

"Kill me, or else you are a murderer."

NIJINSKY

*

In Switzerland in 1919, in a ballroom at the Hotel Suvretta in Saint Moritz, Vaslav Nijinsky danced for the last time.

Before an audience of millionaires, the most famous dancer in the world announced that he would dance the war. And by the light of candelabras, he danced it.

Nijinsky spun in furious whirlwinds and left the ground and broke apart in the air and fell back, thunderstruck, and he rolled about as if the marble floor were mud, and then he began to spin again and, rising once more, again he broke apart, and again, and again, until finally the remains of him, a mute howl, crashed through the window and was lost in the snow.

Nijinsky had entered the realm of madness, his land of exile. He never returned.

ORIGIN OF JAZZ

*

It was 1906. People were coming and going as usual along Perdido Street in a poor neighborhood of New Orleans. A five-year-old child peeking out the window watched that boring sameness with open eyes and very open ears, as if he expected something to happen.

It happened. Music exploded from the corner and filled the street. A man was blowing his cornet straight up to the sky and around him a crowd clapped in time and sang and danced. And Louis Armstrong, the boy in the window, swayed back and forth with such enthusiasm he nearly fell out.

A few days later, the man with the cornet entered an insane asylum. They locked him up in the Negro section.

That was the only time his name, Buddy Bolden, appeared in the newspapers. He died a quarter of a century later in the same asylum, and the papers did not notice. But his music, never written down or recorded, played on inside the people who had delighted in it at parties or at funerals.

According to those in the know, that phantom was the founder of jazz.

RESURRECTION OF DJANGO

❧

He was born in a gypsy caravan and spent his early years on the road in Belgium, playing the banjo for a dancing bear and a goat.

He was eighteen when his wagon caught fire and he was left for dead. He lost a leg, a hand. Goodbye road, goodbye music. But as they were about to amputate, he regained the use of his leg. And from his lost hand he managed to save two fingers and become one of the best jazz guitarists in history.

There was a secret pact between Django Reinhardt and his guitar. If he would play her, she would lend him the fingers he lacked.

ORIGIN OF THE TANGO

❧

It was born in the River Plate, in the whorehouses on the outskirts of the city. Men danced it among themselves to pass the time, while the women attended to other customers in bed. Its slow, stuttering melodies echoed in alleyways where knives and sadness reigned.

The tango wore its birthmark on its forehead, harsh life in the lower depths, and for that reason was not allowed in anywhere else.

But what was unpresentable managed to pry open the door. In 1917, led by Carlos Gardel, the tango turned up downtown in Buenos Aires, climbed onstage at the Esmeralda Theater, and introduced itself by name. Gardel sang *"Mi noche triste"* and tango's isolation was over. Bathed in tears, the snobbish middle class gave it a raucous welcome that washed away its original sin.

That was the first tango Gardel ever recorded. It still gets played and it sounds better and better. They call Gardel "the Magician." It is no exaggeration.

ORIGIN OF THE SAMBA

Like the tango, the samba was not considered respectable: "dime-store music, nigger music."

In 1917, the same year that Gardel ushered tango in the front door, samba burst on the scene during carnival one night in Rio de Janeiro. That night, which went on for years, the mute sang and the street lamps danced.

Not long after that, samba traveled to Paris and Paris went wild. The music, a meeting ground of all the musics of a prodigiously musical country, was irresistible.

But the Brazilian government, which at the time refused to allow blacks on the national soccer team, found Europe's blessing discomfiting. The country's most famous musicians now were black, and Europe might think Brazil was in Africa.

The master muse of those musicians, Pixinguinha, maestro of flute and sax, created an inimitable style. The French had never heard anything like it. More than playing music, he played with music and invited everyone to join the game.

ORIGIN OF HOLLYWOOD

❦

On ride the masked men, wrapped in white sheets, bearing white crosses, torches held high: mounted avengers of the virtue of ladies and the honor of gentlemen strike fear into Negroes hungering for damsels' white flesh.

At the height of a wave of lynchings, D. W. Griffith's film *The Birth of a Nation* sings a hymn of praise to the Ku Klux Klan.

This is Hollywood's first blockbuster and the greatest box office success ever for a silent movie. It is also the first film to ever open at the White House. President Woodrow Wilson gives it a standing ovation. Applauding it, he applauds himself: freedom's famous flag-bearer wrote most of the texts that accompany the epic images.

The president's words explain that the emancipation of the slaves was "a veritable overthrow of Civilization in the South, the white South under the heel of the black South."

Ever since, chaos reigns because blacks are "men who knew none of the uses of authority, except its insolences."

But the president lights the lamp of hope: "At last there had sprung into existence a great Ku Klux Klan."

And even Jesus himself comes down from heaven at the end of the movie to give his blessing.

ORIGIN OF MODERN ART

❦

West African sculptors have always sung while they worked. And they do not stop singing until their sculptures are finished. That way the music gets inside the carvings and keeps on singing.

In 1910, Leo Frobenius found ancient sculptures on the Slave Coast that made his eyes bulge.

Their beauty was such that the German explorer believed they were Greek, brought from Athens, or perhaps from the lost Atlantis. His colleagues agreed: Africa, daughter of scorn, mother of slaves, could not have produced such marvels.

It did, though. Those music-filled effigies had been sculpted a few centuries previous in the belly button of the world, in Ife, the sacred place where the Yoruba gods gave birth to women and men.

Africa turned out to be an unending wellspring of art worth celebrating. And worth stealing.

It seems Paul Gaugin, a rather absentminded fellow, put his name on a couple of sculptures from the Congo. The error was contagious. From then on Picasso, Modigliani, Klee, Giacometti, Ernst, Moore, and many other European artists made the same mistake, and did so with alarming frequency.

Pillaged by its colonial masters, Africa would never know how responsible it was for the most astonishing achievements in twentieth-century European painting and sculpture.

ORIGIN OF THE MODERN NOVEL

❧

A thousand years ago, two Japanese women wrote as if it were today.

According to Jorge Luis Borges and Marguerite Yourcenar, no one ever wrote a better novel than *The Tale of Genji*, Murasaki Shikibu's masterful tale of masculine adventure and feminine humiliation.

Another Japanese, Sei Shōnagon, shared with Murasaki the rare honor of being praised a millennium after the fact. Her *The Pillow Book* gave birth to the *zuihitsu* genre, which means literally "brush drippings." It is a multicolored mosaic made up of short stories, notes, reflections, news items, poems. These seemingly random fragments invite us to penetrate that time and place.

THE UNKNOWN SOLDIER

❧

France lost a million and a half men in the First World War.
Four hundred thousand, nearly a third, were unidentified.

In homage to those anonymous martyrs, the government resolved to build the Tomb of the Unknown Soldier.

For burial, they chose at random one of the fallen at the Battle of Verdun.

Somebody noticed the dead soldier was black, a member of the battalion from the French colony of Senegal.

The error was corrected in time.

Another anonymous soldier, this time white-skinned, was buried under the Arc de Triomphe on November 11, 1920. Wrapped in the nation's flag, he was honored with speeches and medals.

FORBIDDEN TO BE POOR

❧

"A criminal is born, not made," as the Italian physician Cesare Lombroso liked to say, glorying in his ability to identify lawbreakers by their physical traits.

To prove that *homo criminalis* was predestined to do evil, Brazilian physician Sebastião Leão undertook a study of the prisoners in the Porto Alegre jail. But his research revealed

that the source of crime was poverty, not biology;

that the black prisoners, members of a race considered inferior, were as intelligent as the others or more so;

that the mulatto prisoners, members of a race considered weak and degraded, reached old age hale and hearty;

that the verses written on the walls were enough to prove that not all criminals were unintelligent;

that the physical characteristics which Lombroso attributed to friends of the knife, prominent chin, protruding ears, long eyeteeth, were less common in jail than on the outside;

that beardlessness could not be a trait of society's enemies as Lombroso claimed, because among the many prisoners in Porto Alegre, ten at most had little facial hair;

and that the steamy climate did not encourage lawbreaking, for the crime rate did not rise in summer.

INVISIBLE MEN

*

In 1869, the Suez Canal made navigation possible between two seas.

We know that Ferdinand de Lesseps was the project's mastermind,

that Said Pasha and his inheritors sold the canal to the French and the English for practically nothing,

that Giuseppe Verdi composed "Aida" to be sung at the inaugural ceremony,

and that ninety years later, after a long and painful fight, President Gamal Abdel Nasser succeeded in making the canal Egyptian.

Who recalls the hundred and twenty thousand prisoners and peasants, sentenced to forced labor, who died building it, murdered by hunger, exhaustion, and cholera?

In 1914, the Panama Canal sliced open a channel between two oceans.

We know that Ferdinand de Lesseps was the project's mastermind,

that the construction company went belly up in one of the most earth-shattering scandals in French history,

that President Teddy Roosevelt of the United States seized the canal and all of Panama along with it,

and that sixty years later, after a long and painful fight, President Omar Torrijos succeeded in making the canal Panamanian.

Who recalls the West Indian, East Indian, and Chinese workers who were lost building it? For every kilometer, seven hundred died, murdered by hunger, exhaustion, yellow fever, and malaria.

INVISIBLE WOMEN

*

Tradition required that the umbilical cords of newborn girls be buried under the ashes in the kitchen, so that early on they would learn a woman's place and never leave it.

When the Mexican Revolution began, many left their place, but they took the kitchen with them. For better or for worse, out of desire or obligation, they followed their men from battle to battle. They carried babies hanging from their breasts, and pots and pans strapped to their backs. And munitions too: it was women's job to supply tortillas for the belly and bullets for the gun. And when men fell, women took up their weapons.

On the trains, men and horses rode in the cars. Women were on the roof, praying to God it would not rain.

Without the women who came from country and town, who followed the fighters, who rode the rails, who treated the wounded, who cooked the food, who fought the enemy, who braved death, the revolution never would have happened.

None of them got a pension.

FORBIDDEN TO BE A PEASANT

While the euphoric horse thief Pancho Villa set the north of Mexico aflame, the morose muleteer Emiliano Zapata led the revolution in the south.

All over the country, peasant farmers rose up in arms:

"Justice went up to heaven. You won't find it here," they said.

They fought to bring it back.

What else could they do?

In the south, sugar reigned behind its castle walls, while corn eked out a living on the old lava flows. The world market brought the local market to its knees, and the usurpers of land and water advised the men they had dispossessed:

"Plant in flower pots."

The rebels were men not of war but of the earth, and they would suspend the revolution to plant or to harvest.

Sitting in the shade of laurel trees among neighbors who talked of cocks and horses, Zapata said little and listened a lot. But this taciturn man managed to stir up settlements far and wide with the good news of his land reform.

Never was Mexican society so changed.

Never was Mexican society so punished for changing.

A million dead. All or nearly all of them peasants, even if some wore uniforms.

PHOTOGRAPH: THE THRONE

*

National Palace, Mexico City, December 1914.

The countryside, risen in revolution, invades the urban world. The North and the South, Pancho Villa and Emiliano Zapata, conquer Mexico City.

While their soldiers, lost like blind men in a gunfight, wander the streets asking for food and dodging vehicles never before seen, Villa and Zapata enter the seat of government.

Villa offers Zapata the president's golden chair.

Zapata turns him down.

"We ought to burn it," he says. "It's bewitched. When a good man sits here, he turns bad."

Villa laughs as if it were a joke, flops his great humanity over the chair, and poses for Augustín Víctor Casasola's camera.

At his side Zapata appears distant, aloof, while he gazes at the camera as if it shoots bullets, not pictures, and with his eyes he says:

"Nice place to leave."

And in no time at all, the leader of the South returns to the little town of Anenecuilco, his cradle, his sanctuary, and from there he continues directing the recovery of stolen land.

Villa does not take long to do the same:

"This village is too big for us."

Those who later sit in the coveted seat with the gold-leaf design preside over the butchery that reestablishes order.

Zapata and Villa, betrayed, are assassinated.

RESURRECTION OF ZAPATA

He was born, they say, with a little hand tattooed on his chest.

He died with seven bullet holes in his body.

The assassin received fifty thousand pesos and the rank of brigadier general.

The assassinated received a multitude of peasants with hats in hand, who came to pay their respects.

From their indigenous ancestors they inherited silence.

They said nothing, or they said:

"Poor guy."

Nothing else.

But later on in town squares, little by little tongues began to loosen:

"It wasn't him."

"It was someone else."

"I thought he looked too fat."

"The mole above his eye was missing."

"He left on a ship, from Acapulco."

"He slipped away at night, on a white horse."

"He went to Arabia."

"He's over there, in Arabia."

"Arabia's really far away, farther than Oaxaca."

"He'll be back soon."

LENIN

He never wrote the most famous maxim people attribute to him, and who knows if he ever said it:

"The ends justify the means."

In any case, he certainly did what he did because he knew what he wanted to achieve and he lived to achieve it. He spent his days and nights organizing, arguing, studying, writing, conspiring. He allowed himself time to breathe and eat. Never to sleep.

He had been living in Switzerland for ten years, on his second exile. He was austere, dressed in old clothes and ugly boots. He lived in a room over a shoe-repair shop, and the smell of sausages that wafted up from the butcher's next door made him nauseous. He spent all day in the public library, and was more in touch with Hegel and Marx than with the workers and peasants of his own country and his own time.

In 1917, when he got on the train that returned him to St. Petersburg, the city later named for him, few Russians knew who he was. The party he founded, which would soon acquire absolute power, had little popular support and was more or less to the left of the moon.

But Lenin knew better than anyone what the Russian people needed most: *peace and land*. As soon as he got off the train and gave his first speech, a crowd sick and tired of war and humiliation saw in him their interpreter and their instrument.

ALEXANDRA

❧

To be natural and clean, like the water we drink, love must be free and mutual. But men demand obedience and deny pleasure. Without a new morality, without a radical shift in daily life, there will be no real emancipation. If the revolution is not to be a lie, it must abolish in law and in custom men's right of property over women and the rigid social norms that are the enemies of diversity.

Give or take a word, this is what Alexandra Kollontai, the only woman in Lenin's cabinet, demanded.

Thanks to her, homosexuality and abortion were no longer crimes, marriage was no longer a life sentence, women had the right to vote and to equal pay, and there were free child care centers, communal dining halls, and collective laundries.

Years later, when Stalin decapitated the revolution, Alexandra managed to save her neck. But she was no longer Alexandra.

STALIN

❊

He learned to write in the language of Georgia, his homeland, but in the seminary the monks made him speak Russian.

Years later in Moscow, his south Caucasus accent still gave him away.

So he decided to become more Russian than the Russians. Was not Napoleon, who hailed from Corsica, more French than the French? And was not Catherine the Great, who was German, more Russian than the Russians?

The Georgian, Iosif Dzhugashvili, chose a Russian name. He called himself Stalin, which means "steel."

The man of steel expected his son to be made of steel too: from childhood, Stalin's son Yakov was tempered in fire and ice and shaped by hammer blows.

It did not work. He was his mother's child. At the age of nineteen, Yakov wanted no more of it, could bear no more.

He pulled the trigger.

The gunshot did not kill him.

He awoke in the hospital.

At the foot of the bed, his father commented:

"You can't even get that right."

ALIBIS

❊

It was said, is said: social revolutions under attack from the powerful within and from the imperialists without cannot afford the luxury of freedom.

Nevertheless, it was in the first years of the Russian Revolution, when it was beleaguered by enemy harassment, civil war, and foreign invasion, that its creative energy flowed most freely.

In better times later on, when the Communists controlled the entire country, the dictatorship of the bureaucracy imposed its sole truth and condemned diversity as unpardonable heresy.

Painters Marc Chagall and Wassily Kandinsky left and never returned.
Poet Vladimir Mayakovsky put a bullet through his heart.

Another poet, Sergei Yesenin, hanged himself.

Writer Isaac Babel was shot.

Vsevolod Meyerhold, who had made a revolution with his bare theatrical stages, was also shot.

Shot too were Nikolai Bukharin, Grigory Zinoviev, and Lev Kamenev, revolutionary leaders from the beginning, while Leon Trotsky, founder of the Red Army, was assassinated in exile.

Of the revolutionaries who began it all, not one remained. All were purged: buried, locked up, or driven out. And they were removed from official photographs and from history books.

The revolution elevated to the throne the most mediocre of its leaders.

For what you did or what you would do, as punishment or just in case, Stalin sacrificed those who cast a shadow on him, those who said no, those who did not say yes, those who were dangerous today, and those who would be dangerous tomorrow.

PHOTOGRAPH: ENEMIES OF THE PEOPLE

❧

Bolshoi Theater Square, Moscow, May 1920.

Lenin addresses Soviet soldiers before they depart for the Ukrainian front to fight the Polish army.

At Lenin's side on the dais above the crowd are Leon Trotsky, the other orator on the program, and Lev Kamenev.

The photograph by G. P. Goldshtein becomes a symbol of the Communist revolution around the globe.

A few years later, Trotsky and Kamenev would be gone from the photo and from the world.

A little retouching erased them and put five wooden steps in their place, while executioners did the rest.

THE INQUISITION IN STALIN'S TIME

❧

Isaac Babel was an outlawed writer. He explained:

"It's a new genre I've invented: silence."

He was imprisoned in 1939.

The trial lasted twenty minutes.

He confessed to having written books in which his petit bourgeois outlook distorted revolutionary reality.

He confessed to having committed crimes against the Soviet state.

He confessed to having spoken with foreign spies.

He confessed to having contact with Trotskyites during his trips outside the country.

He confessed to knowing about a plot to assassinate Comrade Stalin and not going to the police.

He confessed to feeling attracted to the enemies of the fatherland.

He confessed that all his confessions were false.

They shot him that very night.

His wife learned of it fifteen years later.

ROSA

❧

She was born in Poland, lived in Germany. She dedicated her life to social revolution, right up to the day at the beginning of 1919 when the guardian angels of German capitalism broke her skull with their rifle butts.

Not long before, Rosa Luxemburg wrote an article on the first years of the Russian Revolution. The article, penned in her German jail cell, opposed the divorce of socialism and democracy.

- On the new democracy:
  Socialist democracy is not something which begins only in the promised land after the foundations of the socialist economy are laid. It does not come as some sort of Christmas present for the worthy people who, in the interim, have loyally supported a handful of socialist dictators.

Socialist democracy begins simultaneously with the beginnings of the destruction of class rule and of the construction of socialism.

- On the people's energy:
  The remedy which Trotsky and Lenin have found, the elimination of democracy as such, is worse than the disease it is supposed to cure; for it stops up the very living source from which alone can come correction of all the innate shortcomings of social institutions. That source is the active, untrammeled, energetic political life of the broadest masses of the people.

- On public control:
  Public control is indispensably necessary. Otherwise the exchange of experiences remains only within the closed circle of the officials of the new regime. Corruption becomes inevitable.

- On freedom:
  Freedom for the supporters of the government, only for the members of one party—however numerous they may be—is no freedom at all. Freedom is always and exclusively freedom for the one who thinks differently.

- On the dictatorship of bureaucracy:
  Without general elections, without unrestricted freedom of the press and of assembly, without a free struggle among opinions, life withers in every public institution, becomes a mere semblance of life in which the bureaucracy remains the only active element. Public life gradually falls asleep, as a few party leaders of inexhaustible energy and boundless experience direct and rule. Among them, in reality only a dozen outstanding heads do the leading, and an elite of the working class is invited from time to time to meetings where they are to applaud the speeches of the leaders and to approve proposed resolutions unanimously.

ORIGIN OF TWO COUNTRIES

🗶

They say Churchill said:

"Jordan was an idea I had one spring at about four-thirty in the afternoon."

The fact is that during the month of March 1921, in just three days, British Colonial Secretary Winston Churchill and his forty advisers drew a new map for the Middle East. They invented two countries, named them, appointed their monarchs, and sketched their borders with a finger in the sand. Thus the land embraced by the Tigris and Euphrates rivers, the clay of the very first books, was called Iraq. And the new country amputated from Palestine was called Transjordan, later Jordan.

The task at hand was to change the names of colonies so they would at least appear to be Arab kingdoms. And to divide those colonies, to break them up: an urgent lesson drawn from imperial memory.

While France pulled Lebanon out of a hat, Churchill bestowed the crown of Iraq on the errant Prince Faisal, and a plebiscite ratified him with suspicious enthusiasm: he got 96 percent of the vote. His brother Prince Abdullah became king of Jordan. Both monarchs belonged to a family placed on the British payroll at the recommendation of Lawrence of Arabia.

The manufacturers of countries signed the birth certificates of Iraq and Jordan in Cairo's Semiramis Hotel, and then went out to see the pyramids.

Churchill fell off his camel and hurt his hand.

Fortunately, it was nothing serious. Churchill's favorite artist could continue painting landscapes.

UNGRATEFUL KING

🗶

In 1932, Ibn Saud completed his long war to conquer Mecca and Medina, and proclaimed himself king and sultan of those holy cities and of the vast surrounding desert.

In an act of humility, Ibn Saud named his kingdom Saudi Arabia after his own family. And in an act of amnesia, he gave the country's petroleum to an American company, Standard Oil, forgetting that between 1917 and 1924 he and his family had eaten from the hand of the British, as the account books attest.

Saudi Arabia became a model of democracy in the Middle East. Its five thousand princes waited seventy-three years to hold the first elections. In that vote, for municipal offices only, no political parties took part since they were all outlawed. No women either, since they too were outlawed.

THE AGES OF JOSEPHINE

❧

At nine years old, she works cleaning houses in St. Louis on the banks of the Mississippi.

At ten, she starts dancing for coins in the street.

At thirteen, she marries.

At fifteen, once again. Of the first husband she retains not even a bad memory. Of the second, his last name, because she likes how it sounds.

At seventeen, Josephine Baker dances the Charleston on Broadway.

At eighteen, she crosses the Atlantic and conquers Paris. The "Bronze Venus" performs in the nude, with no more clothing than a belt of bananas.

At twenty-one, her outlandish combination of clown and femme fatale makes her the most popular and highest-paid performer in Europe.

At twenty-four, she is the most photographed woman on the planet. Pablo Picasso, on his knees, paints her. To look like her, the pallid young damsels of Paris rub themselves with walnut cream, which darkens the skin.

At thirty, she has problems in some hotels because she travels with a chimpanzee, a snake, a goat, two parrots, several fish, three cats, seven dogs, a cheetah named Chiquita who wears a diamond-studded collar, and a little pig named Albert, whom she bathes in Je Reviens perfume by Worth.

At forty, she receives the Legion of Honor for service to the French Resistance during the Nazi occupation.

At forty-one and on her fourth husband, she adopts twelve children of many colors and many origins, whom she calls "my rainbow tribe."

At forty-five, she returns to the United States. She insists that everyone, whites and blacks, sit together at her shows. If not, she will not perform.

At fifty-seven, she shares the stage with Martin Luther King and speaks against racial discrimination before an immense crowd at the March on Washington.

At sixty-eight, she recovers from a calamitous bankruptcy and at the Bobino Theater in Paris she celebrates a half century on the stage.

And she departs.

SARAH

❈

"I never stop acting," she said. "Always and everywhere, in all sorts of places, at every instant. I am my own double."

Nobody knew if Sarah Bernhardt was the best actress in the world or the biggest liar in history or both at once.

At the beginning of the twenties, after half a century of unchallenged reign, she remained the queen of theater in Paris and wherever else her endless tours took her. She was nearly eighty, so thin she cast no shadow, and minus a leg. All Paris knew it, but all Paris chose to believe that the irresistible girl, who drew sighs just by walking by, was doing a stupendous job of portraying a poor mutilated elderly woman.

SURRENDER OF PARIS

❈

When he was a barefoot boy kicking soccer balls made of rags down nameless streets, he rubbed his knees and ankles with grasshopper grease. That's what he said, and that was how he got his leg magic.

José Leandro Andrade did not say much. He did not celebrate his goals or his loves. When he danced past defenders with a ball glued to his foot, he moved with the same haughty gait and absent expression as when he danced the tango with a woman glued to his frame.

In the Olympics of 1924, he astonished Paris. The crowds were delirious, the press called him "the Black Marvel." Fame brought dames. Letters rained down on him, none of which he could read. They were written on perfumed paper by ladies who exposed their knees and blew smoke rings from long, gold cigarette holders.

When he returned to Uruguay, he brought back a silk kimono, gray gloves, and a wristwatch.

All this was soon over.

In those days, soccer was played for wine and food and pleasure.

He sold newspapers on the street.

He sold his medals.

He was the first black star of world soccer.

HAREM NIGHTS

❦

In the museums of Paris, writer Fatema Mernissi saw the *Odalisques* painted by Henri Matisse.

They were harem flesh: voluptuous, indolent, obedient.

Fatema looked at the dates on the paintings, compared, and confirmed: when Matisse portrayed Turkish women like that, in the twenties and thirties, they were well on their way to becoming full citizens, gaining entry to the university and Parliament, winning the right to divorce, and tearing off the veil.

The harem, a lockup for women, had been outlawed in Turkey, but not in Europe's imagination. Virtuous gentlemen, monogamous in their wakeful hours and polygamous in their dreams, could enjoy free passes to that exotic paradise, where empty-headed, tight-lipped females delighted in pleasing the male jailer. Any mediocre office worker could close his eyes and become a powerful caliph, caressed by a multitude of naked belly-dancing virgins vying for the favor of a night alongside their lord and master.

Fatema had been born and raised in a harem.

PESSOA'S PERSONS

*

He was one, he was many, he was everyone, he was no one.

Fernando Pessoa, sad bureaucrat, prisoner of the clock, solitary author of love letters never sent, carried an insane asylum around inside himself.

Of the denizens, we know their names, the dates and even hours of their births, their astrological signs, weights, and heights.

And their works, because they were all poets.

Alberto Caeiro, pagan, mocker of metaphysics and other intellectual acrobatics that reduce life to concepts, wrote burps.

Ricardo Reis, monarchist, Hellenist, child of classical culture, who was born several times and had several astrological signs, wrote constructions.

Álvaro de Campos, engineer from Glasgow, vanguardist, who studied energy and feared losing his zest for life, wrote sensations.

Bernardo Soares, master of the paradox, prose poet, scholar, who claimed to be an unwilling aide in some library, wrote contradictions.

And Antonio Mora, psychiatrist and nutcase, interned at Cascais, wrote lucubrations and locobrations.

Pessoa also wrote. When the others slept.

WAR STREET

*

From the start of the twentieth century, a mechanized bell announced each day's opening and closing on the New York Stock Exchange. The pealing tones paid homage to the self-sacrificing labors of the speculators who make the world go round, determine the value of goods and countries, manufacture millionaires and mendicants, and are capable of killing more people than any war, plague, or drought.

On October 24, 1929, the bell rang cheerily as ever on the worst day in the entire history of that cathedral of finance. Its collapse closed banks and factories, sent unemployment skyrocketing, and pushed wages down the basement stairs. The entire world got stuck with the bill.

U.S. Treasury Secretary Andrew Mellon consoled the victims. He said the crisis had its advantages, because "people will work harder and lead a more moral life."

FORBIDDEN TO WIN ELECTIONS

❧

So people would work harder and lead a more moral life, the Wall Street crash brought down the price of coffee and with it the elected government of El Salvador.

The reins of the country were seized by General Maximiliano Hernández Martínez, who liked to use a magic pendulum to find poison in his soup and enemies on the map.

The general called democratic elections, but the people abused the opportunity. The majority voted for the Communist Party. So the general had to annul the vote and a popular revolt erupted, as did Izalco volcano after many years asleep.

Machine guns reestablished the peace. Thousands died. How many, no one knows. They were peons, they were poor, they were Indians: the economy called them "the labor force" and death called them "unidentified."

Indigenous leader José Feliciano Ama had already been killed several times when he was hanged from the branch of an olive tree. And there he was left to swing in the breeze, a civics lesson for schoolchildren brought from all over the country.

FORBIDDEN TO BE FERTILE

❧

So people would work hard and lead a more moral life, the crash on Wall Street also made the price of sugar nosedive.

The disaster severely punished the islands of the Caribbean and gave Brazil's northeast the coup de grâce.

No longer the world's sugar bowl, not nearly, the northeast became the most tragic casualty of sugarcane monoculture.

Some years before it got sacrificed on the altar of the world market, this immense desert was green. Sugar murdered the forest and the fertile lands. Now the northeast produced ever less sugar and ever more thorns and criminals.

In those solitudes lived the dragon of drought and the bandit Lampião.

At the start of each workday, Lampião would kiss his knife:

"Are you feeling brave?"

"Brave? I couldn't say. I'm in the habit."

In the end, he lost his habit and his head. Lieutenant João Bezerra decapitated him for a reward of twelve automobiles, by which time the government had forgotten that it awarded Lampião the rank of army captain so he would hunt down Communists. They displayed triumphantly his confiscated assets: a Napoleon hat covered in little coins, five fake diamond rings, a fifth of White Horse whiskey, a bottle of Fleurs d'Amour perfume, a waterproof cloak, and various other knickknacks.

FORBIDDEN TO BE A COUNTRY

❦

Under his broad-brimmed hat, he disappears.

Since 1926, a flea named Augusto César Sandino has been driving the invading giant crazy.

Thousands of Marines have been in Nicaragua for years, but the heavy military machine of the United States cannot manage to swat the leaping army of patriotic peasants.

"God and the mountains are our allies," Sandino says.

And he says that he and Nicaragua also have the good luck of suffering from a severe case of *latinamericanitis*.

Sandino has two secretaries, his two right hands: one is Salvadorean, Augustín Farabundo Martí, the other Honduran, José Esteban Pavletich. General Manuel María Girón Ruano, a Guatemalan, is the only one who knows how to work the little cannon they call "Cutie," which in his hands can shoot down airplanes. In battle, several men have won positions of command: José León Díaz, a Salvadorean,

Manuel González, a Honduran, the Venezuelan Carlos Aponte, the Mexican José de Paredes, the Dominican Gregorio Urbano Gilbert, and the Colombians Alfonso Alexander and Rubén Ardila Gómez.

The invaders call Sandino a "bandit."

He appreciates the joke:

"So George Washington was a bandit? He fought for the same thing."

And he appreciates the donations: Browning rifles, Thompson submachine guns, and all the weapons and munitions the Marines leave behind in their courageous retreats.

RESURRECTION OF SANDINO

❦

In 1933, the Marines, humiliated, left Nicaragua.

They left, but they remained. They had trained Anastasio Somoza and his troops to be their replacement.

And Sandino, victorious in war, was defeated in an act of treason. He was killed in an ambush in 1934. From behind it must have been.

"You shouldn't take death seriously," he liked to say. "It is but a moment's discomfort."

Although his name was outlawed, and outlawed too was his memory, forty-five years later the Sandinistas overthrew the dictatorship of his assassin and his assassin's children.

And then Nicaragua, little country, barefoot country, managed to commit the insolence of resisting for ten years a mad assault by the greatest military power in the world. That happened from 1979 on, thanks to those secret muscles that do not appear in any book on anatomy.

BRIEF HISTORY OF THE PROPAGATION OF DEMOCRACY IN THE AMERICAS

❦

In 1915, the United States invaded Haiti. In the name of his government, Secretary of State Robert Lansing explained that the Negro race was incapable of governing itself, due to its "inherent tendency to revert to savagery and to cast aside the shackles of civilization, which are irksome to their physical nature." The invaders stayed nineteen years. The leader of the Haitian patriots was nailed to a door, his arms spread out in a cross.

The occupation of Nicaragua lasted twenty-one years and led to the Somoza dictatorship, while the occupation of the Dominican Republic lasted nine years and led to the Trujillo dictatorship.

In 1954, the United States launched democracy in Guatemala with aerial bombardments that put an end to free elections and other perversions. In 1964, the generals who put an end to free elections and other perversions in Brazil received money, weapons, oil, and congratulations from the White House. Something similar occurred in Bolivia, where one studious fellow came to the conclusion that no coup d'état ever occurs in the United States because it has no U.S. Embassy.

That lesson was confirmed when General Augusto Pinochet answered Henry Kissinger's cry of alarm and kept Chile from "going communist due to the irresponsibility of its own people."

Around the same time, the United States bombed three thousand poor Panamanians in order to capture a disgruntled former employee, sent troops to Santo Domingo to frustrate the return of a democratically elected president, and had no choice but to attack Nicaragua to keep Nicaragua from invading the United States through Texas.

At that point, Cuba had already received the affectionate visit of airplanes, ships, bombs, mercenaries, and millionaires sent on a pedagogic mission from Washington. They got no farther than the Bay of Pigs.

FORBIDDEN TO BE A WORKER

❧

Charlie the Tramp picks up a red rag fallen to the pavement from the back of a passing truck. He waves it and shouts to the driver just as a demonstration of workers marches up behind him, and suddenly, without knowing why, he finds himself being chased and beaten by the police.

Modern Times is the last movie that stars this character. And Chaplin, his father, is bidding adieu not only to his loveable creation, but also to silent film.

The movie does not merit a single Oscar nomination. Hollywood does not care one bit for the disagreeable pertinence of the subject matter, the epic of the little guy trapped in the gears of the industrial era in the years following the Crash of 1929.

A tragedy that evokes laughter, an implacable and moving portrait of the times: machines eat people and steal jobs, the human hand is indistinguishable from other tools, and the workers, who imitate machines, do not get sick, they rust.

At the beginning of the nineteenth century, Lord Byron had already concluded:

"It is easier now to manufacture people than machines."

FORBIDDEN TO BE ABNORMAL

❧

People who were physically, mentally, or morally abnormal, murderers, the depraved, imbeciles, crazies, masturbators, drunks, vagrants, beggars, and prostitutes were all lying in wait for their chance to plant a bad seed in the virtuous earth of the United States.

In 1907, the state of Indiana became the first place in the world where the law authorized compulsory sterilization.

By 1942, forty thousand patients in the public hospitals of twenty-eight states had been sterilized against their will. All of them poor or very poor, many of them black, a few Puerto Rican, not a few Native American.

The letters that poured in to the Human Betterment Foundation, a charitable organization dedicated to saving the species, pleaded for assistance. One college student told of being on the point of marrying a young man who appeared normal, but his ears were too small and they looked a bit like they were on upside down:

"I have been advised by a physician that if we have children it may result in something degenerate."

An extremely tall couple asked for help:

"We do not wish to bring abnormally tall children into the world."

In a letter dated June 1941, another college student said that a class-mate was retarded and that she turned her in because she might give birth to idiots.

Harry Laughlin, the foundation's ideological inspiration, received an honorary doctorate in 1936 from the University of Heidelberg for his contribution to the Reich's campaign for racial hygiene.

Laughlin was obsessed with epileptics. He maintained they were the equivalent of the retarded but more dangerous, and that there was no place for them in a normal society. Hitler's "Law for the Prevention of Defective Progeny" imposed obligatory sterilization on the retarded, schizophrenics, manic depressives, the physically deformed, the deaf, the blind . . . and epileptics.

Laughlin himself was epileptic. No one knew.

FORBIDDEN TO BE JEWISH

❧

In 1935, the "Law for the Protection of German Blood and Honor," and other laws brought in simultaneously, laid the foundation for a national identity based on biology.

Anyone who had Jewish blood, even a few drops, could not be a German citizen or marry a German citizen.

According to the authorities, the Jews were not Jews because of their religion or their language, but because of their race. It was not an easy distinction to define. Nazi experts found inspiration in the bountiful history of racism in the world, and they relied on the invaluable assistance of the company IBM.

Engineers at IBM designed forms and perforated cards to record the physical characteristics and genetic history of every person. And they set up a far-reaching high-speed automated system for identifying complete Jews, half-Jews, and those who had more than a sixteenth part Jewish blood circulating in their veins.

SOCIAL HYGIENE, RACIAL PURITY

❧

About a quarter of a million Germans were sterilized between 1935 and 1939.

Then came extermination.

The deformed, the retarded, and the insane were the first to enter the gas chambers in Hitler's camps.

Seventy thousand psychiatric patients were murdered between 1940 and 1941.

Next, "the final solution" was applied to the Jews, the Reds, the Gypsies, the homosexuals . . .

ROAD RAGE

❧

Outskirts of Seville, winter of 1936: the Spanish elections are imminent.

A gentleman is riding about his lands, when a man in tatters crosses his path.

Without getting off his horse, the gentleman calls him over and puts in his hand a coin and a list of candidates.

The man lets them fall, coin and list, and turning his back he says:

"In my hunger, I'm in charge."

VICTORIA

❧

Madrid, winter of 1936: Victoria Kent is elected to Congress.

Her popularity comes from prison reform.

When she first initiated reforms, her numerous enemies accused her of putting a helpless Spain in the hands of criminals. But Victoria, who had worked in prisons and had not just heard about human pain, pressed forward:

she closed prisons that were uninhabitable, which was most of them,
she instituted weekend passes,
she freed all prisoners over seventy years old,
she built sports fields and voluntary workshops,
she shut down the punishment cells,
she melted down the chains, shackles, and bars,
and turned all that iron into a huge sculpture of Concepción Arenal.

THE DEVIL IS RED

*

Melilla, summer of 1936: a coup d'état overthrows the Spanish
Republic.

The ideological motivations would be explained some time later by
Minister of Information Gabriel Arias-Salgado:

"The Devil lives in an oil well in Baku, and from there he sends
instructions to the Communists."

Incense versus sulfur, good versus evil, the Crusades of Christianity
versus the grandchildren of Cain. We must do away with the Reds
before the Reds do away with Spain: prisoners are living like kings,
teachers are booting priests from the classroom, women are voting like
men, divorce is debasing holy matrimony, agrarian reform is threat-
ening the Church's dominion over the land . . .

The coup is born killing, and from its first steps is blatantly open
about it.

Generalissimo Francisco Franco:

"I will save Spain from Marxism at any price."

"What if that means shooting half of Spain?"

"Whatever it takes."

General José Millán-Astray:

"Long live death!"

General Emilio Mola:

"Anyone who defends the Popular Front, openly or secretly, must
be shot."

General Gonzalo Queipo de Llano:

"Start digging graves!"

The Civil War is the name of the bloodbath unleashed by the coup d'état. The term places an equals sign between democracy defending itself and the putsch attacking it, between militia and military, between the government elected by the people and the big shot chosen by the grace of God.

LAST WISH

La Coruña, summer of 1936: Bebel García is shot by a firing squad. Bebel plays lefty, thinks lefty.

In the soccer stadium he wears the jersey of Depor. Outside the stadium he wears the jersey of the Young Socialists.

Eleven days after Franco's coup, having just turned twenty-one, Bebel stands before the firing squad:

"Just a minute," he commands.

And the soldiers, Galicians like him, crazy about soccer like him, obey.

Bebel slowly opens his fly, button by button, and facing the firing squad he takes a long piss.

Then he buttons up.

"Go ahead."

ROSARIO

Villarejo de Salvanés, summer of 1936: Rosario Sánchez Mora heads for the front lines.

She was in sewing class when several militiamen came looking for volunteers. She threw her needlework to the floor and leaped aboard the truck, having just turned seventeen, wearing her brand-new layered skirt, and carrying a fifteen-pound musket like a baby in her arms.

At the front she becomes a dynamiter. In one battle, she lights the fuse of a homemade bomb made from a condensed-milk can filled with nails. The bomb explodes before it gets thrown. She loses her hand but not her life, thanks to a buddy who makes a tourniquet from the straps of his sandals.

After that, Rosario wants to remain in the trenches, but she is not allowed. The Republican militias need to become an army, and an army is no place for a woman. After a lot of arguing she gets permission to deliver mail to the trenches and is given the rank of sergeant.

At the end of the war, people from her town do her the favor of turning her in, and she is condemned to death.

Before dawn each day, she awaits the firing squad.

Time passes.

They do not shoot her.

Years later, when she gets out of jail, she sells contraband cigarettes in Madrid, near the statue of the goddess Cybele.

GUERNICA

❧

Paris, spring of 1937: Pablo Picasso wakes up and reads.

He reads the newspaper while having breakfast in his studio.

His coffee grows cold in the cup.

German planes have razed the city of Guernica. For three hours the Nazi air force chased and machine-gunned people fleeing the burning city.

General Franco insists that Guernica has been set aflame by Asturian dynamiters and Basque pyromaniacs from the ranks of the Communists.

Two years later in Madrid, Wolfram von Richthofen, commander of the German forces in Spain, sits beside Franco at the victory parade: killing Spaniards was Hitler's rehearsal for his impending world war.

Many years later in New York, Colin Powell makes a speech at the United Nations to announce the imminent annihilation of Iraq.

While he speaks, the back of the room is hidden from view, *Guernica* is hidden from view. The reproduction of Picasso's painting, which hangs there, is concealed behind an enormous blue cloth.

UN officials decided it was not the most appropriate backdrop for the proclamation of a new round of butchery.

THE COMMANDER WHO CAME FROM AFAR

❧

Brunete, summer of 1937: in mid-battle Oliver Law takes a bullet in the breast.

Oliver is black and Red and a workingman. He left Chicago to fight for the Spanish Republic in the ranks of the Lincoln Brigade.

In the brigade, blacks do not form a separate regiment. For the first time in the history of the United States, whites and blacks mix. And for the first time in the history of the United States, white soldiers obey the orders of a black commanding officer.

An unusual commander: when Oliver Law gives the order to attack, he does not watch his men through binoculars. He is the first to join the fight.

But then all the volunteers in the international brigades are unusual. They do not fight to win medals or conquer land or capture oil wells.

Sometimes Oliver wonders:

"Since this is a war between whites, who for centuries have held us in slavery, why am I, a Negro, why am I here?"

And he answers:

"We came to wipe out the Fascists."

And laughing he adds, as if it were a joke:

"Some of us must die doing that job."

RAMÓN

❧

Mediterranean Sea, fall of 1938: Ramón Franco explodes in the air.

In 1926 he had crossed the ocean from Huelva to Buenos Aires in an airplane named *Plus Ultra*. And while the world applauded his feat, he celebrated with nights of carousing, toasting his glory, singing the Marseillaise, and cursing kings and popes.

Not long after that, on a drunk, he flew his plane over the Royal Palace in Madrid and refrained from dropping the bombs only because children were playing in the gardens.

He put two and two together and on he went: he raised the Republican flag, took part in an anarchist uprising, was elected to Congress on the Catalan nationalist ticket, and was charged by a woman with bigamy, although in truth it was trigamy.

But when his brother Francisco rebelled against the Republic, Ramón Franco suffered a sudden attack of *familyitis* and joined the ranks of the Cross and the Sword.

After two years of fighting, the remains of a plane, his plane, disappear in the waters of the Mediterranean. Ramón, with a load of bombs, had been headed for Barcelona. He was going there to kill those who had been his comrades, as well as the lovely lunatic he himself had been.

MACHADO

❧

The border, winter of 1939: the Spanish Republic is falling apart.

From Barcelona, from the exploding bombs, poet Antonio Machado manages to flee to France.

He is older than his years.

He coughs, walks with a cane.

He gazes at the sea.

On a scrap of paper he writes:

"This sun of childhood."

It is the last thing he writes.

MATILDE

❧

Palma de Mallorca jail, fall of 1942: the lost sheep.

Everything is ready. Standing in formation, the prisoners wait. The bishop and the civilian governor arrive. Today Matilde Landa, a Red and leader of other Reds, convicted and confessed atheist, will convert to the Catholic faith and will receive the holy sacrament of baptism. The repentant woman will rejoin the flock of the Lord and Satan will lose one of his own.

It grows late.

Matilde does not appear.

She is on the roof, no one sees her.

From way up there, she jumps.

Her body explodes like a bomb against the ground of the prison yard.

No one moves.

The ceremony is carried out as planned.

The bishop makes the sign of the cross, reads a page from the Gospels, exhorts Matilde to renounce evil, recites the Apostles' Creed, and anoints her forehead with holy water.

CHEAPEST JAILS IN THE WORLD

❧

Franco signed death sentences every morning while he had breakfast.

Those not put before a firing squad were locked up. Those who were shot, first dug their own graves. And those who were imprisoned, first built their own jails.

Labor costs were zilch. The Republican prisoners who built the infamous Carabanchel Prison in Madrid, as well as many others throughout Spain, never worked less than twelve hours a day and got a handful of coins, nearly all of them invisible, as payment. What's more, they received other benefits: the satisfaction of contributing to their own political rehabilitation, and a reduced sentence on this earth since tuberculosis would take them sooner.

For years and years, thousands upon thousands of criminals guilty of resisting the military coup did more than construct prisons. They were also forced to rebuild destroyed towns and erect dams, irrigation canals, ports, airports, parks, bridges, highways. They laid new railroad lines and left their lungs in the coal, mercury, asbestos, and tin mines.

And, prompted by bayonet thrusts, they erected the massive Valley of the Fallen monument, in homage to their executioners.

RESURRECTION OF CARNIVAL

*

The sun shone at night,
the dead fled their graves,
every clown was king,
the insane wrote the laws,
the beggars were lords,
and the ladies gave off sparks.

And in the end, when Ash Wednesday arrived, people pulled off their masks, which did not lie, and put on their faces until next year.

In the sixteenth century, Emperor Charles in Madrid decreed the punishment for carnival and its wantonness: "If a lowly person, one hundred lashes in public; if a nobleman, six months in exile . . . "

Four centuries later, one of Generalissimo Francisco Franco's first decrees was to outlaw carnival.

Invincible pagan fiesta: the more they forbade it, the more eagerly it bounced back.

FORBIDDEN TO BE BLACK

*

Haiti and the Dominican Republic are two countries separated by a river called Massacre.

In 1937 it already had the name, which turned out to be prophetic: on the banks of that river thousands of black Haitians who had been cutting sugarcane on the Dominican side were chopped to bits with machetes. Generalissimo Rafael Leónidas Trujillo, mousey face, Napoleon hat, gave the order to exterminate them in order to whiten the race and exorcize his own impure blood.

Dominican dailies did not hear the news. Neither did Haiti's papers. After three months of silence, something was published, a few lines, and Trujillo warned against exaggeration, for the dead numbered no more than eighteen thousand.

A long discussion ensued and in the end he paid twenty-nine dollars a head. In reparations.

INSOLENCE

❧

In the 1936 Olympics, Hitler's country of birth was defeated by the soccer team from Peru.

The referee, who disallowed three Peruvian goals, did what he could and more to avoid displeasing the führer, but Austria lost 4 to 2.

The following day, soccer and Olympic officials set things straight.

The match was annulled. Not because an Aryan defeat at the hands of an attacking line, known for good reason as the Black Steamroller, was inadmissible, but because, the officials said, fans had run onto the field before the end of the match.

Peru left the Olympics and Hitler's country won silver.

Italy, Mussolini's Italy, took the gold.

BLACK WINGS

❧

At the same Olympics, staged by Hitler to consecrate the superiority of his race, the star that shone brightest was black, a grandson of slaves, born in Alabama.

Hitler had no choice but to swallow the bitter pill, four of them actually: the four gold medals that Jesse Owens won in sprinting and long jump.

The entire world celebrated those victories of democracy over racism.

When the champion returned home, he received no congratulations from the president, nor was he invited to the White House. He returned to the usual:

he boarded buses by the back door,

ate in restaurants for Negroes,

used bathrooms for Negroes,

stayed in hotels for Negroes.

For years, he earned a living running for money. Before the start of baseball games he would entertain the crowd by racing against horses, dogs, cars, or motorcycles.

Later on, when his legs were no longer what they had been, Owens took to the lecture circuit. He did pretty well there, praising the virtues of religion, family, and country.

BLACK STAR

❧

Baseball was for whites only.

In the spring of 1947, Jackie Robinson, grandson of slaves, broke that unwritten rule, played in the major leagues, and became one of the best.

He paid dearly for it. His errors were twice as costly, his good plays worth only half. His teammates would not speak to him, the fans told him to go back to the jungle, and his wife and children received death threats.

He swallowed his bile.

After two years, the Ku Klux Klan decreed that the game that Jackie's team, the Brooklyn Dodgers, was to play in Atlanta would not take place. The move backfired. Blacks and whites cheered Jackie Robinson as he came on to the field, and when he went off a crowd chased after him.

To hug him, not to lynch him.

BLACK BLOOD

❧

The first transfusions used blood from lambs. Rumor had it that they made you sprout wool. In 1670, such experiments were outlawed in Europe.

Much later on, around 1940, Charles Drew came up with new techniques for processing and storing plasma. In light of his discoveries, which were to save millions of lives during the Second World War, Drew was named the first director of the Red Cross blood bank in the United States.

He lasted eight months in the job.

In 1942, a military directive prohibited mixing black blood with white blood in transfusions.

Black blood? White blood? "This is utter stupidity," Drew said, and he would not discriminate against blood.

He understood the matter: he was a scientist, and he was black.

So he resigned, or was resigned.

BLACK VOICE

❧

Columbia Records refused to record the song and the composer had to use a pseudonym.

But when Billie Holiday sang "Strange Fruit," the walls of censorship and fear came down. She sang it with her eyes closed, and the grace of her voice, born to sing that very song, turned it into a hymn. From then on, every black man lynched became much more than a strange fruit swinging from a tree, rotting in the sun.

Billie,

who at age fourteen achieved the miracle of rapt attention in the whorehouses of Harlem where she sang for her supper,

who hid a jackknife in her stocking,

who did not know how to defend herself from the beatings of her lovers and husbands,

who lived a prisoner of drugs and jail,

whose body was a map of needle pricks and scars,

who always sang like never before.

IMPUNITY IS THE DAUGHTER OF OBLIVION

❧

The Ottoman Empire was falling to pieces and the Armenians paid the price. While the First World War thundered on, government-sponsored butchery did away with half of the Armenians in Turkey:

homes ransacked and burned,

columns of people fleeing without clothes, water, or anything else,

women raped in town squares in broad daylight,
mutilated bodies floating on the rivers.

Whoever escaped thirst or hunger or cold died by the knife or the bullet. Or the gallows. Or by smoke: in the Syrian desert, Armenians driven out of Turkey were forced into caves and suffocated with smoke, in what foreshadowed the Nazi gas chambers to come.

Twenty years later, Hitler and his advisers were planning the invasion of Poland. Weighing the pros and cons, Hitler realized there would be protests, diplomatic outrage, loud complaints, but he was certain the noise would not last. And to prove his point, he asked:

"Who remembers the Armenians?"

THE GEARS

❧

German battalions swept through Poland, village by village, exterminating Jews by the light of day or in the glow of truck headlamps.

The soldiers, nearly all civilians, bureaucrats, workers, students, were actors in a tragedy scripted in advance. They would become executioners. They might feel violently ill, but when the curtain rose and they went onstage, they would play their parts.

In the town of Josefów, in July 1942, Reserve Police Battalion 101 had its first taste of combat against fifteen hundred old folks, women, and children, who offered no resistance at all.

The commanding officer gathered his troops, all novices in this sort of battle, and told them if anyone did not feel up to the task, he could give it a pass. Just step forward. The commander spoke and waited. Very few stepped forward.

The victims, naked, awaited death lying face down.

The soldiers bayoneted them between the shoulder blades, then they all fired at once.

FORBIDDEN TO BE INEFFICIENT

❈

Home was next door to the factory. The bedroom window looked out on the chimneys.

The manager went home every day at noon, sat with his wife and five children, recited the Our Father, ate lunch, and then went for a stroll in the garden filled with trees, flowers, chickens, and songbirds, never for an instant losing sight of the industry chugging on.

He was first to arrive at the factory and last to leave. Respected and feared, he could appear without warning anywhere, anytime.

He would not tolerate waste. High costs and low productivity made him despair. Lack of hygiene and clutter made him ill. He forgave any sin except inefficiency.

It was he who substituted the lethal gas Zyklon B for sulfuric acid and carbon monoxide. It was he who built crematoria ten times as productive as the ovens at Treblinka. It was he who managed to produce the greatest quantity of death in the shortest possible time. And it was he who devised the best death camp in the entire history of humanity.

In 1947, Rudolf Höss was hanged at Auschwitz, the concentration camp he built and ran, amidst the flowering trees about which he wrote a number of poems.

MENGELE

❈

For reasons of hygiene, the threshold to the gas chambers was an iron grating. There, the attendants wiped the mud from their boots.

The condemned, in contrast, entered barefoot. They entered by the door and left by the chimney, after being dispossessed of their gold teeth, fat, hair, and anything else of value.

There, in Auschwitz, Dr. Josef Mengele carried out his experiments.

Like other Nazi sages, he dreamed of nurseries for growing the super-race of the future. To learn how to eradicate hereditary defects, he worked with four-winged flies, legless mice, midgets, and Jews. But nothing excited his scientific passion like twin children.

Mengele used to give chocolates and affectionate pats to his child guinea pigs, even though most of them turned out to be useless for the progress of science.

He tried to turn several pairs into Siamese twins, slicing open their backs to connect their veins: they died, apart, howling in pain.

With others he tried to change their sex: they died mutilated.

With others still he tried to change their voices by operating on their vocal chords: they died mute.

To beautify the species, he injected blue dye into the eyes of dark-eyed twins: they died blind.

GOD

❦

Dietrich Bonhoeffer is imprisoned in the concentration camp at Flossenbürg.

The guards make all the prisoners watch the execution of three condemned men.

Someone standing next to Bonhoeffer whispers:

"So, where is God?"

And Bonhoeffer, who is a theologian, points to the hanged men swinging in the dawn light:

"There."

A few days later, it is his turn.

LOVE ME DO

❦

Adolf Hitler's friends have lousy memories, but the Nazi enterprise would not have been possible without their help.

Like his colleagues Mussolini and Franco, Hitler got approval early on from the Catholic Church.

Hugo Boss dressed his troops.

Bertelsmann published the training manuals for his officers.

His airplanes flew thanks to fuel from Standard Oil, and his soldiers traveled in Ford trucks and jeeps.

The maker of those vehicles and author of *The International Jew,* Henry Ford, was his muse. Hitler thanked him with a medal.

He also decorated the president of IBM, the company that made it possible to track and identify Jews.

The Rockefeller Foundation financed Nazi medicine's racial and racist research.

Joe Kennedy, father of the president, was the U.S. ambassador in London, but might as well have been the German one. And Prescott Bush, father and grandfather of presidents, was an associate of Fritz Thyssen, who used his fortune to further Hitler's cause.

Deutsche Bank financed the construction of the concentration camp at Auschwitz.

IG Farben, the giant chemical conglomerate, which later on changed its name to Bayer, BASF, and Hoechst, used concentration camp prisoners as guinea pigs and workers. These slave laborers made everything, even the gas that killed them.

The prisoners also worked for other companies, like Krupp, Thyssen, Siemens, VARTA, Bosch, Daimler-Benz, Volkswagen, and BMW, which provided an economic foundation for the Nazi madness.

Swiss banks made a killing buying the gold jewelry and teeth of Hitler's victims. The gold crossed the border with astonishing ease, while the gates remained hermetically sealed to flesh and blood trying to escape.

Coca-Cola came up with Fanta for the German market smack in the middle of the war. During that period, Unilever, Westinghouse, and General Electric also boosted their investments and profits in the country. When the war ended, ITT received a multimillion-dollar settlement for damages to its factories in Germany caused by Allied bombing.

PHOTOGRAPH: THE FLAG OF VICTORY

❧

Mount Suribachi, Iwo Jima, February 1945.

Six Marines plant the flag of the United States at the summit of the volcano they have taken after a bitterly fought battle with the Japanese.

The photograph by Joe Rosenthal will become a symbol of the victorious homeland in this war and wars to follow, and will be reproduced by the millions on posters and postage stamps and even on Treasury bonds.

In reality, it shows the second flag of the day. The first, much smaller and hardly appropriate for an epic image, was planted a few hours earlier without any showmanship. And the moment it records as victory occurs when the battle is not yet over; in fact it is just beginning. Three of the six soldiers in the picture will not come out alive, and seven thousand more Marines will die on this minuscule island in the South Pacific.

PHOTOGRAPH: MAP OF THE WORLD

❧

Yalta, Crimean Coast, February 1945.

The victors of the Second World War meet.

Churchill, Roosevelt, and Stalin sign secret agreements. The great powers decide the fate of several countries, whose people will not learn of it for two years. Some will remain capitalist and others will become communist, as if such a tremendous historic leap could be achieved by a name change decided from outside and from above.

Three people draw a new world map, establish the United Nations, and give themselves veto power, which guarantees they will remain in charge.

Richard Sarno's and Robert Hopkins's cameras record Churchill's impassive smile, Roosevelt's face already visited by death, and Stalin's shrewd eyes.

Stalin is still Uncle Joe, but in a movie soon to be released, called *The Cold War*, he will take on the role of the villain.

PHOTOGRAPH: ANOTHER FLAG OF VICTORY

❧

Reichstag, Berlin, May 1945.

Two soldiers raise the flag of the Soviet Union over the pinnacle of German power.

This photograph by Yevgeny Khaldei portrays the triumph of the nation that lost more sons in the war than any other.

The news agency TASS distributes the picture. But before doing so, it makes a correction. The Russian soldier wearing two wristwatches now has only one. The warriors of the proletariat do not loot dead bodies.

FATHER AND MOTHER OF PENICILLIN

❧

He made light of his own fame. Alexander Fleming said penicillin was invented by a microbe that took advantage of the chaos in his laboratory to sneak into a different culture. And he said that the honors for antibiotics should go not to him but to the researchers who turned a scientific curiosity into a useful medicine.

With the help of the interloping microbe, Fleming discovered penicillin in 1928. No one paid any attention. It was developed years later, a daughter of the Second World War. More people were dying from infections than from bombs, and the Germans were a step ahead ever since Gerhard Domagk invented sulfa drugs. For the Allies, producing penicillin was a matter of urgency. The chemical industry, converted to military production, was obliged to save lives as well as destroy them.

RESURRECTION OF VIVALDI

❧

Antonio Vivaldi and Ezra Pound left indelible footprints in their passage through time. The world would be a much less livable place if it weren't for the music of one and the poetry of the other.

But Vivaldi lay silent for two centuries.

Pound brought him back. The strains the world had forgotten opened and closed the poet's radio show from Italy, which broadcast Fascist propaganda in English.

The program earned Mussolini few if any sympathizers. But the Venetian musician gained worldwide adoration.

When Fascism collapsed, officers from the United States put Pound in a barbed-wire cage outdoors so that people would lob coins at him and balls of spit, and later on they sent him to an asylum for the insane.

PHOTOGRAPH: A MUSHROOM BIG AS THE SKY

*

Sky over Hiroshima, August 1945.

The B-29 is called *Enola Gay,* after the pilot's mother.

Enola Gay has a baby in her belly. The infant, named Little Boy, is ten feet long and weighs more than four tons.

At a quarter past eight in the morning, it drops. It takes a minute to reach the ground. The explosion is equivalent to forty million sticks of dynamite.

From where Hiroshima lay, an atomic cloud rises. From the tail of the airplane, military photographer George R. Caron snaps the picture.

The immense, beautiful white mushroom becomes the logo of fifty-five companies in New York and of the Miss Atomic Bomb pageant in Las Vegas.

A quarter of a century later, in 1970, several photographs of the victims of radiation are published for the first time. They had been a military secret.

In 1995, the Smithsonian Institution in Washington announces a large exhibit on the explosions at Hiroshima and Nagasaki.

The government quashes it.

THE OTHER MUSHROOM

❧

Three days after Hiroshima, another B-29 flies over Japan.

The gift it bears, larger, rounder, is called Fat Man.

After testing uranium in Hiroshima, the experts want to try their luck with plutonium. A dense cloud cover blankets Kokura, the chosen city. After circling three times in vain, the airplane changes course. Bad weather and low fuel decide the extermination of Nagasaki.

As in Hiroshima, the thousands upon thousands of victims are all civilians. As in Hiroshima, many thousands more will die later on. The nuclear age is dawning and giving birth to a new disease, the final cry of civilization: radiation poisoning, which after each explosion continues to kill for centuries upon centuries.

FATHER OF THE BOMB

❧

The first bomb was tried out in the desert of New Mexico. The sky caught fire and Robert Oppenheimer, who led the tests, felt proud of a job well done.

But three months after the explosions at Hiroshima and Nagasaki, Oppenheimer said to President Harry Truman:

"I feel I have blood on my hands."

And President Truman told Secretary of State Dean Acheson:

"I don't want to see that son of a bitch in this office ever again."

PHOTOGRAPH: SADDEST EYES IN THE WORLD

❧

Princeton, New Jersey, May 1947.

Photographer Philippe Halsman asks him:

"Do you think there will be peace?"

And while the shutter clicks, Albert Einstein says, or rather mutters:

"No."

People believe that Einstein got the Nobel Prize for his theory of relativity, that he was the originator of the saying "Everything is relative," and that he was the inventor of the atom bomb.

The truth is they did not give him a Nobel for his theory of relativity and he never uttered those words. Neither did he invent the bomb, although Hiroshima and Nagasaki would not have been possible if he had not discovered what he did.

He knew all too well that his findings, born of a celebration of life, had been used to annihilate it.

HOLLYWOOD HEROES THEY WERE NOT

The Soviet Union contributed the dead.

On that, all the Second World War statistics agree.

In this war, the bloodiest in history, the people who had humiliated Napoleon made Hitler taste the dust of defeat. The price was high: the Soviets suffered more than half of all the Allied deaths and more than twice all the Axis deaths.

Some examples, in round numbers:

in the siege of Leningrad, half a million died of hunger,

the battle of Stalingrad left a mountain of eight hundred thousand Soviet dead or wounded,

seven hundred thousand died defending Moscow, and another six hundred thousand in Kursk,

in the assault on Berlin, three hundred thousand,

the crossing of the Dnieper River cost a hundred times as many lives as the invasion of Normandy, yet is a hundred times less famous.

TSARS

Ivan the Terrible, the first tsar of all the Russias, began his career in childhood killing the prince who cast a shadow on his road to throne. He ended it forty years later crushing his own son's skull with his cane.

Between those two feats, he gained fame for

his black guard warriors, black horses, long black capes, of whom even the stones were terrified,

his enormous cannons,

his invincible fortresses,

his habit of calling a traitor anyone who did not bow as he passed,

his tendency to sever the heads of his most talented courtiers,

his Cathedral of St. Basil, the symbol of Moscow, erected to offer his imperial conquests to God,

his will to be the bastion of Christianity in the Orient,

and his long mystical torments, when he repented and wept tears of blood, beat his breast, scraped his fingernails against the walls, and howled, begging to be forgiven for his sins.

Four centuries later, during the most tragic hours of the Second World War, in the middle of the German invasion, Stalin asked Sergei Eisenstein for a movie about Ivan the Terrible.

Eisenstein made a work of art.

Stalin did not like it one bit.

He had asked for a piece of propaganda and Eisenstein had not understood: Stalin the Terrible, the last tsar of all the Russias, implacable scourge of his enemies, wanted to turn the patriotic resistance to the Nazi avalanche into a personal exploit. The sacrifice of all was not an epic struggle of collective dignity, rather the ingenious inspiration of the chosen one, the masterpiece of the highest priest of a religion called the Party and a god called the State.

ONE WAR DIES, OTHERS ARE BORN

❧

On April 28, 1945, while Mussolini swung by his feet in a square in Milan, Hitler prowled his Berlin bunker. The city burned and bombs fell nearby, but he hammered his fist on his desk and shouted orders to no one. His finger on the map, he ordered the deployment of troops that no longer existed, and over a telephone that no longer worked he summoned his dead or fleeing generals.

On April 30, when the Soviet flag rose over the Reichstag, Hitler shot himself, and on the night of May 7 Germany surrendered.

Very early the following morning, crowds filled the streets of cities across the world. It was the end of a global nightmare that had lasted six years and caused fifty-five million deaths.

Algeria was also one big party. In the two World Wars, many Algerian soldiers had given their lives for freedom, the freedom of France.

In the city of Sétif, in mid-celebration, the flag outlawed by the colonial power was raised alongside the flags of the victors. The green and white standard, the national symbol of Algeria, drew cheers from the crowd, and a young Algerian named Saâl Bouzid wrapped himself in it and was peppered with bullets, killed from behind.

And the rage exploded.

In Algeria and in Vietnam and everywhere.

The end of the world war sparked rebellions in the colonies. The subjugated, cannon fodder in Europe's trenches, rose up against their masters.

HO

❦

No one was missing.

All of Vietnam in a single square.

A skinny, bony peasant with a goatlike beard spoke to the multitude gathered in Hanoi.

He had gone by many names. Now they called him Ho Chi Minh.

He was a man of words as soft and measured as his gait. Unhurried, he had visited many places and survived many misadventures. It was as if he were talking to his neighbors in the village when he said to the immense crowd:

"Under the banner of liberty, equality, and fraternity, France built more prisons than schools in our country."

He had barely eluded the guillotine, and several times had been shackled and thrown in prison. His country remained imprisoned, but not for long, not anymore: that very morning in September 1945, Ho Chi Minh declared independence. Serenely, simply, he said:

"We are free."

And he announced:

"We will never again be humiliated. Never!"

The crowd erupted.

Ho Chi Minh's powerful fragility embodied the energy of his homeland, armed like him with pain and with patience.

From his cabin made of wood, Ho led two long wars of liberation. Tuberculosis killed him before the final victory.

He wanted his ashes scattered freely in the wind, but his comrades mummified him and enclosed him in a glass sarcophagus.

IT WAS NO GIFT

❧

During thirty years of war, Vietnam gave two imperial powers a terrific thrashing: it defeated France and it defeated the United States.

Here is the grandeur and horror of national independence:

Vietnam withstood more bombs than all the bombs dropped in the entire Second World War,

its jungles and fields were drenched with twenty million gallons of chemical defoliants,

two million Vietnamese perished,

and innumerable were the people mutilated, the villages annihilated, the forests razed, the lands left sterile, and the poisonings bequeathed to future generations.

The invaders acted with the impunity bestowed by history and guaranteed by might.

A belated revelation: in the year 2006, following nearly forty years of secrecy, a detailed nine-thousand-page report by the Pentagon became public. The report confirmed that *all* U.S. military units operating in Vietnam had committed war crimes against the civilian population.

OBJECTIVE NEWS

❧

In democratic countries, the overriding duty of the mass media is objectivity.

Objectivity consists of conveying the points of view of both sides of a conflict.

During the years of the Vietnam War, the mass media in the United States made the public aware of the stance of their government and of that of the enemy.

George Bayley, who is curious about such things, added up the time allotted to one side or the other on the television networks ABC, CBS, and NBC between 1965 and 1970: the point of view of the invading nation took up 97 percent, while that of the nation invaded got 3 percent.

Ninety-seven to three.

For the invaded, the obligation to suffer through the war; for the invaders, the right to tell the story.

The news makes reality, not the other way around.

SALT OF THE EARTH

❧

In 1947, India became an independent country.

India's big English-language newspapers, which had called Mahatma Gandhi "a ridiculous little man" when he launched his salt march in 1930, changed their tune.

The British Empire had erected a barrier of trees and thorn bushes, known as the Great Hedge, two thousand miles long, between the Himalayas and the coast at Orissa, to stand in the way of the salt of the earth. Free competition forbade freedom: India was not free to consume its own salt, even though it was better and cheaper than salt imported from Liverpool.

Over time, the hedge grew old and died. But the prohibition lived on, and against it marched a tiny, bony, nearsighted man who went about half-naked, leaning on a bamboo cane.

Mahatma Gandhi began his march to the sea leading a handful of pilgrims. Within a month, after a lot of walking, a multitude marched with him. When they reached the sea, each of them picked up a fistful of salt. By so doing, they broke the law. It was civil disobedience against the empire.

A few of the disobedient were shot and killed and more than a hundred thousand were imprisoned.

Imprisoned too was their country.

Seventeen years later, disobedience freed it.

EDUCATION IN FRANCO'S DAY

❧

Flipping through his schoolbooks, Spanish writer Andrés Sopeña Monsalve found this:

- On Spaniards, Arabs, and Jews:
  Let us loudly proclaim that Spain has never ever been a backwards country. Since the earliest of times Spain produced useful inventions such as the horseshoe, which it taught to the most advanced peoples on earth.

  Though when they first came to Spain the Arabs were simple and ferocious desert warriors, contact with Spaniards awoke in them dreams of art and knowledge.

  On several occasions, the Jews made martyrs of Christian children, torturing them horrendously. For all that the people hated them.

- On America:
  One day a sailor named Christopher Columbus introduced himself to Doña Isabella the Catholic, saying he wanted to sail the seas and find what lands there were and teach all peoples to be good and to pray. Spain felt very sorry for those poor people in America.

- On the world:
  English and French are such diluted languages that they are on the verge of completely disappearing.

The Chinese do not observe a weekly rest and are physiologically and spiritually inferior to other men.

- On rich and poor:
  Since everything is covered in snow and ice, the little birds cannot find anything and now they are poor. That is why I feed them, and in the same way the rich maintain and feed the poor.

  Socialism organizes the poor so they can destroy the rich.

- On the mission of Generalissimo Franco:
  Russia dreamed of stabbing its bloody sickle into this beautiful corner of Europe, and all the communist and socialist masses of the earth, together with Masons and Jews, sought to triumph in Spain . . . And then came the man, the savior, the Great One.

  To give responsibility for running the state to the people, who have not studied or learned the complicated art of governing, is foolish and evil.

- On good health:
  Stimulants, like coffee, tobacco, alcohol, newspapers, politics, movies, and luxuries, relentlessly undermine and wear down our organism.

JUSTICE IN FRANCO'S DAY

❧

On the uppermost part of the dais, wrapped in his black toga, sits the presiding judge.

To his right, the defense lawyer.

To his left, the prosecutor.

Steps below and still empty, the bench for the accused.

A new trial is about to begin.

Speaking to the bailiff, Judge Alfonso Hernández Pardo orders: "Bring in the guilty man."

DORIA

❧

In Cairo in 1951, fifteen hundred women invaded Parliament.

They stayed for hours and there was no getting them out. They shouted that Parliament was a lie because half the population could neither vote nor be elected.

Religious leaders, representing heaven, raised their cries heavenwards: "Voting degrades women and goes against nature!"

Nationalist leaders, representing the fatherland, denounced the proponents of women's suffrage for treason.

Winning the right to vote was costly, but in the end it was won, along with other triumphs of the Union of the Daughters of the Nile. Then the government forbade the union from becoming a political party, and sentenced Doria Shafik, the movement's living symbol, to house arrest.

That was not out of the ordinary. Nearly all Egyptian women were sentenced to house arrest, and many a woman left the house on three occasions only: to go to Mecca, to attend her wedding, and to attend her funeral.

FAMILY PORTRAIT IN JORDAN

❧

One day in the year 1998, Yasmin Abdullah came home in tears. All she could say over and over was:

"I'm not a girl anymore."

She had gone to visit her older sister.

Her brother-in-law had raped her.

Yasmin ended up in the Jweidah prison, where she remained until her father put up the bail and promised to take care of her.

By that time, the father, mother, uncles and aunts, and the entire neighborhood had resolved at an assembly to cleanse the family honor with blood.

Yasmin was sixteen.

Her brother, Sarhan, put four bullets in her head.

Sarhan spent six months in prison. He was treated as a hero. As were the twenty-seven other men imprisoned in similar cases.

One out of every four crimes committed in Jordan is a "crime of honor."

PHOOLAN

❧

Phoolan Devi had the terrible idea to be born poor and female and a member of one of India's lowest castes.

In 1974, at the age of eleven, her parents married her to a man from a caste not quite as low, and gave him a cow for a dowry.

Since Phoolan knew nothing of conjugal duties, her husband taught her by torture and rape. And when she fled, he went to the police, and the police tortured and raped her. And when she returned to the village, the ox, her ox, was the only one who did not accuse her of being impure.

And she left. And she met a thief with a long and impressive record. He was the only man who ever asked if she was cold and if she felt all right.

Her thieving lover was shot down in the village of Behmai and she was dragged through the streets and tortured and raped by a number of landowners. And some time later, Phoolan returned to Behmai at night leading a gang of strongmen. She searched for those landowners house-to-house and found twenty-two of them. And she woke them up, one by one, and killed them.

By then Phoolan was eighteen. Along the entire length of the Yamuna River people knew she was the daughter of the goddess Durga, and as beautiful and violent as her mother.

MAP OF THE COLD WAR

❧

A tough guy, a he-man with hair on his chest, is Senator Joseph McCarthy. In the middle of the twentieth century he bangs his fist on the table and bellows that his country is on the verge of being taken over by Communist totalitarianism, like the reigns of terror behind the Iron Curtain, where

freedom is suffocated,

books are banned,

ideas are banned,

people turn others in before they get turned in themselves,

anyone who thinks is a threat to national security,

and anyone who dissents is a spy for the imperialists.

Senator McCarthy sows fear across the United States. And under the sway of fear, which rules by terrifying,

freedom is suffocated,

books are banned,

ideas are banned,

people turn others in before they get turned in themselves,

anyone who thinks is a threat to national security,

and anyone who dissents is a spy for the Communists.

FATHER OF THE COMPUTER

❧

Alan Turing was sneered at for not being a tough guy, a he-man with hair on his chest.

He whined, croaked, stuttered. He used an old necktie for a belt. He rarely slept and went without shaving for days. And he raced from one end of the city to the other all the while concocting complicated mathematical formulas in his mind.

Working for British intelligence, he helped shorten the Second World War by inventing a machine that cracked the impenetrable military codes used by Germany's high command.

At that point he had already dreamed up a prototype for an electronic computer and had laid out the theoretical foundations of today's information systems. Later on, he led the team that built the first computer to operate with integrated programs. He played interminable chess games with it and asked it questions that drove it nuts. He insisted that it write him love letters. The machine responded by emitting messages that were rather incoherent.

But it was flesh-and-blood Manchester police who arrested him in 1952 for gross indecency.

At the trial, Turing pled guilty to being a homosexual.

To stay out of jail, he agreed to undergo medical treatment to cure him of the affliction. The bombardment of drugs left him impotent. He grew breasts. He stayed indoors, no longer went to the university. He heard whispers, felt stares drilling into his back.

He had the habit of eating an apple before going to bed.

One night, he injected the apple with cyanide.

MOTHER AND FATHER OF CIVIL RIGHTS

❧

Rosa Parks, a black passenger on a city bus in Montgomery, Alabama, refused to give up her seat for a white passenger.

The driver called the police.

The officers arrived, said, "The law is the law," and arrested Rosa for disturbing the peace.

Then a little-known pastor named Martin Luther King launched a bus boycott from his church. He put it this way:

> Cowardice asks the question:
> "Is it safe?"
> Expediency asks the question:
> "Is it politic?"
> Vanity asks the question:
> "Is it popular?"
> But Conscience asks the question:
> "Is it right?"

And he too went to jail.

The boycott lasted more than a year and unleashed an unstoppable tide of protest against racial discrimination from coast to coast.

In 1968, in the southern city of Memphis, a bullet tore into Reverend King's face after he had criticized the military machine for feeding on Negro flesh in Vietnam.

According to the FBI, he was a dangerous sort.

Like Rosa and the many other lungs behind the wind.

SOCCER CIVIL RIGHTS

❧

The grass was getting long in the empty stadiums.

Strikers on strike, and defenders too: Uruguay's soccer players, slaves of their teams, were simply demanding acknowledgment of their union and its right to exist. Their cause was so scandalously just that people supported them, even as time wore on and each soccerless Sunday became an insufferable yawn.

The owners would not yield, and just sat on their hands and waited for hunger to exact surrender. But the players held firm, their spirits boosted by the example of a proud man of few words, Obdulio Varela, a black, all-but-illiterate soccer player and bricklayer. He lifted up the fallen and urged on the weary.

And that was how, at the end of seven long months, Uruguay's players won the strike of crossed legs.

A year later, in 1950, they also won the World Cup.

Brazil, playing at home in Maracanã Stadium, was the indisputable favorite. It had just trounced Spain 6–1 and Sweden 7–1. Fate's verdict named Uruguay as the last lamb to be sacrificed on its altar in the final. And so it was shaping up, Uruguay losing and two hundred thousand fans roaring in the stands, when Obdulio, playing with a swollen ankle, gritted his teeth. Then the captain of the strike became captain of an impossible victory.

MARACANÃ

❧

The moribund held off their death and babies hurried up their birth.
Rio de Janeiro, July 16, 1950, Maracanã Stadium.
The night before, no one could fall asleep.
The morning after, no one wanted to wake up.

PELÉ

❧

Two British teams were battling out the championship match. The
final whistle was not far off and they were still tied, when one player
collided with another and fell, out cold.

A stretcher carried him off and the entire medical team went to
work, but the man did not come to.

Minutes passed, centuries passed, and the coach was swallowing the
clock, hands and all. He had already used up his substitutions. His boys,
ten against eleven, were defending as best they could, which was not
much.

The coach could see defeat coming, when suddenly the team doctor
ran up and cried ecstatically:

"We did it! He's coming around!"

And in a low voice, added:

"But he doesn't know who he is."

The coach went over to the player, who was babbling incoherently
as he tried to get to his feet, and in his ear informed him:

"You are Pelé."

They won five–nil.

Years ago in London, I heard this lie that told the truth.

MARADONA

Never before had a star soccer player openly criticized the lords of the industry. But the most famous and popular athlete of all time took to the ramparts to defend players who were neither famous nor popular.

This generous and caring idol managed to score, in the space of five minutes, the two most contradictory goals in the entire history of soccer. His devoted fans venerated him for both: for the goal of the artist, embroidered by his legs' devilish tricks, and perhaps even more for the goal of the thief, pickpocketed by his hand.

They adored Diego Armando Maradona for his prodigious acrobatics and because he was a dirty god, a sinner, the most human of the deities. Anyone could see in him a walking synthesis of human, or at least masculine, weaknesses: he was a womanizer, a glutton, a drunk, a hustler, a liar, a braggart, and utterly irresponsible.

But gods, no matter how human, do not retire.

He could never return to the anonymous crowd from whence he came.

Fame, which saved him from poverty, held him like a prisoner.

Maradona was condemned to believing he was Maradona, obliged to be the hub of every party, the baby at every christening, the deceased at every wake.

Neither urine analysis nor blood tests can detect the drug of success, but it is far more devastating than cocaine.

PHOTOGRAPH: THE SCORPION

London, Wembley Stadium, fall of 1995.

The Colombian soccer team is challenging venerable old England in its holiest house of worship, and goalkeeper René Higuita makes an incomparable save.

His body flying horizontal, the keeper lets a deadly blast from an

English striker sail past and then sends it back with his heels, flexing his legs the way a scorpion flips its tail.

It is worth looking closely at this piece of Colombian I.D. Its revelatory power resides not in the athletic prowess, but in the grin splitting Higuita's face from ear to ear while he commits his unforgivable sacrilege.

BRECHT

❧

Bertolt Brecht loved unmasking reality.

In 1953, raucous protests broke out across Communist Germany. Workers took to the streets and Soviet tanks moved quickly to shut their mouths. The official press then published a letter from Brecht in support of the ruling party. The letter, chopped up and switched around, did not say what he had written. But Brecht managed to slip past the censors with a poem spread via the underground:

> *After the uprising of June 17*
> *the Secretariat of the Writers' Union*
> *handed out a few leaflets on Stalin Avenue*
> *in which one could read that the people*
> *had lost the government's trust*
> *and that only with great effort*
> *could they recover it.*
> *Would it not be easier*
> *for the government to dissolve the people*
> *and elect another?*

A HUNDRED FLOWERS AND
ONLY ONE GARDENER

❦

In China, during Mao's final years, anyone who dared to show what reality was and not what the Party ordered it to be committed an act of treason.

But in other times, Mao was not the person he ended up being. In his early twenties, he proposed a melding of Lao Tse and Karl Marx, and he dared to formulate it like this: "Imagination is thought, the present is the past and the future, the past and the future are the present, small is big, male is female, the many are one, and change is permanence."

At that point, there were sixty Communists in all China.

Forty years later, the revolution took power with Mao at the helm. Women no longer had to hobble along on bound feet as commanded by appalling tradition, nor were there parks with signs warning:

CHINESE AND DOGS NOT ALLOWED.

The revolution changed the lives of one-fourth of humanity and Mao did not hide his differences with the practices bequeathed by Stalin, for whom contradictions were not proof of life or winds of history, but bothers that existed only to be crushed.

Mao said:

"Discipline that stifles creativity and initiative should be abolished."

And he said:

"Fear is no solution. The more afraid you are, the more ghosts will come to visit you."

And he put forth the slogan:

"Let a hundred flowers bloom, let a hundred schools of thought contend."

But the flowers did not last.

In 1957, the Great Helmsman launched the Great Leap Forward and announced that the Chinese economy would soon humble the richest economies in the world. From then on, difference and doubt were forbidden. Belief was obligatory in the lying numbers that bureaucrats churned out to keep their jobs.

Mao listened only to the echoes of his own voice telling him what he wished to hear. The Great Leap Forward leapt into the abyss.

RED EMPEROR

*

I was in China three years after the failure of the Great Leap Forward. No one talked about it. It was a state secret.

I saw Mao paying homage to Mao. In Tiananmen Square, the Gate of Heavenly Peace, Mao presided over an immense parade led by an immense statue of Mao. The plaster Mao held his hand high, and the flesh-and-blood Mao answered the greeting. From an ocean of flowers and colored balloons, the crowd cheered both.

Mao was China and China was his shrine. Mao exhorted all to follow the example set by Lei Feng and Lei Feng exhorted all to follow the example set by Mao. Lei Feng, a young Communist apostle of dubious existence, spent his days consoling the sick, helping widows, and giving his food away to orphans. His nights he spent reading the complete works of Mao. When he slept, he dreamed of Mao, his guide for every step. Lei Feng had no girlfriend or boyfriend because he did not waste time on frivolities, and it never occurred to him that life could be contradictory or reality diverse.

YELLOW EMPEROR

*

Pu Yi was three years old in 1908 when he first sat on the throne reserved for the Sons of Heaven. The minuscule emperor was the only person in China allowed to wear yellow. The great crown of pearls slipped over his eyes, but there was not much to look at anyway. Swimming inside tunics of silk and gold, he was bored with the immensity of the Forbidden City, his palace, his prison, forever surrounded by a throng of eunuchs.

The monarchy fell and Pu Yi became Henry, christened by the English. Later on, the Japanese sat him on the throne of Manchuria, and he had three hundred courtiers who ate the leftovers from his ninety dishes.

Tortoises and cranes symbolize eternal life in China. Though Pu Yi was neither a tortoise nor a crane, he managed to keep his head on his shoulders, something quite uncommon in his line of work.

In 1949, when Mao took power, Pu Yi crowned his career by converting to Marxism-Leninism.

At the end of 1963, when I interviewed him in Beijing, he was dressed like everyone else, blue uniform buttoned to the collar, his worn shirt cuffs protruding from the sleeves of his coat. He made his living by pruning plants in the Beijing Botanical Garden.

He was surprised that anyone would be interested in talking to him. He recited his mea culpa, "I am a traitor, I am a traitor," and in an unwavering monotone he repeated slogans for a couple of hours.

Every so often, I was able to interrupt him. Of his aunt, the empress, the phoenix, all he recalled was her deathlike face, which so frightened him he cried. She gave him a candy and he threw it on the floor. The women in his life he met via photographs that the mandarins or the English or the Japanese gave him to choose from. Until at last, thanks to President Mao, he had been able to marry the woman he truly loved.

"Who is she, if you don't mind my asking?"

"A worker, a hospital nurse. We got married on May 1st."

I asked him if he was a member of the Communist Party. No, he was not.

I asked him if he would like to be.

The interpreter was named Wang, not Freud, and he must have been exhausted, because he translated:

"For me, that would be a tremendous horror."

FORBIDDEN TO BE INDEPENDENT

*

In the middle of 1960, the Congo, until then a Belgian colony, celebrated its independence.

Speech followed speech, and the audience was melting from heat and boredom. Belgium, a strict teacher, warned of the dangers of freedom. The Congo, grateful pupil, promised to behave.

Then Patrice Lumumba's speech exploded and ruined the party. He spoke out against the "empire of silence," and through him the silenced found a voice. He paid homage to the fathers of independence, the murdered, the imprisoned, the tortured, and the exiled, who throughout so many years had fought "to bring to an end the humiliating slavery imposed on us by force."

His words, received in icy silence by the Europeans present, were interrupted eight times by ovations from the Africans in the audience.

That speech sealed his fate.

Lumumba, recently released from prison, had won the first free elections in the Congo's history, and headed up its first government. But the Belgian press called him a "delirious and illiterate thief." In Belgian intelligence cables, Lumumba was dubbed Satan. The director of the CIA, Allen Dulles, sent instructions to his agents:

"The removal of Lumumba must be an urgent objective."

Dwight Eisenhower, president of the United States, told British Foreign Secretary Lord Alec Douglas-Home:

"I wish Lumumba would fall into a river full of crocodiles."

Lord Douglas-Home took a week to reply:

"Now is the time to get rid of Lumumba."

And the minister for African affairs of the Belgian government, Harold d'Aspremont Lynden, offered his own opinion:

"Lumumba must be eliminated once and for all."

At the beginning of 1961, a firing squad of eight soldiers and nine policemen commanded by Belgian officers shot him along with his two closest collaborators.

Fearing a popular uprising, the Belgian government and its Congolese tools, Mobutu Sese Seko and Moise Tshombe, covered up the crime.

Two weeks later, the new president of the United States, John Kennedy, announced:

"We will not allow Lumumba to return to the government."

And Lumumba, who by then had already been killed and dissolved in a barrel of sulfuric acid, did not return to the government.

RESURRECTION OF LUMUMBA

❧

The assassination of Lumumba was an act of colonial reconquest.

The Congo's mineral wealth, copper, cobalt, diamonds, gold, uranium, oil, gave the orders from the depths of the earth.

The sentence was carried out with the complicity of the United Nations. Lumumba had good reason to mistrust the officers of troops that claimed to be international, and he denounced "the racism and paternalism of people whose only vision of Africa is lion hunting, slave markets, and colonial conquest. Naturally they would understand the Belgians. They have the same history, the same lust for our wealth."

Mobutu, the free-world hero who trapped Lumumba and had him crushed, held power for more than thirty years. The international financial institutions recognized his merits and showered him with generosity. By the time he died, his personal fortune was nearly equal to the foreign debt of the country to which he had devoted his best energies.

But Lumumba had announced:

"History will one day have its say. It will not be the history taught in the United Nations, Washington, Paris, or Brussels. Africa will write its own history."

The tree where Lumumba was executed still stands in the woods of Mwadingusha. Riddled with bullets. Like him.

MAU MAU

❧

In the fifties, terrorism was black, its name was Mau Mau, and it hid out in the shadows of the Kenyan jungle.

According to world opinion, the Mau Mau danced as they slit the throats of the English. Then they chopped them to pieces, and in satanic ceremonies drank their blood.

The supposed leader of those savages, Jomo Kenyatta, fresh out of prison, became the first president of his free country in 1964.

Later on, it came out: during the years of struggle for independence, fewer than two hundred British citizens, civilians or soldiers, had been slain. More than ninety thousand natives were hanged, shot, or killed in concentration camps.

EUROPE'S LEGACY

❧

When Belgium left the Congo, a total of three Congolese held positions of responsibility in government.

When Great Britain left Tanzania, the country had but two engineers and twelve doctors.

When Spain left Western Sahara, the country had one doctor, one lawyer, and one specialist in commerce.

When Portugal left Mozambique, the country had a 99 percent illiteracy rate, not a single high school graduate, and no university.

SANKARA

❧

Thomas Sankara changed Upper Volta's name. The old French colony came to be called Burkina Faso, "land of honest men."

Following the long period of colonial domination, honest men inherited a desert: fields exhausted, rivers gone dry, forests devastated. One of every two newborns did not survive beyond three months old.

Sankara headed up the transformation. Community energies were marshaled to produce more food, teach literacy, replant native forests, and protect the scarce and sacred water.

The voice of Sankara echoed around Africa and out to the world:

"We propose that at least one percent of the fabulous sums spent studying life on other planets be used to save life on this planet."

"The World Bank and the International Monetary Fund deny us financing to dig down three hundred feet for water, but they offer it to dig down nine thousand feet for oil."

"We want to create a new world. We refuse to choose between hell and purgatory."

"We accuse those men whose selfishness causes the misfortune of their fellows. In the world, no one is yet held to account for the murderous attacks on the land and the air that destroy the biosphere."

In 1987, the so-called international community decided to rid itself of this new Lumumba.

The mission was assigned to his best friend, Blaise Campaoré.

The crime placed Campaoré in power for life.

ORIGIN OF CUBA

❧

Revolution, revelation: blacks set foot on beaches formerly closed to any whose skin might stain the water, and all of the Cubas that Cuba held exploded into the light of day.

Deep in the mountains, deep inside Cuba, children who had never seen a movie made friends with Charlie Chaplin, and volunteers brought reading and writing to far-flung places where such strange wonders were unknown.

In an attack of tropical lunacy, the entire National Symphony Orchestra took Beethoven and his cohorts to villages that had fallen off the map, and the euphoric residents scrawled posters that invited:

"Come dance to the National Symphony! It's hot!"

I was out in the East, where colorful snails fall like rain from the trees, and the blue mountains of Haiti peek over the horizon.

On a dusty path, I met up with a couple.

She was on a donkey, riding under an umbrella.

He, on foot.

The two were dressed for a party, queen and king of these hamlets, invulnerable to time or mud: not a wrinkle, not a stain violated the whiteness of their attire, which had been waiting years if not centuries in the back of a closet ever since the day of their wedding.

I asked them where they were going. He answered:

"We're headed for Havana. To the Tropicana Cabaret. We've got tickets for Saturday."

And he patted his pocket.

'I CAN SO

❧

In 1961, a million Cubans learned how to read and write, and thousands of volunteers erased the mocking smiles and pitying looks they got whenever they said what they planned to accomplish. Some time later, Catherine Murphy collected their stories:

- Griselda Aguilera:
  My parents taught literacy here in Havana. I asked to go along, but they wouldn't let me. Every morning very early, the two of them would head off until nighttime and I'd stay home. One day, after so much whining, they finally let me. I went with them. Carlos Pérez Isla was the name of my first student. He was fifty-eight. I was seven.

- Sixto Jiménez:
  They didn't let me go either. I was twelve, I knew how to read and write, and every day I'd ask and argue, but no. It's really dangerous, my mother said. And right then was when the invasion took place at the Bay of Pigs, those criminals came to take revenge, they came with blood in their eyes, those people, the ones who used to own Cuba. We knew who they were. In the old days they set our house on fire twice up there in the mountains. That was when my mother packed my knapsack. Bye-bye, she said.

- Sila Osorio:
  My mother taught literacy in the mountains beyond Manzanillo. She was assigned a family with seven children. None of them knew how to read or write. My mother lived in their house for six months. During the day she harvested coffee, carried water . . . At night, she taught. Once everyone had learned, she left. She arrived there by herself, but she didn't leave by herself. Imagine that: if it hadn't been for the literacy campaign, I wouldn't exist.

- Jorge Oviedo:
  I was fourteen when the volunteers turned up in Palma Soriano. I'd never been to school. But I went to the first literacy class. I drew a few letters and I realized: this is for me. And the next morning I slipped out

of the house and took to the road. I had the volunteers' manual under my arm. I walked a long way until I came to a town deep in the mountains of the East. I introduced myself as a literacy teacher. I gave the first class, repeating everything I'd heard back in Palma Soriano. I remembered every detail. For the second class I studied the manual, or rather I guessed at what it said. And for the following ones . . .

I taught literacy before I was literate. Or maybe it happened all at once, I don't know.

PHOTOGRAPH:
THE WORLD'S MOST POPULATED EYES

❋

Havana, Plaza of the Revolution, March 1960. The bearded ones have been in power a little more than a year.

A ship has been blown up in the port. Seventy-six workers dead. The ship carried weapons and munitions for Cuba's defense, and the Eisenhower administration would not permit Cuba to defend itself.

A multitude fills the streets of the city.

From the podium, Che Guevara observes so much rage concentrated in one place.

He has the crowd in his eyes.

Alberto Korda snaps the picture.

His newspaper does not publish it. The editor sees nothing special. Years will pass. The photograph will become a symbol of our times.

COMEBACK KID

❋

What is it about Che Guevara? The more they manipulate and betray him, the more he rises anew. There is no comeback kid like him.

Could it be because Che said what he thought and did what he said? In this world words and deeds so rarely meet, and when they do they fail to say hello, because they do not recognize each other. Perhaps that is why he is still so dangerous.

FIDEL

His enemies say he was an uncrowned king who confused unity with unanimity.

And in that his enemies are right.

His enemies say that if Napoleon had a newspaper like *Granma,* no Frenchman would have learned of the disaster at Waterloo.

And in that his enemies are right.

His enemies say that he exercised power by talking a lot and listening little, because he was more used to hearing echoes than voices.

And in that his enemies are right.

But some things his enemies do not say: it was not to pose for the history books that he bared his breast to the invaders' bullets,

he faced hurricanes as an equal, hurricane to hurricane,

he survived six hundred and thirty-seven attempts on his life,

his contagious energy was decisive in making a country out of a colony,

and it was not by Lucifer's curse or God's miracle that the new country managed to outlive ten U.S. presidents, their napkins spread in their laps, ready to eat it with knife and fork.

And his enemies never mention that Cuba is one rare country that does not compete for the World Doormat Cup.

And they do not say that the revolution, punished for the crime of dignity, is what it managed to be and not what it wished to become. Nor do they say that the wall separating desire from reality grew ever higher and wider thanks to the imperial blockade, which suffocated a Cuban-style democracy, militarized society, and gave the bureaucracy, always ready with a problem for every solution, the alibis it needed to justify and perpetuate itself.

And they do not say that in spite of all the sorrow, in spite of the external aggression and the internal high-handedness, this distressed and obstinate island has spawned the least unjust society in Latin America.

And his enemies do not say that this feat was the outcome of the sacrifice of its people, and also of the stubborn will and old-fashioned sense of honor of the knight who always fought on the side of the losers, like his famous colleague in the fields of Castile.

PHOTOGRAPH: FISTS HELD HIGH

❧

Mexico City, Olympic Stadium, October 1968.

The Stars and Stripes waves triumphantly on the highest flagpole, while the strains of the national anthem of the United States ring out.

The Olympic champions mount the podium. Then at the climactic moment, gold medalist Tommie Smith and bronze medalist John Carlos, both black, both Americans, raise their black-gloved fists against the night sky.

Life photographer John Dominis captures the scene. Those raised fists, symbols of the Black Panther Party, denounce before the entire world racial bigotry in the United States.

Tommie and John are immediately expelled from the Olympic Village. Never again will they be allowed to take part in any sports competition. Race horses, fighting cocks, and human athletes have no right to spoil the party.

Tommie's wife divorces him. John's wife commits suicide.

Back home, no one will hire these troublemakers. John gets by as best he can, and Tommie, who holds eleven world records, washes cars for tips.

ALI

❧

He was butterfly and bee. In the ring, he floated and stung.

In 1967, Muhammad Ali, born Cassius Clay, refused to put on a uniform.

"Got nothing against no Viet Cong," he said. "Ain't no Vietnamese ever called me nigger."

They called him a traitor. They sentenced him to a five-year jail term, and barred him from boxing. They stripped him of his title as champion of the world.

The punishment became his trophy. By taking away his crown, they anointed him king.

Years later, a few college students asked him to recite something. And for them he improvised the shortest poem in world literature: "Me, we."

THE GARDENER

❧

At the end of 1967, in a hospital in South Africa, Christian Barnard carried out the first human heart transplant and became the most famous doctor in the world.

In one of the pictures sent around the world, a black man appears among his assistants. The head of the hospital explained that he had snuck in.

At the time, Hamilton Naki lived in a hut without electricity or running water. He had no degree, but he was Dr. Barnard's right-hand man. He worked by his side in secret. Law or custom forbade a black man from touching the flesh or blood of whites.

Shortly before he died, Barnard admitted:

"He probably had more technical skill than I had."

In the final analysis, Barnard's achievement would not have been possible without the man of magic fingers who had rehearsed the heart transplant several times with pigs and dogs.

On the hospital payroll, Hamilton Naki was listed as a gardener.

He retired on a gardener's pension.

THE NINTH

❧

Deafness kept Beethoven from ever hearing a note of his Ninth Symphony, and death kept him from learning of his masterpiece's adventures and misadventures.

Bismarck proclaimed the Ninth an inspiration for the German race, Bakunin heard it as the music of anarchy, Engels declared it would become the hymn of humanity, and Lenin thought it more revolutionary than "The Internationale."

Von Karajan conducted it for the Nazis, and years later he used it to consecrate the unity of free Europe.

The Ninth accompanied Japanese kamikazes who died for their emperor, as well as the soldiers who gave their lives fighting against all empires.

It was sung by those resisting the German blitzkrieg, and hummed by Hitler himself, who in a rare attack of modesty said that Beethoven was the true führer.

Paul Robeson sang it against racism, and the racists of South Africa used it as the soundtrack for apartheid propaganda.

To the strains of the Ninth, the Berlin Wall went up in 1961.

To the strains of the Ninth, the Berlin Wall came down in 1989.

WALLS

❧

The Berlin Wall made the news every day. From morning till night we read, saw, heard: the Wall of Shame, the Wall of Infamy, the Iron Curtain . . .

In the end, a wall which deserved to fall fell. But other walls sprouted and continue sprouting across the world. Though they are much larger than the one in Berlin, we rarely hear of them.

Little is said about the wall the United States is building along the Mexican border, and less is said about the barbed-wire barriers surrounding the Spanish enclaves of Ceuta and Melilla on the African coast.

Practically nothing is said about the West Bank Wall, which perpetuates the Israeli occupation of Palestinian lands and will be fifteen times longer than the Berlin Wall. And nothing, nothing at all, is said about the Morocco Wall, which perpetuates the seizure of the Saharan homeland by the kingdom of Morocco, and is sixty times the length of the Berlin Wall.

Why are some walls so loud and others mute?

PHOTOGRAPH: THE WALL FALLS

❧

Berlin, November 1989. Ferdinando Scianna photographs a man pushing a wheelbarrow. It holds, just barely, an enormous bust of Stalin. The bronze head was liberated from its body when a furious people armed with sledgehammers brought down the wall that had divided Berlin in two.

The wall is not all that falls. With it crumbles the regimes that started out proclaiming the dictatorship of the proletariat and ended up running the dictatorship of the bureaucracy. And with it falls political ideology reduced to religious faith, and parties that invoked Marx but acted like churches inspired by the old dictum of Pope Gregory VII: "The Roman Church has never erred, nor will it err to all eternity, the Scripture bearing witness."

Without shedding a tear or a single drop of blood, Eastern Europeans watch the death throes of the powers that acted in their name.

Meanwhile in China, Mao's successor Deng Xiaoping launches the slogan "To grow rich is glorious." And to enrich her glorious leaders, China offers the world market her millions of cheap and very obedient workers, and her air, land, and water, a natural bounty all too willing to immolate itself on the altars of success.

Communist bureaucrats become businessmen. That must be why they studied *Das Kapital*: to live off the dividends.

DIVINE LIGHT, MURDEROUS LIGHT

❧

The flames crackle.

On the pyre burn discarded mattresses, discarded easy chairs, discarded tires.

A discarded god also burns: the fire blackens the body of Pol Pot.

At the end of 1998, the man who killed with such abandon died at home, in his bed.

No plague had ever so reduced the population of Cambodia. Invoking the sacred names of Marx, Lenin, and Mao, Pol Pot erected a colossal slaughterhouse. To save time and money, every charge came complete with sentence, and every jail had a door to a common grave. The entire country was a great burial mound and a temple to Pol Pot, who purified society to make it worthy of him.

Revolutionary purity demanded liquidating the impure.

The impure: those who thought, those who dissented, those who doubted, those who disobeyed.

CRIME PAYS

❧

At the end of his many years in power, General Suharto could not keep track of either his victims or his money.

He began his career in 1965 by exterminating Indonesia's Communists. How many, no one knows. Not less than half a million, perhaps more than a million. Once the military gave the green light to kill, anyone with a cow or a few chickens coveted by the neighbors suddenly became a Communist worthy of the noose.

U.S. Ambassador Marshall Green conveyed his government's "sympathy and admiration for what the army is doing." *Time* reported that dead bodies impeded navigation on the rivers, but went on to celebrate the events as "the best news for years."

A few decades later, the same magazine revealed that General Suharto had "a tender heart." By then, he had lost count of the many dead, and was about to turn the gardens of Timor Island into cemeteries.

His savings account was not negligible either by the time he was forced to resign, after more than thirty years of service to his country. Deep pockets: Abdurrahman Wahid, his successor as president, estimated Suharto's personal fortune to be equal to everything Indonesia owed the International Monetary Fund and the World Bank.

We know he loved Switzerland and enjoyed walking along the streets of Zurich and Geneva, but he never managed to recall precisely where he had left his money.

In the year 2000, a medical team examined General Suharto and declared him physically and mentally unfit to stand trial.

ANOTHER CASE OF AMNESIA

A medical report ruled that General Augusto Pinochet was suffering from senile dementia.

Incapable of judgment, he could not be judged.

Pinochet maneuvered past three hundred criminal charges without losing his cool, and died without ever doing time. Chile's reborn democracy, meanwhile, was saddled with paying his debts and forgetting his crimes. He joined in the official amnesia.

He had killed, he had tortured, but he said:

"It wasn't me. Besides, I don't remember. And if I do remember, it wasn't me."

In the international language of soccer, bad teams are still called "Pinochets" because they fill stadiums in order to torture people, but the general does not lack admirers. Santiago's September 11 Avenue was christened, not in memory of the victims of the Twin Towers, but in homage to the terrorist coup that brought down Chile's democracy.

In an unintended endorsement, Pinochet died on December 10, International Human Rights Day.

By then, thirty million dollars stolen by him had turned up in one hundred and twenty accounts in various banks around the world. The revelation somewhat tarnished his prestige. Not because he was a crook, but because his take was so meager.

PHOTOGRAPH: THIS BULLET DOES NOT LIE

❧

Santiago de Chile, Government House, September 1973.

We do not know the name of the photographer. It is the last image of Salvador Allende: he wears a helmet, walks with rifle in hand, looks up at the airplanes spitting out bombs.

The freely elected president of Chile said:

"I won't get out of here alive."

In the history of Latin America, that is an oft-heard expression.

Many presidents say it, but at the moment of truth they decide to go on living in order to go on saying it.

Allende did not get out of there alive.

A KISS OPENED THE DOORS TO HELL

※

The kiss was the signal of betrayal, just as in the Gospels: "Whomsoever I kiss, that same is the one."

In Buenos Aires at the end of 1977, the Blond Angel kissed, one by one, the three founders of the Mothers of the Plaza de Mayo, Esther Balestrino, María Ponce, and Azucena Villaflor, as well as the nuns Alice Domon and Léonie Duquet.

And the earth swallowed them. Spokesmen for the dictatorship denied holding the mothers and said the sisters were in Mexico working as prostitutes.

Later on it came out: all of them, mothers and sisters alike, had been tortured and thrown, still alive, from an airplane into the sea.

And the Blond Angel's identity came out too. The papers published a photograph of Captain Alfredo Astiz, his head bowed, surrendering to the English, and despite his beard and cap he was recognized. It was the end of the Falklands War and he had not fired a shot. He was a specialist in another sort of heroism.

FAMILY PORTRAIT IN ARGENTINA

※

Argentine poet Leopoldo Lugones proclaimed:

"For the good of the world, the hour of the sword has struck!" In this way he applauded the 1930 coup d'état, which installed a military dictatorship.

In the service of that dictatorship, the poet's son, Police Chief Polo Lugones, devised new uses for the cattle prod and other instruments of coercion by experimenting on the bodies of the disobedient.

Forty-some years later, a disobedient named Piri Lugones, granddaughter of the poet, daughter of the police chief, endured her father's techniques firsthand in the torture chambers of a more recent dictatorship.

That dictatorship disappeared thirty thousand Argentines.

Among them, her.

THE AGES OF ANA

❧

In her first years, Ana Fellini believed her parents had died in an accident. That was what her grandparents told her. They said that her parents were on their way to pick her up when their plane went down.

At the age of eleven, someone else told her that her parents had died fighting Argentina's military dictatorship. She asked nothing, said nothing. She had been a bubbly child, but from then on she said little or nothing.

At the age of seventeen, she had trouble kissing. There was a sore under her tongue.

At the age of eighteen, she had trouble eating. The sore was growing deeper.

At the age of nineteen, they operated.

At the age of twenty, she died.

The doctor said it was cancer of the mouth.

Her grandparents said it was the truth that killed her.

The neighborhood witch said she died because she did not scream.

THE NAME MOST TOUCHED

❧

In the spring of 1979, the archbishop of El Salvador, Oscar Arnulfo Romero, traveled to the Vatican. He asked, pleaded, begged for an audience with Pope John Paul II:

"Wait your turn."

"We don't know."

"Come back tomorrow."

In the end, by lining up with the faithful waiting to be blessed, just one among the many, he surprised His Holiness and managed to steal a few minutes with him.

Romero tried to deliver a voluminous report with photographs and testimony, but the pope handed it back:

"I don't have time to read all this!"

And Romero sputtered that thousands of Salvadoreans had been tortured and murdered by the military, among them many Catholics and five priests, and that just yesterday, on the eve of this audience, the army had riddled twenty-five people with bullets in the doorway of the cathedral.

The head of the Church stopped him right there:

"Mr. Archbishop, do not exaggerate!"

The meeting did not last much longer.

Saint Peter's successor demanded, commanded, ordered:

"You must reach an understanding with the government! A good Christian does not look for trouble with the authorities! The Church wants peace and harmony!"

Ten months later, Archbishop Romero was shot down in a parish of San Salvador. The bullet killed him as he was saying Mass, at the moment he raised the host.

From Rome, the pontiff condemned the crime.

He forgot to condemn the criminals.

Years later, in Cuscatlán Park, names on an infinitely long wall commemorate the civilian victims of the war. Thousands upon thousands of names are etched in white on black marble. The letters of Archbishop Romero's name are the only ones that show wear.

From the touch of so many fingers.

THE BISHOP WHO DIED TWICE

❧

Memory is held prisoner in museums and is not allowed out.

Bishop Juan Gerardi led an investigation into Guatemala's terror.

One spring night in 1998, in the courtyard of the cathedral, the bishop presented the results, fourteen hundred pages, testimony from over a thousand witnesses. And he said:

"We all know that this path, the path of memory, is dangerous."

Two nights later, he was found lying in his own blood, his skull smashed with a chunk of concrete.

As if by magic, the blood and fingerprints were immediately wiped away. Several people confessed, but their confessions were more like confusions, the advance party of a gigantic international operation to turn the murder into an impenetrable maze.

And thus occurred the second death of the bishop. Lawyers, journalists, writers, and criminologists for hire did the dirty work. New culprits and new evidence appeared and disappeared at a dizzying pace, shovelfuls of infamy were heaped onto the body of the victim to safeguard the untouchable impunity of the authors of this crime and of two hundred thousand murders more:

"It was one of the Communists who infiltrated the Church."

"It was the cook."

"It was the woman who kept the keys."

"It was that drunk who slept in the park across the street."

"It was jealousy."

"Among fags, busting heads happens all the time."

"It was revenge, a priest had sworn to get him."

"It was that priest, and his dog."

"It was . . ."

GLOBAL TAXES

❧

Love wanes, life weighs, death wastes.

Some griefs are inevitable. That is the way it is, and not much can be done about it.

But those in charge of the planet pile grief on top of grief, and then charge us for the favor.

We pay the value-added tax every day in cold hard cash.

And every day, in cold hard misfortune, we pay the grief-added tax.

The added grief comes disguised as fate or destiny, as if the anguish born of the fleeting nature of life were the same as the anguish born of the fleeting nature of jobs.

THEY ARE NOT NEWS

*

In the south of India, at the Nallamada hospital, a failed suicide revives.

Around his bed, smiles from the ones who brought him back to life.

The survivor eyes them and says:

"What are you expecting, a thank-you? I owed a hundred thousand rupees. Now I'm also going to owe for four days in the hospital. Some favor you imbeciles did me."

We hear a lot about suicide bombers. The media blather on about them every day. But we hear nothing about suicide farmers.

According to official figures, India's farmers have been killing themselves steadily, at a rate of a thousand a month since the end of the twentieth century.

Many suicide farmers die from drinking the pesticides for which they cannot pay.

The market drives them into debt, then unpayable debt drives them into the grave. They spend more and more, earn less and less. They buy at penthouse prices and sell at bargain-basement markdowns. They are held hostage by the foreign chemical industry, by imported seeds, by genetically modified crops. Once upon a time, India worked to eat. Now India works to be eaten.

CRIMINOLOGY

*

Every year, chemical pesticides kill no fewer than three million farmers.

Every day, workplace accidents kill no fewer than ten thousand workers.

Every minute, poverty kills no fewer than ten children.

These crimes do not show up on the news. They are, like wars, normal acts of cannibalism.

The criminals are on the loose. No prisons are built for those who rip the guts out of thousands. Prisons are built as public housing for the poor.

More than two centuries ago, Thomas Paine wondered:

"Why is it that scarcely any are executed but the poor?"

Texas, twenty-first century: the last supper sheds light on the cellblock's clientele. Nobody chooses lobster or filet mignon, even though those dishes figure on the farewell menu. The condemned men prefer to say goodbye to the world with the usual: burgers and fries.

LIVE AND DIRECT

❧

All Brazil is watching.

A reality show in real time.

From the moment the criminal, he had to be black, takes the passengers of a Rio bus hostage one morning in the year 2000, television broadcasts every detail.

The commentators treat it as a mixture of soccer and war, the heartbreaking emotion of a World Cup final narrated in the tragic-epic tone of the invasion of Normandy.

The police lay siege to the bus.

In a long exchange of gunfire, a girl is killed. The crowd in the street shouts curses at the beast for whom innocent lives mean nothing.

At last, after four hours of shooting and other dramatics, a bullet from the forces of order brings the public enemy down. The police show off their trophy, critically wounded, bathed in blood, to the camera.

Everyone wants to lynch him, the thousands present and the millions watching.

The policemen pull him free from the angry crowd.

He gets into the patrol car alive. He comes out strangled.

In his brief passage through the world, he was Sandro do Nascimento, one of many children sleeping on the steps of the cathedral on a night in 1993, when it rained bullets. Eight died.

Of the survivors, nearly all were killed soon thereafter.

Sandro was lucky, but he was a dead man on leave.

Seven years later, the sentence was carried out.

He always dreamed of becoming a TV star.

DIRECT AND LIVE

*

All Argentina is watching.

A reality show in real time.

From the moment the bull, he had to be black, turns up in a Buenos Aires suburb one morning in 2004, television broadcasts every detail.

The commentators treat it as a mixture of bullfighting and war, the heartbreaking emotion of a corrida in Seville narrated in the tragic-epic tone of the fall of Berlin.

The morning passes and the police do not show up.

The animal eats grass, threateningly.

The people watch from afar, fearfully.

"Watch out," warns a journalist walking through the crowd, microphone in hand. "Careful, he might get nervous."

Off on his own, the beast nibbles and chews, focused on the little piece of greenery he discovered amid the gray buildings.

At last police cars filled with officers arrive and they take up positions around the animal. They watch him, unsure what to do.

Then a few brave souls break out of the crowd and, demonstrating great courage and skill, leap on the wild bull. Kicking and punching, they knock him over and wrap him in chains. The camera records the moment when one of them puts his foot triumphantly on the trophy.

They take him away in a cart. His head hangs over the side. Whenever he raises it, blows rain down on him. Voices scream:

"He's trying to escape! He's trying to escape again!"

And thus ends the life of this little calf, an escapee from the slaughterhouse whose horns are barely beginning to show.

The plate was his fate.

He never dreamed of becoming a TV star.

DANGER IN PRISON

❧

In 1998, the National Directorate of the Penitentiary System of the Republic of Bolivia received a letter signed by every prisoner in a jail in the Cochabamba Valley.

The letter respectfully requested that the prison wall be made higher, for as it was, people from the neighborhood were climbing over and stealing the clothes the prisoners hung out to dry.

Since no budget was available, there was no response. And since there was no response, the prisoners had no choice but to get to work. With bricks and straw they raised the wall high enough to protect themselves from their neighbors on the other side.

DANGER IN THE STREET

❧

For half a century, Uruguay has not won a single world soccer championship, but during the military dictatorship the country won other titles: relative to its population, it had the most political prisoners and the most victims of torture.

"Libertad" was the name of the biggest jail. Perhaps inspired by the name, imprisoned words sometimes broke out. Through the bars slid poems written on tiny cigarette papers. Like this one:

> *Sometimes it rains and I love you.*
> *Sometimes it's sunny and I love you.*
> *The prison is sometimes.*
> *I love you always.*

DANGER IN THE ANDES

※

The fox was on his way back from the heavens when parrots pecked through the rope he was sliding down.

The fox fell onto the high peaks of the Andes and burst apart. The quinoa in his belly, stolen from celestial banquets, sprayed everywhere.

Thus the food of the gods came to be planted in this world.

Ever since, quinoa lives in the highest lands, where it alone can withstand the dryness and the cold.

The world market ignored this useless Indian feed until two researchers at Colorado State University learned that the tiny wholesome grain, which grows where nothing else will, is not fattening and builds resistance to several diseases. And in 1994, they obtained U.S. patent number 5304718 for it.

The farmers were furious. Quinoa's patent-holders assured them they would not use their legal rights to stop them from growing it or to charge them a fee, but the farmers, indigenous Bolivians, responded:

"We don't need some professor from the United States to come here and donate to us what is ours."

Four years later, the scandal was such that Colorado State University had to give up the patent.

DANGER ON AIR

※

Radio Paiwas was born in the heart of Nicaragua on the eve of the twenty-first century.

The early morning program attracts the largest audience. *The Messenger Witch,* heard by thousands of women, frightens thousands of men.

The witch introduces women to friends they have never met, including one named Pap Smear and an old lady named Constitution. And she talks to them about their rights, "zero tolerance for violence in the street, in the home, and in bed too," and she asks them:

"How did it go last night? How did he treat you? Did it feel good or was it a little forced?"

And when men rape or beat women, she names names. At night, the witch flies house to house on her broom, and before dawn she rubs her crystal ball. Then she reveals on-air the secrets she has learned:

"Angel? You're out there, I can see you. Beating your wife, are you? That's awful, you scumbag!"

The radio receives and broadcasts the complaints the police ignore. The police are busy chasing cow thieves, and a cow is worth more than a woman.

BARBIE GOES TO WAR

There are more than a billion Barbies. Only the Chinese outnumber them.

The most beloved woman on the planet would never let us down. In the war of good against evil, Barbie enlisted, saluted, and marched off to Iraq.

She arrived at the front wearing made-to-measure land, sea, and air uniforms reviewed and approved by the Pentagon.

Barbie is accustomed to changing professions, hairdos, and clothes. She has been a singer, an athlete, a paleontologist, an orthodontist, an astronaut, a firewoman, a ballerina, and who knows what else. Every new job entails a new look and a complete new wardrobe that every girl in the world is obliged to buy.

In February 2004, Barbie wanted to change boyfriends too. For nearly half a century she had been going steady with Ken, whose nose is the only protuberance on his body, when an Australian surfer seduced her and invited her to commit the sin of plastic.

Mattel, the manufacturer, announced an official separation.

It was a catastrophe. Sales plummeted. Barbie could change occupations and outfits, but she had no right to set a bad example.

Mattel announced an official reconciliation.

'ROBOCOP'S CHILDREN GO TO WAR

In the year 2005, the Pentagon disclosed that its dream of an army of automatons is coming true.

According to spokesman Gordon Johnson, the wars in Afghanistan and Iraq have been tremendously valuable for the robots' progress. Now robots equipped with night vision and automatic weapons are able to locate and destroy enemy emplacements with practically no margin of error.

No trace of humanity diminishes their optimum efficiency:

"They don't get hungry, they're not afraid, they don't forget their orders," Johnson said. "They don't care if the guy next to them has just been shot."

CAMOUFLAGED WARS

At the beginning of the twentieth century, Colombia suffered through a thousand-day war.

In the middle of the twentieth century, the war lasted three thousand days.

At the outset of the twenty-first century, the days of the war have become too numerous to count.

But this war, fatal for Colombia, is not so fatal for Colombia's owners:

the war feeds fear, and fear turns injustice into an inescapable fate;

the war feeds poverty, and poverty supplies hands that will work for little or nothing;

the war drives peasants off their land, which then gets sold for little or nothing;

the war lines the pockets of arms smugglers and kidnappers, and grants sanctuary to drug traffickers for whom cocaine remains a venture in which Americans up north invest their noses and Colombians invest their dead;

the war murders so many labor activists that trade unions organize more funerals than strikes, and they stop bothering companies like Chiquita Brands, Coca-Cola, Nestlé, Del Monte, or Drummond Limited;

and the war murders those who point out the causes of the war, making the war as inexplicable as it is inevitable.

The experts, known as violentologists, say Colombia is a country in love with death.

It is in the genes, they say.

A WOMAN ON THE BANKS OF A RIVER

❦

It rains death.

In the deathmill, Colombians die by bullet or by knife,

by machete or by club,

by noose or by fire,

by falling bomb or by buried mine.

In the jungle of Urabá, on the banks of the Perancho River or the Peranchito, in her home made of sticks and palm leaves, a woman named Eligia fans herself to chase off the mosquitoes and the heat, and the fear as well. And while her fan flutters, she says out loud:

"Wouldn't it be great to die a natural death?"

LIED≠ABOUT WARS

❦

Advertising campaigns, marketing schemes. The target is public opinion. Wars are sold the same way cars are, by lying.

In August 1964, President Lyndon Johnson accused the Vietnamese of attacking two U.S. warships in the Tonkin Gulf.

Then the president invaded Vietnam, sending planes and troops. He was acclaimed by journalists and by politicians, and his popularity sky-rocketed. The Democrats in power and the Republicans out of power became a single party united against Communist aggression.

After the war had slaughtered Vietnamese in vast numbers, most of them women and children, Johnson's secretary of defense, Robert McNamara, confessed that the Tonkin Gulf attack had never occurred.

The dead did not revive.

In March 2003, President George W. Bush accused Iraq of being on the verge of destroying the world with its weapons of mass destruction, "the most lethal weapons ever devised."

Then the president invaded Iraq, sending planes and troops. He was acclaimed by journalists and by politicians, and his popularity skyrocketed. The Republicans in power and the Democrats out of power became a single party united against terrorist aggression.

After the war had slaughtered Iraqis in vast numbers, most of them women and children, Bush confessed that the weapons of mass destruction never existed. "The most lethal weapons ever devised" were his own speeches.

In the following elections, he won a second term.

In my childhood, my mother used to tell me that a lie has no feet. She was misinformed.

ORIGIN OF THE EMBRACE

❧

Thousands of years before its devastation, Iraq gave birth to the first love poem in world literature:

> *What I tell you*
> *Let the weaver weave into song.*

The song, in Sumerian, told of the encounter of a goddess and a shepherd.

That night, the goddess Ianna loved as if she were mortal. Dumuzi the shepherd was immortal as long as the night lasted.

LYING WARS

❧

The war in Iraq grew out of the need to correct an error made by Geography when she put the West's oil under the East's sand. But no war is honest enough to confess:

"I kill to steal."

"The devil's shit," as oil is called by its victims, has caused many wars and will certainly cause many more.

In Sudan, for instance, a huge number of people lost their lives between the final years of the twentieth century and the first years of the twenty-first, in an oil war that disguised itself as an ethnic and religious conflict. Derricks and drills, pipes and pipelines sprouted as if by magic in villages turned to ashes and in fields of ruined crops. In the Darfur region, where the butchery continues, the people, all Muslim, began to hate each other when they discovered there might be oil under their feet.

The killing in the hills of Rwanda also claimed to be an ethnic and religious war, even though killers and killed were all Catholics. Hatred, a colonial legacy, stemmed from the time when Belgium decreed that those who raised cattle were Tutsis and those who grew crops were Hutus, and that the Tutsi minority ought to dominate the Hutu majority.

In recent years, another multitude lost their lives in the Democratic Republic of the Congo in the service of foreign companies fighting over coltan. That rare mineral is an essential ingredient in cell phones, computers, microchips, and batteries, all of which are staples of the mass media. The media, however, forgot to mention coltan in their scant coverage of the war.

VORACIOUS WARS

❧

In 1975, the king of Morocco invaded the homeland of the Saharan people and expelled the majority of the population.

Today Western Sahara is the last colony in Africa.

Morocco denies it the right to determine its own future, and thus admits to having stolen a country it has no intention of returning.

The Saharans, "children of the clouds," pursuers of rain, have been handed a life sentence of constant anguish and perpetual nostalgia. In the desert, independence is harder to come by than water.

A thousand and one times, the United Nations has spoken out against the Israeli occupation of the Palestinian homeland.

In 1948, the founding of the state of Israel led to the expulsion of eight hundred thousand people. The Palestinians took with them the keys to their homes, as had the Jews kicked out of Spain centuries before. The Jews were never able to return to Spain. The Palestinians were never able to return to Palestine.

Those who stayed behind were condemned to live humiliated in territories that are nibbled away at daily by relentless incursions.

Susan Abdallah, a Palestinian, knows the recipe for making a terrorist:

Deprive him of food and water.

Surround his home with the machinery of war.

Attack him with all means at all times, especially at night.

Demolish his home, uproot his farmland, kill his loved ones.

Congratulations: you have created an army of suicide bombers.

'WORLD-KILLING WARS

*

In the middle of the seventeenth century, Irish bishop James Ussher revealed that the world began in the year 404 before Christ, between dusk on Saturday, October 22, and nightfall the following day.

Regarding the end of the world, we don't have such precise information. For sure, we fear its demise is not far off, given the feverish pace at which its murderers labor. The technological advances of the twenty-first century will no doubt equal the progress of the previous twenty thousand years of human history, but no one knows on which planet they will be celebrated. Shakespeare foretold it: "'Tis the times' plague when madmen lead the blind."

Machines built to help us live are helping us die.

Breathing and walking are forbidden in our great cities. Chemical bombardments melt the polar icecaps and the mountain snows. A California travel agency sells goodbye-glacier tours to Greenland. The sea eats away the shore and fishermen's nets catch jellyfish instead of cod. Natural forests, riots of diversity, are turned into industrial forests or into deserts where not even the stones multiply. Since the beginning of this century, drought has put a hundred million peasant farmers in twenty countries at God's mercy. "Nature has grown very tired," wrote Spanish monk Luis Alfonso de Carvallo. That was in 1695. If only he could see us now.

When it isn't drought, it's flood. Year after year the number of never-ending floods, hurricanes, and cyclones grows. They call them natural disasters, as if nature were the aggressor and not the victim. World-killing disasters, poor-killing disasters: in Guatemala they say natural disasters are like old cowboy movies, because only the Indians die.

Why do the stars tremble? Perhaps they sense that soon we shall invade other heavenly bodies.

THE GIANT AT TULE

❧

In the year 1586, Spanish priest Josep de Acosta caught sight of it in the town of Tule, three leagues from Oaxaca. "A bolt of lightning wounded this tree from the crown through its heart to the base. Before it was hit by lightning, they say it offered shade for a thousand men."

And in 1630, Bernabé Cobo wrote that the tree had three doors wide enough to ride through on horseback.

It is still there. It was born before Christ, and it is still there. The oldest and largest living thing in the world. In the dense foliage of its branches, thousands of birds make their home.

This green god is doomed to solitude. No jungle is left to keep it company.

ORIGIN OF ROAD RAGE

❧

Horses whinnied, coachmen cursed, whips whistled through the air.

The noble gentleman was in a fury. He had been waiting for what felt like centuries. His carriage was blocked by another carriage that was vainly trying to turn around amid many other carriages. He lost the little patience he had left, got out, unsheathed his sword, and sliced open the first horse he saw.

That happened one Saturday at dusk in the year 1766 at the Place des Victoires in Paris.

The noble gentleman was the Marquis de Sade.

Today's traffic jams are even more sadistic.

RIDDLE

❧

They are the most important members of our family.

They are gluttons, devouring gas, oil, corn, sugarcane, and anything else that comes their way.

They own our time: bathing them, feeding and sheltering them, talking about them, and opening the way for them.

They reproduce faster than we do, and are ten times as numerous as they were half a century ago.

They kill more people than do wars, but no one condemns the murders, least of all the newspapers and television channels that live off their advertisements.

They steal our streets. They steal our air.

They laugh when they hear us say: "I drive."

BRIEF HISTORY OF THE
TECHNOLOGICAL REVOLUTION

❧

Be fruitful and multiply, we said, and machines were fruitful and they multiplied.

They promised they would work for us.

Now we work for them.

The machines we invented to produce more food now produce more hunger.

The weapons we invented to defend ourselves now kill us.

The cars we invented to transport us now paralyze us.

The cities we invented so we could meet each other now keep us apart.

The mass media we invented so we could communicate now neither hear nor see us.

We are the machines of our machines.

They claim innocence.

And they are right.

BHOPAL

❧

In the middle of the night, people woke up to a nightmare: the air was on fire.

The year was 1984, and in the city of Bhopal, India, a Union Carbide Corporation factory exploded.

None of the security systems worked. Or better put: profitability sacrificed safety by imposing drastic cost reductions.

A crime termed an accident killed many thousands, and left many more ill for life.

In the south of the world, human life is priced according to supply. After a lot of tussling, Union Carbide paid three thousand dollars for each person killed, and a thousand for each left incurably ill. Its prestigious lawyers rejected the demands of the survivors, arguing that illiterates were incapable of understanding what their thumbprints had signed. The company did not clean up the water or the air of Bhopal, which remain contaminated, nor did it clean up the earth, which remains poisoned with mercury and lead.

Instead, Union Carbide cleaned up its image, paying millions to the priciest makeup specialists in the world.

A few years later, another chemical giant, Dow Chemical, bought the company. The company, that is, not its account book: Dow Chemical washed its hands, denied any responsibility in the matter, and sued the women protesting at its doors for disturbing the peace.

ANIMAL MEDIA

*

One spring night in 1986, the nuclear power plant at Chernobyl blew up.

The Soviet government decreed silence.

Many died, a multitude survived as walking bombs, but TV, radio, the newspapers heard nothing, said nothing. And at the end of three days, when they did mention it, they did not violate the gag order. No one warned that we faced a new Hiroshima. On the contrary, they insisted it had been a minor accident, nothing at all, everything under control, nobody get upset.

The farmers and fishermen on lands and waters both near and far knew that something very serious had occurred. They heard the bad news from the bees, wasps, and birds that took flight and vanished over the horizon, and from the worms that burrowed several feet underground, leaving the fishermen without bait and the chickens without food.

A couple of decades later, a tsunami struck South Asia and gigantic waves swallowed another multitude.

As the tragedy was brewing, when the earth had barely begun to move deep under the sea, elephants raised their trunks and blared desperate laments. No one understood when the beasts broke their chains and stampeded into the jungle.

Flamingos, leopards, tigers, boars, deer, water buffalo, monkeys, and snakes also fled before the disaster.

The only ones to die were the humans and the turtles.

ARNO

❧

Nature had not yet been committed to the insane asylum, but it already suffered from periodic nervous breakdowns that warned of things to come.

At the end of 1966, the Arno River's dream of having a flood all its own came true, and the city of Florence faced the worst inundation in its entire history. In a single day, Florence lost more than it had in all the bombings of the Second World War.

Soon after, Florentines knee-deep in mud set to rescuing whatever might have survived the shipwreck. There they were, men and women, dripping wet, working, cursing the Arno and all its relatives, when a long truck came barreling past.

The truck carried an enormous body mortally wounded by the flood: the head bounced along over the rear wheels and a broken arm hung over the side.

As the wooden giant passed, men and women put aside their shovels and pails, uncovered their heads, crossed themselves. And in silence they watched it disappear from view.

He too was a son of the city of Florence.

This Jesus crucified, Jesus broken, had been born here seven centuries ago from the hand of Giovanni Cimabue, teacher of Giotto.

GANGES

❧

The great river of India used to bathe not the earth, but the heavens above and beyond. The gods refused to give up the river that brought them water and cool air.

And thus it was until the Ganges decided to move. It moved to India, where it now flows from the Himalayas to the sea, so the living can purify themselves in its waters, and the ashes of the dead may find their destiny.

The sacred river, which took pity on the earthborn, never imagined that it would receive offerings of garbage and poison that would make its life in the world impossible.

THE RIVER AND THE FISH

❧

An old proverb has it that teaching fishing is better than handing out fish.

Bishop Pedro Casaldáliga, who lives in the Amazon, says yes, that is correct, a very good thought. But suppose someone buys the river that had belonged to all and outlaws fishing? Or suppose toxic waste pollutes the river and poisons the fish? In other words, suppose what happens is what is happening now?

THE RIVER AND THE DEER

❧

The oldest book on education was written by a woman.

Dhouda of Gascony wrote *Liber Manualis,* a manual for her son, in Latin at the beginning of the ninth century.

She did not impose a thing. She suggested, she advised, she showed. One of the pages invites us to learn from deer that "ford wide rivers swimming in single file, one after the other, with the head and shoulders of each resting on the rump of the deer ahead; they support one another and thus are able to cross the river more easily. And they are so intelligent and clever that when they realize the one in the very front is tiring, they send him to the end of the line and another takes the lead."

THE HANDS OF THE TRAIN

*

Mumbai's trains, which transport six million passengers a day, break the laws of physics: more passengers enter them than fit.

Suketu Mehta, who knows about these impossible voyages, says when every jam-packed train pulls out, people run after it. Whoever misses the train, loses his job.

Then the cars sprout hands out of windows or from roofs, and they help the ones left behind clamber aboard. And these train hands do not ask the one running up if he is foreign or native-born, nor do they ask what language he speaks, or if he believes in Brahma or in Allah, in Buddha or in Jesus, nor do they ask which caste he belongs to, if he is from a cursed caste or no caste at all.

DANGER IN THE JUNGLE

*

Savitri left.

The savage who had heard her call trampled the fence, knocked over the guards, and entered the tent. Savitri broke free of her chains and the two of them disappeared, together, into the jungle.

The owner of the Olympic Circus calculated the loss at about nine thousand dollars and said, to make matters worse, Savitiri's friend Gayatri was very depressed and refused to work.

At the end of 2007, the fugitive couple was located at the edge of a lake, 150 miles from Calcutta.

The pursuers dared not approach. The male and female elephants had intertwined their trunks.

DANGER AT THE TAP

※

According to Revelation 21:6, God will create a new world and say: "I will give unto him that is athirst of the fountain of water of life freely."

Freely? Meaning the new world won't make room for the World Bank or the private companies that ply the noble trade in water?

So it seems. Meanwhile, in the old world where we all still live, sources of water are as coveted as oil reserves, and are becoming battlegrounds.

In Latin America, the first water war was the invasion of Mexico by Hernán Cortés. More recently, combat over the blue gold took place in Bolivia and Uruguay. In Bolivia, the people took to the streets and won back their lost water. In Uruguay, the people voted in a plebiscite and kept their water from being lost.

DANGER ON THE LAND

※

One afternoon in 1996, nineteen landless peasants were shot in cold blood by members of the military police of Pará state in the Brazilian Amazon.

In Pará and in much of Brazil, the lords of the land reign over empty vastnesses, thanks to the right to inheritance or the right to thievery. These property rights give them the right to impunity. Ten years after the massacre, no one is in jail. Not the lords, not their thugs.

But the tragedy did not frighten or discourage the landless farmers. The membership of their organization mushroomed, and so did their will to work the land, even though that is a capital offense and an act of incomprehensible madness.

DANGER IN THE SKY

❧

In the year 2003, a tsunami of people washed away the government of Bolivia.

The poor were sick and tired. Everything had been privatized, even the rainwater. A "for sale" sign had been hung on Bolivia, and they were going to sell it, Bolivians and all.

The uprising shook El Alto, perched above the incredibly high city of La Paz, where the poorest of the poor work throughout their lives, day after day, chewing on their troubles. They are so high up they push the clouds when they walk, and every house has a door to heaven.

Heaven was where those who died in the rebellion went. It was a lot closer than earth. Now they are shaking up paradise.

DANGER IN THE CLOUDS

❧

According to incontrovertible testimony that has reached the Vatican, Antoni Gaudí merits sainthood for his numerous miracles.

The artist who founded Catalan modernism died in 1926, and since then he has cured many who were incurable, found many who were unfindable, and sprinkled jobs and housing everywhere.

The beatification process is under way.

Heaven's architecture had better watch out, for this chaste puritan who never missed a procession had a pagan hand, evident in the carnal labyrinths he designed for homes and parks.

What will he do with the cloud he is given? Will he not invite us to stroll through Adam and Eve's innards on the night of the first sin?

INVENTORY OF THE WORLD

❧

Arthur Bispo do Rosario was black and poor, a sailor, a boxer, and, on God's account, an artist.

He lived in the Rio de Janeiro insane asylum.

There, seven blue angels delivered an order from the divine: God wants an inventory taken of the world.

The mission was monumental. Arthur worked day and night, every day, every night, until the winter of 1989 when, still immersed in the task, death took him by the hair and carried him off.

The inventory, incomplete, consisted of scrap metal,
broken glass,
bald brooms,
walked-through sneakers,
emptied bottles,
slept-in sheets,
road-weary wheels,
sea-worn sails,
defeated flags,
well-thumbed letters,
forgotten words, and
fallen rain.

Arthur worked with garbage, because all garbage is life lived and from garbage comes everything the world is or has ever been. Nothing intact deserved a listing. Things intact die without ever being born. Life only pulsates in what bears scars.

THE ROAD GOES ON

٭

When someone dies, when his time is up, what happens to the wanderings, desirings, and speakings that were called by his name?

Among the Indians of the upper Orinoco, he who dies loses his name. His ashes are stirred into plantain soup or corn wine and everybody eats. After the ceremony no one ever names the dead person again: the dead one, now living in other bodies, called by other names, wanders, desires, and speaks.

DANGER IN THE NIGHT

❧

Sleeping, she saw us.

Helena dreamed we were waiting in line at an airport.

A long line where every passenger had under the arm the pillow on which he or she had slept the night before.

The pillows were sent through a dream-reading machine.

The machine detected any dangerous dreams that threatened to disturb the peace.

LOST AND FOUND

❧

The twentieth century, which was born proclaiming peace and justice, died bathed in blood. It passed on a world much more unjust than the one it inherited.

The twenty-first century, which also arrived heralding peace and justice, is following in its predecessor's footsteps.

In my childhood, I was convinced that everything that went astray on earth ended up on the moon.

But the astronauts found no sign of dangerous dreams or broken promises or hopes betrayed.

If not on the moon, where might they be?

Perhaps they were never misplaced.

Perhaps they are in hiding here on earth. Waiting.

LIST OF ILLUSTRATIONS

INDEX OF NAMES

CONTENTS

CPSIA information can be obtained at www.ICGtesting.com
Printed in the USA
LVOW10s2249190914

404899LV00002B/6/P